Edward Upward was born in 1903 in Romford, Essex. He was educated at Repton School and Corpus Christi College, Cambridge, where he won the Chancellor's medal for English Verse and where he and Christopher Isherwood wrote stories for each other about the imaginary village of Mortmere, described in the latter's *Lions and Shadows*. He took a degree in History and English and became a schoolmaster. In the 1930s he was a contributor to *New Country*, *New Writing* and *Left Review* and had a significant influence on young writers such as Auden, Spender, Day Lewis and Rex Warner. His first novel, *Journey to the Border* was published in 1938.

In the Thirties, the first volume of *The Spiral Ascent*, was published in 1962. Simultaneously with the next volume, *The Rotten Elements*, he published a collection of short stories, *The Railway Accident and Other Stories*. The trilogy was completed in 1977 with *No Home But the Struggle*.

Now retired, Edward Upward lives on the Isle of Wight.

No Home But The Struggle

Struggle

Volume Three of THE SPIRAL ASCENT

Edward Upward

QUARTET BOOKS
LONDON   MELBOURNE   NEW YORK

Published by Quartet Books Limited 1979
A member of the Namara Group
27 Goodge Street, London W1P 1FD

First published by William Heinemann Limited, London, 1977

ISBN 0 7043 3277 9

Printed in Great Britain

To my son Christopher and my daughter Kathy
and to both their families

No Home But The Struggle

I have arrived home for good at last. There will never again be a morning now when I shall say to myself here: 'To-morrow the guillotine descends. Tomorrow I must return to London and to my job as a teacher.' Until I die or until I am kept in bed by a serious illness I shall be able every day after breakfast to come into this pleasant white and yellow room which is still called the 'drawing-room' both by me and Elsie just as it was by my parents before us and my grandparents before them; I shall be able to look through the large panes of the French window at the verandah and the lawn and the flint wall beneath the holly tree where on fine days an oblong of sunlight is reflected as now from one of the other windows of this house, or to sit out on the verandah in spring and autumn when the weather is neither too cool nor too warm; and every day I shall be free to write poetry. But in spite of my having retired from teaching more than a month ago I still can't easily believe that the life I have always wanted to live has become fully possible for me at last. I don't seem even to have convinced myself absolutely that I am not due back in London for the beginning of the Easter term. At nights I still dream fairly often that I am in school, though the type of nightmare I've had recently hasn't been quite as bad as the type I recurrently had during my years of teaching: then, long after I'd 'matured' as a teacher and did not have serious 'disciplinary' difficulties any more, I used to dream I was standing powerless in the middle of a crowd of boys who had got outrageously out of control; whereas during the past few weeks I've dreamt three or four times that I am hurriedly going up a concrete staircase to take a class I am disgracefully late for, and when I eventually reach the classroom I find there are no boys in it — or only a few, who drift out as soon as I begin to speak to them. Perhaps I must expect such lesser nightmares for a while yet after more than thirty years in a job which, however honourable and necessary it may be, cannot in present conditions be without heavy strain even for teachers far more capable than I ever was. Let me try to dissolve from my mind all disagreeable residues of my working years by remembering often how, as I walked out of the school building for the last time, I imagined myself arriving home here and saying to my mother and father: 'It has been a bad patch, but it's all finished with now.' I had forgotten for an instant that they were both dead and that this patch had covered more than half of my life so far, but my mood was the right one. Let me revive it. Those years are done with for ever and for ever, and I am free.

I have come back to the house and the town where I have always wanted to live. I am sitting in the room whose details I have so many times visually remembered when I have been where I did not want to be, and I am able to see in actuality now the gold and white pattern on the damask chair coverings and curtains — more faded than they already were when my mother and father retired to this house thirty years ago — and the slightly less old though equally faded gold and rose and white Indian carpet, and on the mantelpiece made of the white marble which my grandfather brought back from Italy the two Sheffield-plated candlesticks with their underlying copper beginning to show through the worn silver of their surfaces. It would be absurd if what has been preventing me this morning from being sure that I'm at last going to live the life I've always longed for has partly been a feeling of guilt about my not having earned this house: even supposing I had inherited huge wealth and aesthetic luxury instead of a richness which is entirely in the poetic childhood and boyhood associations this house has for me, I could still have justified·my inheritance by using it, as I intend to use what I actually have inherited, to attack the social system that denies to most other people the economic freedom I've eventually got. Only opponents of socialism would believe that a socialist with money ought to give it away to the poor rather than use it in aid of the revolutionary abolition of poverty. Not that Elsie and I have much money, and at present there is no political organisation we would want to help except the Campaign for Nuclear Disarmament, but the poetry I shall write will be for revolution. And though I could have written it if I had inherited nothing from my parents and if Elsie and I had stayed on in London after our retirement from teaching, this house is the place where poetry came most easily to me in the past and where I shall best be able to continue writing it now.

Nowhere else I have ever been has seemed more beautiful to me than this house and this town. Admittedly they are no longer quite all that they were to me when Elsie and I were not yet living here and when I was able to come down from London only during school holidays for visits which became shorter, though not less frequent, as my parents grew too old to want interruptions of more than a day or two at a time in the routine of their lives. During those visits the sight of sunlight on the bookcase in the dining-room could fill me with a boundless joy, and in the loved town no detail seemed accidental or meaningless. Smears on the pavement, fallen holly leaves in summer, even frozen dog's urine against a wall at Christmas time, were no less interesting to the doting observer than were the chalk cliffs of the bay in the light of a September evening or the startlingly tall monkey-puzzle tree rising dark green above the middle of the town against a sky shading to cobalt at the zenith. As in a stage set, every item had significance; and yet how incomparably more moving to me than anything I had ever seen at the theatre was this reality. I can hardly expect, now that I am here for good, to appreciate this place as ecstatically as when I used to come to it briefly after starving for it through weeks of teaching in London. But I can find compensation in aspects of it which ecstasy might overlook, one of them being the friendliness that Elsie and I have been discovering everywhere here: as a small instance of this, when either of us goes into a shop we are called Mr or Mrs Sebrill, not sir or madam as in London; and I don't doubt that a number of people in this town whom we've not yet met will be calling us Elsie and Alan before the end of the year. We have become inhabitants, and we are conscious of being welcome.

The air here and the sea may not have quite the marvellousness they seemed to have in my boyhood, but my sense of well-being is steadier if less exalted than then. It's true that yesterday evening, for a while, a different feeling came over me. I had opened the drawing-room door and switched on the light and I saw the French windows — their curtains not having been drawn across them yet — and they looked absolutely black and blank. There was no sound at all from outside the house. I was aware that my personal annihilation was less far off than it had been during my working years. But the fear soon passed, and I know that my own everlasting death cannot face me with any problems — only my unfinished life can do that. And there is no real reason whatsoever why it should do so at present.

I have come home to this place to live the poetic life, the life of imagination and of poetic creation, which I was able to live in the past here for brief periods — and which I was able to live elsewhere too at times, though perhaps never with such intensity as here, and always this house and this town were the inspiration and the headquarters of that life. I shall be living it all the time now, instead of trying, as I have only half-successfully tried for the last few years, to live it during school holidays and in free hours after a day's teaching. I know I am late — though how late I can't know — in returning to it here. Yet my lateness isn't the chief cause of my uneasiness. (And I'd better not spend any more of this morning in efforts to conceal from myself that I am uneasy.) No, the chief cause is far more likely to be that the successive attempts I made here and elsewhere thirty and more years ago to live that life resulted finally in my being unable to write poetry. I would have committed suicide or become insane if I hadn't decided to join the Communist Party and to regard the political struggle rather than poetic creation as my first concern. But the new poetic life, which I have been aiming to live since I gave up the political life twelve years ago after recognising at last that the Party had become a revisionist and non-revolutionary organisation, will avoid the mistakes of the old. My freedom, now that I have retired on a pension, is not an illusion which I have temporarily procured for myself by abandoning an unpleasant job and closing my mind to the necessity of having to find another and perhaps still more unpleasant one in a few months' time. The poems I shall write will not be evading a reality which when it irresistibly asserts itself in my life will prove them to be unreal and worthless. They will be poems for the struggle against capitalism. And if they are to avoid becoming tainted with insincerity I must take part in direct political activity too — Elsie and I mean to get in touch with the local C.N.D. group very soon — though I must never again let political activity involve me to the extent that I have hardly any time or energy left for poetry, as happened when I was in the Party. I have returned not to what was bad in the earlier poetic life, not to its disastrous anti-political unrealism, but to what was good in it, to its uncompromising love of poetry.

Then why am I no less and perhaps more uneasy than when I sat down here twenty minutes ago? At this moment as I look through the window at the flint wall below the holly tree I know why. The uneasiness isn't caused by my not having thrown off the effects of thirty-five years of teaching yet, nor by a guiltiness about my having inherited this

13

house, nor by the prospect of death, nor by my inability to feel as ecstatically as I once could here, but by the absence in me of any poetic feelings whatsoever about this place now. The oblong reflection on the alternate banded rows of rounded grey and white flints is as if it were totally external to me, as if it existed solely in itself; it has no emotional or scientific significance for me, does not enchant or interest me at all. There is a fear in me that now I've come here for good this house and this town will never again excite me poetically, that as a result I shall before long begin to have difficulty in continuing to write poetry, that the new poetic life will end even more disastrously than the old because there will be no Party I can turn to for refuge this time but only death.

I am being unnecessarily, as well as self-demoralisingly pessimistic. It's not true that I've lost the ability to be poetically excited by this place. I am disregarding what happened only two days ago as I was walking along the cliff path in the afternoon. I saw the building which looks like a small powerhouse and which stands half-screened now by a row of holm-oaks about a hundred and fifty yards inland from the cliff edge. I remembered the impression it had made on me as a boy of sixteen and the poem I had conceived about it then. I remembered not so much the poem itself as the extraordinary exhilaration this supposed power-house — it is an ice-cream factory now, whatever it may have been forty-four years ago — had aroused in me because of the strangeness of its presence there not far from the cliff edge with no other tall-chimneyed building visible inland for miles around, and because of the look its large round-headed windows had given it of being an apparition from the mid-nineteenth century, half Beulah chapel and half industrial mill, and because of the heavy flywheel and glistening piston and whirling brass-balled governor and big horizontal boiler I had imagined to be concealed behind the long high stretch of windowless wall below the windows.

In remembering that past poetic exhilaration I felt a similar exhilaration, as an iron core is magnetised by the electric current running through a coil of wire that surrounds it. The old poetic life gave potency to the new; and through my surroundings here it will do so again, often. This is why I have come to live here.

Must I passively wait for the next time when the past will vivify the present? What is to prevent me from deliberately — this morning, this instant — stimulating poetic imaginativeness in myself by thinking of other occasions here years ago when I felt the kind of excitement that the sight of the power-house near the cliff path gave me? One other occasion was on a summer afternoon in the dining-room here as I was standing in front of the bookcase, reading a book I had just taken down from the shelf. I had walked up to the house quite soon after having lunch with the rest of my family — except my father, who always had his holidays on his own — at the lodgings in Victoria Road where we stayed when we visited this seaside place for three weeks every August; and after spending the morning on the beach we used to come up to this house for tea with my grandmother each day, though that summer I often came up earlier than Hugh or Vaughan or Laura or my mother. I was nineteen and had returned to England a fortnight before from Rouen where I had lived for six months after leaving my Public school, and I was due to start my first term at Cambridge in the autumn. The book I took down from the shelf was an anthology of poems. But am I going to spend the rest of the morning thinking about the past? I seem to be forgetting that to-day is the day when without fail, after the five weeks' holiday I've felt I could afford to allow myself at the beginning of my retirement, I was to have started work again on the poem I began last November. Isn't my remembering of former imaginative experiences merely a means of postponing a duty I am afraid will be a difficult one, and mightn't the postponement — if I allow myself to make it — be continued to-morrow and the day after? No, there is no real danger of that. I have a clear conception of the whole of the first section of the poem, and I know how to go on from the opening I wrote in November, which was a good opening. I may be much less sure about some of the subsequent sections — I've not even decided whether there will be seven sections or eight or how long I want each of them and the poem as a whole to be — but all problems not connected with the first section can be dealt with later. Whenever I choose to start work on the poem again I shall have no difficulty in continuing from where I left off two months ago. And my postponing writing for a little while longer in order to think of past imaginative experiences will improve my morale and make me more eager to get on with this poem in the present.

The anthology I took down from the book-case had a well known poem in it by John Clare that I had not discovered anywhere before. I read the first verse, and when I was in the middle of reading the second I returned to the first and re-read it twice and then re-read it again a third and a fourth time till it became for me something that was no longer on the printed page but wholly in my mind and feelings:

> Love lies beyond
> The tomb, the earth, which fades like dew —
> I love the fond,
> The faithful, and the true.

The simplicity, even obviousness, of the words made their power seem all the more miraculous to me. But soon the emotion they evoked in me became such that I was hardly conscious of the words themselves; it became physical, a movement in the throat as of a rising sob of joy. At this moment my grandmother, with a suddenness which suggested that she might have been standing quite still for a while outside the half-open door, came rustling into the room in her black dress — I think she always wore black after my grandfather died, though I don't know whether she wore it because of his death or because it may have been the fashion for women of her age even if they weren't widows — and I was astonished that she did not look at me. I had become so accustomed over years to being an object of her loving interest that I could not easily think she was purposely ignoring me. She moved hurriedly yet uncertainly about the room, turning first towards the sideboard, then towards the mantelpiece and then towards the window. She gave a little moan. I could not suppose she was ill: she walked very upright as usual, and in her large eyes under her high-arched eyebrows there was no sign of physical pain but only the sadness they were never quite without. The thought came to me that she might be upset by something I had done; and immediately and with shame I knew what it could be. Almost every afternoon during this holiday I had come up early to the house on my own in order to look into as many of the books here as I could, and I had never once gone to talk to her until tea time when my mother and brothers and sister were here too. Now perhaps she had come into the room because she wanted to talk to me, but on seeing me reading she had felt I might not like to be interrupted. I painfully needed to say something to her that would make amends, that would express my contrition, but I could think of nothing that would excuse the lack of attention to her which I had been guilty of for the last fortnight. However, she spoke first:

'I am playing the last game.' She gave me rather a weak smile. She did not explain what she meant, and I felt that she expected me to ask.

'What game is that?' I did ask, with embarrassment.

'Looking for my spectacles.'

I stood there with nothing to say, and she was out of the room again before I thought of offering to help her to find them. I did not follow her out. I felt that she would not expect any help from me and might not welcome it now. A mood of self-accusation came upon me. I believed that her moan after she had hurried into the room had been due not just to her having mislaid her spectacles but also to an unhappiness at my no longer showing towards her the affection I had shown as a child. I recognised, as I stood with the book still open in my hand, how selfish my feelings towards her had always been. I had regarded her as a person for myself and never as having a life of her own. I had been aware quite early of the nervousness she chronically suffered from but had never imagined what this condition of hers must feel like to her. When she sewed up with needle and cotton the last two pages of a child's picture book of mine called *The Merry Mad Motor* in order to hide the motor car's total explosion which was depicted on the final page and which had frightened me, her action seemed to me simply a warm kindness; and when later on she used to break off the bayonets and swords of the lead soldiers that she sent me or my brothers or sister as presents, I found her anxiety for our eyes comic, and also annoying because it spoilt the soldiers. Children, I realised as I continued holding the anthology open at Clare's poem which I was now wholly unconscious of, sometimes find a cosiness even in the feebleness and deformities of old people who are affectionate towards them. I knew for the first time that my idea of my grandmother, and also of my grandfather and of my uncle Vernon and of the life that had been lived in this house, must be very unlike the reality, and that I ought to try to think of them differently.

I put the anthology back on the shelf but I remained standing in front of the bookcase. I thought of my grandfather, who had been dead for twelve years. In himself, and for others than me, he had never been simply the person whom once, when I as a child of three or four had gone out into the garden here on my own, I had seen running playfully towards me from the verandah, his gait seeming neither that of an adult nor of another child. Nor had he ever been simply the white-bearded smiler towards whose armchair — I suppose less than a year after his first paralytic stroke — I had run with a piece of torn paper in order to ask him 'Will you sign this cheque?' and who gave me a look in which fondness was mixed with an amused knowingness that made me feel a little shy. (Perhaps he thought I might have heard my parents talk of him in connection with the signing of cheques.) Nor had he been simply the interesting 'character' that my father's stories about him had led me to think he had been. There was the story for instance of how he, a Calvinist with religious objections to card-playing, had once said to my father, 'Harold, I am very sorry to hear that you have been playing cards for money at Cambridge', and when my father had answered 'Oh but, father, I nearly always win', my grandfather had said 'Ah well, that puts rather a different complexion on the matter'. There was the story of how on finding in a restaurant that there were not enough chairs free for him and his family to sit on he had said to the owner of a Pekinese which was occupying one chair, 'Human beings first, madam', and had tipped the dog on to the floor. And there was the other story about a dog, a continually barking dog next door here which had disturbed him intolerably and which he had paid a man to come and poison while he himself would be abroad in Italy. Remembering this story as I stood in front of the bookcase I did not think my grandfather's action reprehensible at all: I am shocked by it now, though I suppose that the general treatment of animals in my grandather's day was less humane than it has since become, and also that among the middle-class a Miller of Dee attitude — 'I care for nobody, no not I/If nobody cares for me' — towards inconsiderate neighbours was more usual then. Anyway my grandfather's dog-poisoning by proxy was not as bad as Charles Dickens' ordering an offending dog to be shot and to be flogged before it was shot. At nineteen I was amused as I thought of this story about my grandfather and I more or less approved of what he had done. I certainly approved of the humane attitude I believed he had had towards human beings. He had never beaten or struck his children, my father had told me, and he had sent my father and my uncle Vernon to a Noncomformist boarding-school where corporal punishment hadn't been used, a very different kind of school from socially-superior 'Rugtonstead' (as I named it in a satirical poem I wrote there) to which my mother had wished and where my father had consented that I should go. My grandfather, however, had not been an unauthoritarian parent, and he had given my father and my uncle no choice at all of the jobs they were to do in life: he had decided that my father, the elder son, should be the one to begin to clear the family name of what was in those days the social slur of being connected with trade, and should become a doctor, and that Vernon should go into the family wholesale grocery business so that its profits would remain in the family. (My father would have done well in the family firm but hated being a doctor, though he made quite a successful business out of his medical practice and took on three partners before he finished, whereas Vernon disliked business even more than he would have disliked being a doctor.) But of all the things my father had told me about my grandfather much the most important, so it seemed to me as I stood facing his books on the shelves in the dining-room, was that at the age of forty after considerably improving the profitability of the family business, he had taken on a partner to do most of the work while he himself went into a semi-retirement which gave him the leisure to learn languages and to visit many of the countries of Europe including Russia (where he was arrested temporarily in Nijni Novgorod because of a mis-understanding about his passport) and to accumulate these books here nearly all of which he had read, as was evident from his pencilled notes in their margins. He had made money not for the sake of making money but to become free from the servitude of making money and to enable himself to live the only kind of life that I, at nineteen, thought worth living. I was not yet aware of another side of his character which later on I was to consider even more important — his political radicalism, though I was aware that there were suprisingly many books about Cromwell and the Commonwealth period of English history on the shelves of the bookcases in this house.

I was still thinking with admiration of my grandfather's early semi-retirement from business when my grandmother came into the room again.

'I have found them,' she said, holding out towards me her spectacle-case which was open with the spectacles inside it.

Her smile now, like her moan earlier, seemed to be not just about the spectacles. It forgave me for omitting to come and talk to her first before occupying myself with the books. Perhaps, almost, it apologised to me for the moan. And immediately, as if she did not want me to begin to think that she would like me to stop looking at the books and to talk to her now, she turned and still smiling went out of the room. But this time instead of feeling guilt about her I felt absolved of it. Or, rather, it became transformed into a guilt about my Uncle Vernon, whose voice I thought I heard coming suddenly from the direction of the front door, though I soon realised that he couldn't have returned from work as early as this and that the voice was really Hugh's, strangely similar to Vernon's in spite of its being so much younger than his, speaking to our grandmother. Hugh did not come into the dining-room. I recognised that up to this moment my attitude to Uncle Vernon had remained almost as it had been in my childhood: I had hardly ever considered him as someone who had an existence other than for myself and Hugh. He had continued in my feelings to be the Uncle Vernon who had always understood so well what would please us, who had played bat-and-trap with us in the garden, who had made paper boats for us, who had rushed down the hill outside this house so fast holding the hand of Hugh on one side of him and of myself on the other that we expected to be run off our feet at any moment, who had sent us all presents both on our birthdays and at Christmas, who had brought out from cupboards in the basement here — and had joined us in playing with — the toys and games that he and my father had had as boys, the lead soldiers which unlike our own were flat instead of three-dimensional and were much smaller than ours (though some he brought out were much bigger, flat also but wooden: green-uniformed Russians and busbied British of the time of the Crimean War, perhaps belonging once to my grandfather as a boy), the beautifully made Victorian table games, ivory spillikins, polished wooden squails, and above all the game called Cannonade or Castle Bagatelle which consisted of a large circular wooden tray-board surrounded by a six inch-high wall of green wire gauze and sloping down to a centre where a number of small marbles were placed and from where, by means of an ivory teetotum that each player spun in turn with the aid of string wound round its stem, these marbles would be violently propelled against the castles of ivory that stood only partly protected behind hoops of wire at the edge of the board. I had seldom thought of Uncle Vernon as someone whose experience when a young man of working in the family firm had turned him against capitalism and had caused him to refuse for the rest of his life to occupy any position in the firm other than that of an ordinary employee. I had been no more than moderately interested in him as the pacifist who would not fight in the Great War and had narrowly avoided being sent to prison then, and I had not been curious to know how he had avoided it. I am curious about this now and I think perhaps he may have been found medically unfit for military service: he was never a politically militant person, but I don't doubt he would have chosen to go to prison on principle if there had been no other way for him to get exempted from conscription. I had not appreciated him as the locally well-known amateur botanist he became, though I had been impressed when he had taken Hugh and myself once to a marshy field to see a sticky-looking sundew with a half-digested fly caught in it, nor had I thought of the relief and eagerness he must have felt in the evenings when after returning home here from work he had settled down to fill his notebooks — which he kept on a bookshelf in the old nursery, and I had several times surreptitiously looked into some of them — with notes not only on botany but on various other scientific and literary subjects too, including aeronautics, and also with drawings and short stories and poems, apparently not intended for publication. I had been aware that he had plenty of friends in the district and that on the mantelshelf in his bedroom there were many signed photographs, more than half of them from girls, yet I had not wondered why he had remained a bachelor and continued living here in his childhood home, nor why he attended morning and evening service every Sunday at the local Congregational chapel although he didn't give the impression of having religious beliefs (later he was to tell me he was an atheist and attended the services solely for social reasons), nor whether he was happy in his life. But my feeling of guilt about my past attitude towards Uncle Vernon didn't continue for long after my grandmother went out of the room. I believed he wouldn't have been in the least upset by my self-centred view of him if he had become aware of it, as he very probably had become years ago. Resolving that in future I would try to see and value him as he truly was, I was about to take down the anthology from the bookshelf once again when the sharply disturbing realisation came to me that the poems I had been writing during my months at Rouen, and had been well satisfied with there, were just as superficial and immature in their own way as were the ideas I had hitherto formed of my Uncle Vernon and my grandmother and grandfather and of the life that had been lived in this house.

I became sure that these poems, which I had believed to be better than anything I had written before I had finally left Rugtonstead, though they used much the same deliberately decadent imagery that my revulsion against the false healthiness and arduous optimism of the official Public school ethos had led me to use in the later poems of my Rugtonstead period, were in fact worse than these. Perhaps I had achieved certain technical improvements, but the feeling in the Rouen poems was shallower, no doubt because I had experienced none of the bitterness there which had given some force to the images of putrefaction and deformity that my late Rugtonstead poems had been full of. Now for a moment I had the belief that in future I would be able to change my poetry in the same way that I had already begun to change my attitude towards my Uncle Vernon and my grandmother and grandfather: I would purge it of fantasy, make it truer to life. But I soon knew that this change would be too great for me to be able to manage yet: it would mean an almost total abandonment of poetry as I had hitherto practised it, and I couldn't even vaguely imagine what the new truer-to-life poems would be like. A fear, much stronger than the guilt I had felt about my attitude towards my grandparents and my uncle, came upon me for my future as a poet. However within less than a minute this fear, as though it had been of no more significance than the shadow which a temporary clouding of the sun outside caused to pass across the bookcase in front of me, was dissolved by a hope that I need not completely abandon my present kind of poetry, that I could still make something good of it if while maintaining the technical advance I had made at Rouen I could at the same time deepen my poems both emotionally and intellectually. I became increasingly certain that my hope was realisable, and as I at last took down the anthology from the bookshelf again I had the elating conviction that I was at one of the most important turning-points I had yet reached in my development as a poet.

This conviction may have arisen in some way from my discovery of Clare's poem. I wasn't really at a turning-point otherwise in my poetic development at all, or if I was it was a very minor one compared with several previous turning-points I had reached during the four or five years since I had first begun writing poetry. For instance the one when at the age of fifteen, not long after I had fallen in love with a girl for the first time, I was in the nursery — as the room was still called — of our home in Essex. Hugh was sitting up at the large gate-legged table, getting his soldiers out of the long cardboard boxes in which they were kept, and I was sitting as I am now in an armchair, thinking. But ought I to let this episode come back into my mind now? My purpose in remembering the emotions of that afternoon when my grandmother came into the dining-room looking for her spectacles was to induce in myself the kind of mood which would make poetic creation easier for me at present. Have I perhaps been trying to evade my decision of last November that to-day should be the day when I would without fail start work again on the poem I had already begun writing then? There is still at least an hour of the morning left. How glad I would be later to-day if in spite of my having lost two-thirds of the morning I were to make a start at this moment. I will do that. There will be many later opportunities for remembering my life of forty and more years ago. I can think of it during afternoon walks, or in bed, or at almost any time except during mornings when I ought to be writing. And I shall need to think of it often if I am to be able to live the new poetic life in the present.

2

Hugh was sitting at the gate-legged oak table, getting his soldiers out of their boxes and expecting that very soon I would fetch mine from the toy-cupboard and would join him at the table. The room we were in seems almost nearer to me this afternoon than the chalk cliffs at the northern end of the bay towards which I am walking along the seashore at low tide now, and I can hardly believe that to return to it as it used to be is no less impossible for me in physical actuality than to travel to a self-contained galaxy millions of light years away in cosmic space. How and when did I leave it and become excluded from it for ever? My loss of it did not happen suddenly on the day when I went out of it and out of our home in Essex for the last time but was gradual and began on that morning years earlier when I continued sitting in the armchair, thinking, while Hugh at the oak table was assembling his Argyll and Sutherland Highlanders, the regiment he liked more than any other of his at that period.

He was too much occupied with standing the soldiers up on the table to wonder why I was delaying so long before bringing mine and joining him there. He was arranging his Highlanders not in lines but in a loose crowd as though they were waiting for the order to fall in on parade. He seemed not to have made up his mind yet what he most wanted to do this morning; he probably intended to let that be decided by some suggestion which might come to him from a chance grouping of a few of the soldiers, or by some idea I might put to him when I had brought mine out. He could just line them up in platoons and drill them, or perhaps he would prefer social visits between his officers and mine, or he might like me to propose Highland Games with tossing the caber (represented by a wooden pencil placed against the moveable arm of each officer-competitor in turn and then flung forward as Hugh or I vigorously manipulated the arm) and with long-jumping (which meant our sliding each competitor in turn on his lead 'stand' along a specially furniture-polished strip of the table surface, the winner being the one we managed to slide farthest without his falling over), or Hugh might have the idea of our arranging a rebellion by one of his or my officers and of our transferring all our troops on to the floor for a battle of the sophisticated kind (with dice and with measuring tape) which we had developed as we had grown from childhood into boyhood and which, because we would both be on the same side against the rebellion, could not lead to the overheated feelings there had been in some earlier battles when we had taken opposite sides. Hugh now, having got out as many of his soldiers as he for the moment needed, put their cardboard boxes away out of sight below the table on the seat of an unoccupied chair: he did not want the boxes to interfere with the illusion that the soldiers on the table were living individuals. He took hold of a kilted officer whom we had named Eyeglassy and who had binoculars which could be raised and lowered, and he inspected him intently, never lifting him from the surface of the table but lowering his own head until one eye was almost on a level with Eyeglassy's face, examining with happy fascination — as I knew because I had so often looked at individual soldiers of mine in just the same way — every distinctive detail of the face, the exact positioning of the black dots of Eyeglassy's eyes and of the pinker blobs in the middle of the paler pink of his cheeks and the precise slant of the scarlet streak of his mouth. Yet however absorbed Hugh at the moment was I knew he would very soon look up inquiringly at me, wondering why I hadn't got my soldiers out yet. I was becoming increasingly sure that I did not want to get them out.

They would not suit my mood, would on the contrary jar with it, and I needed above all else to continue to indulge fully in it. It had been a constantly recurring mood for the last three months ever since the Christmas holidays and through the Easter term at my Public school. It had begun after a Christmas party where I had met a girl of my own age whom I had not seen since we had been children at kindergarten together, or if I had seen her since then my being unable to remember any occasion on which I had done so showed that she had not made a deeper impression on me than when I had known her at the kindergarten. It was a mood of love. Her name — which had become so numinous for me that sometimes I hardly dared speak it to myself even in my thoughts — was Christine. And although as I speak it in my present thoughts it revives for me not the emotion but only a memory of the emotion it once aroused, I feel for the first time now during my walk along the beach how beautiful the sea, calm and faintly hazy with a matt bronze sheen on it towards the horizon, is looking this afternoon. At that Christmas party she seemed at first, with her dark hair plaited as formerly into two pigtails which had a ribbon tied in a bow at the end of each of them, and with her clear pink and white complexion so childlike still, not to have changed very greatly from the girl I had known at the kindergarten — where I had liked her as I had liked all the other children except John Wheeler, who was too aggressively boisterous, but I doubt whether I was aware that she was prettier than the other girls there though I did know she was cleverer and quicker at learning to read than the rest of us. By the end of the party, after I had danced with her and talked with her, she was transformed for me, and when I got home that evening I knew I had fallen totally in love with her. I met her at one more party afterwards during the same Christmas holidays, but I remember nothing about it except the feelings whose power in me it must have helped to increase. At nights I kept

28

myself awake for hours with exquisitely happy thoughts of her and I made vows to myself that whatever obstacles I might have to overcome I would marry her when I was old enough. In the daytime I often sang *Annie Laurie* to myself — her parents were Scottish, or 'Scotch' as I would have said then, and she spoke gently with a Scottish accent which had a slight childish huskiness in it still. Before I went back to Rugtonstead for the Easter term I wrote out Burns's poem *O My Luve's Like a Red, Red Rose* in my blood on a small piece of good writing-paper which I could always carry secretly about with me, though I found that my blood was not easy to write with. (In order to prevent it from coagulating too quickly I should have had to cut my hand more deeply than I wanted to.) I kept the paper folded up in a compartment of the leather purse my grandmother had sent as one of her Christmas presents to me; but after a week or two back at Rugtonstead I lost the purse, which however someone found and it was returned to me by one of the House prefects who had had no means of identifying its owner other than guesswork based on the poem and on his knowledge of my interest in poetry: he handed it to me with a perfectly straight face that I couldn't help admiring him for in spite of my loathing of the Rugtonstead prefect and fagging system. My love for Christine was sustaining to me in the life of exile which I regarded myself as living at this repulsive boarding-school more than a hundred miles away from her and from my home. My love for her was also before long the cause of my beginning to write poetry, and poetic creation became a happiness in itself which strengthened me further against the wretchedness of school. There had been very few days during the Easter term when I had failed to think of her, and now that I was back home for the holidays and within a quarter of a mile of where she lived she was in my feelings if not in my thoughts all the time. The question of how and when I would be able to meet her did not seem urgent to me yet: as she was on holiday from her day-school she would often be at home in the mornings and afternoons, and I had only to bicycle along Western Road and sooner or later I should catch sight of her at one of the windows of her house there, or more wonderful still she might happen to be coming out of the front gate just as I was passing. The thought of that was so exciting as almost to inhibit me from taking the action which might make it a reality; however I decided that this afternoon I would bicycle past her house. Meanwhile the only occupation — other than thinking of her — that I wouldn't find jarring or savourless would be to write poetry. I could write another poem about her.

'Aren't you going to get your soldiers out?' Hugh at last said.

'I don't think I will.' I tried to sound neither too wholly disinclined nor too indefinite. I explained: 'I rather want to do some writing.'

I brought out from my pocket the small notebook which I had used for writing my other poems in and which I always carried about with me. Hugh showed only a little surprise at my not wanting to join him, and no sign of being aggrieved. But I soon found that I had no eagerness to write a poem. I hesitated to open my notebook. By declining to join Hugh I had upset not him but myself. He was already wholly occupied with Eyeglassy once more. He no doubt supposed that my unwillingness to play with my soldiers was merely temporary, that I would be willing to-morrow or that perhaps I might get them out this morning in half an hour's time. But I knew that I would never play with them again; or if I did he would soon detect that I was a hypocrite playing not for my own enjoyment but to please him. I felt a painful regret. I was conscious of how much I was losing, a whole childhood of warm imagination which we had shared and which he, being nearly two years younger than me, would not lose yet even though it might be impaired for him a little by my defection. Our soldiers, or at least our officers, had been to us — and still were to him — individuals who could engage in many different kinds of human-seeming activity besides battles and rebellions, though not in any activity requiring female participation, such as weddings, because women soldiers or even Red Cross nurses, so far as we could discover, weren't obtainable; and, as I recognise now, our happy parading and drilling of our soldiers had not caused me to become in the least military-minded, had on the contrary made the reality of the Officers' Training Corps at Rugtonstead by contrast even less likeable than it would otherwise have been to me. But I was losing much more than the pleasure we had got from our soldiers; I was losing the whole life of our childhood; I was abandoning nearly everything that our home, and this room especially, had meant for us; I was renouncing the imaginings we had projected on to and incorporated into almost every object here. The big coloured map of the world hanging unrolled on the wall would no longer have the charm for me it had had when Hugh and I, not knowing the names of many of the countries, called Baffin Island the land of the Good Bobbies and Spitzbergen the land of the Bad Bobbies (I have forgotten why) and invented stories about these peoples as we ate our bread and milk for breakfast at the gate-legged table. The high black brass-railed fire-guard which, when Hans Andersen's story *The Constant Tin Soldier* was first read to me, I pictured as being in the nursery where the one-legged tin soldier had stood beside the looking-glass lake gazing at the beautiful ballet dancer, and which often afterwards evoked for me something of the feeling of that story, would from now on be nothing more than a fireguard. I was renouncing a life that four terms at Rugtonstead had failed to alienate me from and that I had been able to resume with ease during each of my three previous holidays away from that foul place.

I felt a nostalgia momentarily so strong that it might have

enabled me to get out my soldiers and to join Hugh at the table without revealing any sign of the treachery I had been nurturing in my mind against the imaginings we had shared; but a better way, less unconsonant with my mood of love, occurred to me of re-affirming my loyalty. I would write a poem about our soldiers, a short epic telling their history from the day when each of us was given his first box with nine of them in it. Love and poetic creation were cognate for me, had been born together; and any poem I wrote, whether about Christine or not, would be consonant with love. I would begin by describing our first soldiers as we saw them brightly new in their boxes, their legs and necks tied with cotton to a strip of white cardboard which could be taken out of the box. Or, no, perhaps I would say nothing about the boxes, because this might make our soldiers seem less alive than they soon became for us. Hugh's first ones were Marines and mine were Grenadiers, and each of us had an officer and eight men. (Some of the boxes we were given later contained ten soldiers, but the advantage of the larger number was outweighed by the disadvantage that there was no officer among the ten.)When we had each been given soldiers of several regiments we crowned Hugh's first Marine officer with a Plasticine or coloured wax crown as King Marine, and my Grenadier officer — I think because we had once involved him in a sea battle on the nursery floor — we crowned as King Seagren. Later we arranged a rebellion by General Loutro, a soldier made of solid lead and bigger than any of our others, whom we allowed temporarily to overthrow both our kings. My poem would rigorously avoid condescension towards our past imaginings: there would be no suggestion in it of a childish story told by an adult for the amusement of adults. I would try to present our imaginings just as they had been to us, in all their warmth and comfortable excitement. They were entirely worthy of being put into a poem, I believed, because though they belonged to a pre-poetic stage of my life they were a preparation without which not even my love for Christine could have caused me to become a poet.

As I opened my notebook, eagerly, I not only felt freed from nostalgic regret for · lost childhood but also I was conscious once more of the incomparable happiness of being in love. The need to savour this happiness for a while again after having half-forgotten it during the past two or three minutes made me delay starting to think how my poem would begin. I recognised that I would rather be in love than return to even the happiest games and imaginings I had had in my childhood, and a poem about them — however good it might be as a poem — couldn't satisfy me as much as my poems about love. Nevertheless I was determined to write it, if only out of loyalty to Hugh. But mightn't I be able to give it greater strength and depth if I wrote it about Hugh's and my childhood as a whole instead of solely about our soldiers? I looked at the map on the wall behind Hugh's head and then at the window with its white-painted iron bars that had been put up across its lower sash for our safety long ago but had not been removed yet although Vaughan and Laura had become old enough to be in no danger of tumbling out, and a clear awareness came to me such as I had not had at any time before of how protectively enclosed and also how self-sufficient our life in childhood here had been — not that we hadn't had quite friendly contact with several other families in the town, but we had felt we were in some way special and different from them. I did not want my poem to be about this.

The sight of the two narrow bands of embroidered white material looped round the lower part of the curtains to hold them drawn back from the window reminded me of why my mother had substituted these bands some years ago for the tasselled silk cords that had been there before. She had chosen the silk cords when the house next to ours was being built. It belonged to a prosperous draper named Peterson, and my mother was critical of the taste exhibited by several

33

features of its design as it went up; but when it was finished and there were curtains in every window with tasselled silk cords round them exactly like her own she was angered, not flattered as my father suggested to her she should have been. She removed, and threw away, all the cords from her curtains on the same day that she noticed the imitation, as if they had become unwashably soiled, and within a week she had put up the embroidered bands in place of them. This action of hers, although I couldn't have been older than seven at the time, had seemed rather absurd to me even then, but now my love for Christine made me think of it as revealing an attitude which typified the way my mother regarded too much of the world outside our home. She might not feel towards any of the other families we knew in the town the kind of antagonism she showed towards the Petersons — an antagonism that had no doubt played its part in causing Hugh and me not to become friendly with the two Peterson boys who were about the same age as ourselves, and they and we had once had a stone-throwing battle in which they, less ignorant of the world than we were, had got the better of us because they had already learned to throw overhand while we were still only able to throw underhand; however there were families that, though she never spoke to us unfavourably of them and was willing for us to meet them, I sensed she had reservations about, and one of these families was Christine's.

Sitting in the nursery with my notebook open in my hand I still did not begin the poem I intended to write about Hugh's and my soldiers. I thought of my mother's outlook on the world. I felt no, or very little, resentment against her. Such a negative emotion could not easily have co-existed in me with my love for Christine, and if I did feel it a little it was incomparably weaker than the resentment I had sometimes felt against her while I had been a child without any general ideas at all, as for instance in quite early infancy when because of something she'd done which I've since forgotten I had revengefully and secretly torn out several of the gilt-edged pages of her white kid-leather-bound Book of Common Prayer, a book I believed she treasured; or on another occasion when she had been getting Hugh and myself ready for a party we'd been invited to by a family called the Cullises, who'd never invited us before and who lived in a big house, and she had been making a greater fuss than usual about our clothes and hair, I had said to her with a child's venomous percipience 'You only want us to go there because they are rich'; or more recently when after she'd discovered with disproportionate horror that small patches of the hair of both Vaughan and Laura had inexplicably become infested with nits, and after she'd scrubbed the patches frenetically enough to produce small rawnesses on the children's scalps, she had warned me that unless I kept myself cleaner I would certainly get lice too, and I had been stung into retorting 'I would rather get those than the mental lice you've got.' Although remembrance of these incidents did not give me any such feelings of remorse and sadness as I was to have forty-five years later when soon after I retired to my present home I found the kid-leather-covered prayer book in the room which used to be my mother's bedroom, my love for Christine helped to bring me a little nearer than I had been before to a sympathetic understanding of my mother. I asked myself why she had come to have the outlook she had, and I thought it might be because of experiences of hers during that younger part of her life which she had never been willing to tell us anything much about. I knew from my father that her parents had owned a large public house and that the sale of this had provided most of the considerable sum of money which a few years after their early deaths (from occupational phthisis, as I now suppose) had enabled her to travel on her own in Europe and Palestine and the United States, and in Egypt too where she had met my father travelling with his father. Had she perhaps, as a young girl living in the upstairs rooms of the pub, glimpsed and been unable to forget something of the sordidness of the lives of the men and women who came into the bar-rooms below? Or perhaps when, after trying for a short while to become an actress, she had trained to be a nurse at a hospital in the East End of London, she had seen what poverty was, and ever since then her ruling concern had been to ensure that her own life and the lives of those she loved should be as unlike the lives of the poor as possible. I knew she loved me and her other children, though no doubt there were times when she regretted losing the freedom which we had caused her to lose. Her frequent reproving of us for not caring enough about our appearance, for not cleaning our teeth properly, for being round-shouldered (at one time in my childhood she got me to wear, though not for long, a contraption made of corset-like material to pull my shoulders back), was due not to any anxiety about what other people might think of her as our mother but to a fear that unless we were kept on the right path we might when we grew older slip further and further down toward the social abyss which since her first glimpses of it she had never been able to become wholly unaware of. And her own children were not the only ones whose physical well-being she worried about: more than once when I had opened the door to go into the downstairs room which we called the morning-room I had come upon a group of children brought in by her from the street who were eating the bread and dripping she had provided for them and who gave me looks of not unfriendly curiosity very different from the looks of scorn accompanied by jeers I sometimes got from similar-seeming children outside in the street. And weren't there many other things she had done since her own childhood which were to her credit? Had she been wrong to travel, and to educate herself, and to engage fräuleins and later on mademoiselles as nurses or governesses for us so that we should learn some French and German early, and to admire the Indians and the Chinese, and, together with my father, to make our home a place where we could not grow up ignorant of the great musicians or painters or writers? I knew that but for my home I might never have begun to be a poet. In spite of its causing us to feel we were somehow special and different from other people in the town, a fault which my love for Christine had helped me recognise for the first time that morning as I sat in the nursery with my notebook in my hand, I would never repudiate my childhood home. And a few minutes after telling myself this I started to write the poem about Hugh's and my soldiers.

I do not repudiate my childhood home now. Here at the foot of the chalk cliff which during my summer holidays when I was a child I used to see in the distance but never walked as far as, let me decide that in future I will think more often of my childhood. By remembering my earliest imaginings, just as much as by remembering my adolescent life after I had begun to write poetry, I can help myself to sustain a state of mind which will be favourable to poetic creation in the present; and how would I be able to think of my poetically creative adolescence with true understanding if I didn't first think of the pre-poetic childhood out of which it developed?

My will to create in the present certainly needs strengthening. Not that I haven't made progress during the last three of the eight weeks since I retired: I have managed to produce almost as many lines of my poem as I had hoped to in the time, and their quality is adequate. Yet every morning I seem to have a harder struggle to get started, because of the disgust and anger agitating me after I've read the newspaper at breakfast. This morning I lost nearly threequarters of an hour, though there was nothing outstandingly vile in the news — no reference to American imperialism's nuclear bombers which are said to be in the air 'all round the clock' and to be loaded up with bombs ready for use at any moment (the sound of heavy aero-engines I can hear out to sea at this instant could be from one of these bombers), nothing to remind me that the Soviet leaders have broken the moratorium on bomb-testing which they unilaterally declared not long ago (and which gave me hopes of them once again for a while) and have thereby presented the American imperialists with a colourable pretext for starting up their tests again, no reference to orbital fighters or to the preparations for chemical and biological warfare that are being made at Porton not so very many miles from here, none or hardly any of the nauseously euphemistic phrases that capitalist newspapers normally use in articles about weapons of mass murder, as for instance 'the teething troubles of guided missiles'; no, the loathing and fury which delayed my getting down to work this morning were due not to anything the newspaper said but to what it did not say, to the absence in it of any hint of protest against the mega-massacres that capitalism is planning for us. But if I suppose that by deciding not to read the newspaper at breakfast, and by thinking more about my childhood, I could insulate the act of poetic creation from feelings of hatred and horror such as have been making it more of a struggle for me every morning, then I am contemptibly deceiving myself.

This small seaside town to which I've retired is not a fairyland where hydrogen bombs have no significance. The new poetic life I came here to live must fail from the start if, like the earlier poetic life I tried to live before I joined the Communist Party, it does not include political action against the external causes of feelings which obstruct creativity in me. Why haven't Elsie and I got in touch with the C.N.D. group here yet? Elsie isn't to blame: she did find that small advertisement in the local paper giving the name and address of the secretary of the group, but I threw the paper into the dustbin by mistake along with last week's rubbish. By mistake? I suspect I may have been motivated by a fear that my return to organised political activity will inhibit me as a poet in the same way as my joining the Party did eventually. But there can be no grounds for such a fear, both because I am absolutely determined never to become so involved in C.N.D. activities as to have no energy left for poetry and also because the theoretical line adopted by C.N.D., however far short of Marxism it may be and therefore incompletely compatible with the line I need to take in my poems, cannot produce an anti-creative conflict in me between my loyalty to the organisation and my poetic conscience — as the Party, which I had totally committed myself to, did during the period when it was becoming increasingly revisionist and non-revolutionary. Of course there is always the risk that in spite of my firmest intentions my C.N.D. activities will become so demanding that they will encroach upon my poetry-writing, but there is a certainty that if I remain politically inactive the external world will arouse such intolerable feelings in me that sooner or later they will bring my writing to a stop.

I will walk back along the beach and instead of returning directly to the house I will go into the town. I will call in at the newsagent's. I will try to avoid looking anxious. I will ask him if he can get me a copy of the issue of the local paper in which the C.N.D. advertisement appeared. He may even have a copy still in the shop.

3

I find it difficult this afternoon to think of anything except yesterday evening at Dan and Myra's house, where Elsie and I met the local C.N.D. group for the first time. Twenty minutes ago I left Elsie at work in our garden weeding the flower-beds, as she especially enjoys doing while the soil is wet enough to make the weeds easy to uproot, and I came to walk by myself along this cliff path (always preferable to most other paths after heavy rain, because it's asphalted) with the intention of trying to remember everything I could about my imaginings and imaginative impressions in early childhood; but even my awareness at this moment of the Beulah-chapel ice-cream factory behind the row of holm oaks not far from the path here cannot help to get me into a mood for remembering anything before yesterday. My mind seems capable of seeing and hearing only Dan and Myra and the boys and girls who were in their front room. And why shouldn't I allow myself to go on thinking of them all? Yesterday evening's meeting has already done more than any of my recallings of my remoter past to stimulate me poetically in the present. This morning although I read the newspaper at breakfast I was able to get down to work on my poem almost immediately afterwards, and I progressed better with it than during any previous morning since my retirement began.

On our way to Dan and Myra's house I was nervous, in spite of our having taken a liking to them both when they had called at our house three days before in response to the letter Elsie had written to Myra saying we wanted to join the local C.N.D. group. My nervousness was not unlike what I felt thirty years ago when I first contacted the Communist

Party, though at that time it was more intense and was due to my wondering whether I might be regarded as a middle-class interloper by the Party members, whereas yesterday evening it was a delayed after-effect of my experience of being driven eventually to leave the Party. The shock of that experience was still strong enough in me, twelve years afterwards, to make me doubt whether I would be capable of becoming politically active ever again. But Myra, who came to open the front-door to us when we arrived at her house, did not look in the least like a Party member. This wasn't because of the gaiety of the smile she gave us, almost as though she was welcoming us to some lively social celebration rather than to a serious political meeting (I can remember Party members whose manner of welcome would have been much the same), nor was it merely because the fashion of the clothes she wore and the way she had done her hair were strikingly different from anything to be seen among women Party members when Elsie and I had been in the Party: no, what made her unlike a Party member was the *obviousness* of the interest she took in her appearance, and one indication of this interest was how different she looked from when we had first met her three days before. Although she had seemed just as beautiful then, her high backward-slanting hair-do was much smoother now and it reminded me not of a beehive but of the head of Queen Nefertiti, as did the skin of her face which — even if I discounted the orange light upon it from a shaded electric bulb in the hall passage — gave the impression of being more deeply coloured than before. But however changed she might appear, I felt once again, as I had after she'd been at our house three days before, that we'd known her for months rather than for only two or three hours. Elsie and I have re-discovered what we were so well aware of years ago when we were still in the Party — that people who share our views about things that matter seem closer to us on the day we first meet them than other people we've known for a

41

very long time who are not opposed to imperialism or to nuclear weapons. There seemed no difference in Dan, who came out from the doorway of the front sitting-room to welcome us as we began to follow Myra along the hall passage. The orange light did not make his longish wavy hair and curly beard appear any less golden, and this time I was not automatically disconcerted by these as I had for an instant been when we'd first met him. My brief dismay then had probably been a transient reversion not to a prejudice unconsciously retained from my Public School upbringing but to a belief I had accepted during my Party years that a left-wing militant ought not to risk antagonising possible political converts by flouting conventional ideas about unimportant things — such as fashions in clothes and appearance. But after Dan and Myra had been at our house the thought came to me that beards were not as unconventional or unfashionable now as they had been during my university days when the upper-class young had played a game of exclaiming 'Beaver' at the sight of a bearded man, and that young men with short hair and neat clothes were beginning to look odd. Dan's hair and beard, as he brought Elsie and me into the front-room where other members of the local C.N.D. group were sitting, seemed entirely proper and right.

About fifteen members were there, most of them seeming even younger than Dan and Myra. A large coal fire was alight in the fireplace. Myra coming in behind us said, 'Here are Mr and Mrs Sebrill.' She emphasised the 'are', as if to let us know that she and Dan had just been telling the others about the two of us who were now, very welcomely and rather wonderfully, present in actuality. There were many smiles of pleasure. Dan led us to two chairs which unlike most of the others in the room were upholstered and had evidently been reserved specially for us. As soon as we'd sat down, a boy, who might have been seventeen or perhaps younger and who would certainly have been described by some middle-aged opponents of C.N.D as looking like a real tough, asked Myra, 'What about slogans?' Myra answered, 'We'd better decide on those this evening, and we shall need to have another meeting before the end of this week for volunteers to help in painting them on placards and banners.' 'Yes,' the same boy said, 'but what I meant was' — he hesitated — 'should we shout the slogans when we're marching in the demonstration?' Myra considered this, then said, 'Well, Kevin, my own feeling is that a completely silent march would have a better effect on people in this part of the country.' Kevin accepted her opinion, without arguing, and so did the other boys and girls in the room. I got the impression, which was strengthened as the meeting went on, that they regarded Myra with very great respect and admiration. Next, a dark-haired girl who had an extraordinarily lovely face asked when the printer would have the leaflets ready; and sitting beside her a good-looking boy with strangely tidy hair and clothes made the suggestion, as soon as Myra had answered the girl's question, that it would be useful if local shopkeepers could be got to display the leaflet in their windows. I realised that Elsie and I must have arrived after the meeting had begun — evidently Myra had made a mistake three days before in telling us that it would begin at eight o'clock — and when we had arrived punctually at that time she and Dan had interrupted the meeting to come and greet us at the front door. I soon realised also that the interruption had been typical of the informality with which the meeting was being conducted. There seemed to be no one acting as chairman — though Dan and Myra were obviously regarded by the others as leaders in the discussion about arrangements for the coming demonstration — and no one was taking down minutes. I could guess what Elsie must be thinking about this. I too was rather shocked by it at first. The necessity of conducting meetings in a business-like way had been deeply impressed upon us when we had been members of the

Communist Party. But formal correctness had not saved the Party from becoming infected with revisionism. As the meeting continued I wondered whether the kind of spontaneity which Dan and Myra seemed to be encouraging in this C.N.D. group might not be healthier than the Party's correctness had eventually turned out to be.

The discussion got on to the subject of dress and personal appearance. The line that both Myra and Dan took about this was more like what I would have expected from them if they had been Party members and it was a line that wasn't altogether in keeping with their own dress and appearance. Myra asked whether the girls thought a good impression might be made if they wore hats while they were marching, but they soon showed that they didn't think so, and the boys agreed with them. Everyone however accepted the idea put forward by Dan that any oddity in clothes or aggressiveness in behaviour which might distract attention from the serious purpose of the demonstration ought to be avoided, and he evidently felt encouraged to go on to say — though mildly and with a smile — to a girl sitting next to Elsie: 'I think perhaps it might be better not to wear jeans.' She had a maturely pretty face, her hair seemed deliberately unkempt, her clothes had a look of studied drabness, and she wore a heavy chain-like necklace. She answered him with a similar mildness, and without the faintest hint of pertness, 'But you wear a beard.' Dan appeared to be on the point of arguing that this was quite different and then to realise that it wasn't, and he smiled again, this time in admission that she was right. I thought of my relationship as a schoolmaster with pupils of her age whom I had taught during my working years — how far short it had fallen, despite all my efforts, of the equality which I saw demonstrated between this girl and Dan. Almost always the school had come between me and them: I had seldom been able entirely to forget they were part of an institution to which I had been forced by economic need to sacrifice my

44

freedom and which required that I should exercise authority over them, and they in turn couldn't help seeing me primarily as a master at the school and as being in some degree responsible for whatever the school did to them. But after ten minutes among the boys and girls at the meeting in Dan and Myra's sitting-room I already felt sure there was nothing unfree about my attitude towards them or about theirs towards me. We had come together voluntarily because we were opposed to nuclear weapons. We were equals in a campaign which was the only good thing politically that had come out of England since the second world war — a campaign, I went on to think as I sat listening to them, that had already spread to other countries and could be the first step towards the development of a consciously anti-imperialist movement among the young all over the capitalist world.

They discussed arrangements for the public meeting which would be held immediately after the demonstration. One important aim of the march, Myra said, would be to advertise the meeting and attract people along to it. They discussed how much they could afford to spend on advertisements in the local press. Elsie asked about local churches and chapels: whether the vicars and ministers had been circularised. Myra said that they hadn't been yet, but that it was a very good idea, and she would circularise them, though there were a surprisingly large number of them and the postage would be quite costly. I wanted to say that Elsie and I would like to contribute towards the cost, but I felt that this might sound ostentatious and that no doubt finance would be discussed later, so I said nothing. Several times before the meeting finished I came near to adding something to the discussion, but I never succeeded in bringing myself to the point of actually doing so. I wondered whether the others might think my silence odd, though they showed no sign that they did. I hoped Dan and Myra would find an explanation of it in what I had told them about myself when they had come to our house.

I had told them I would not want to take too prominent a part in the local group because of my past membership of the Communist Party, which if it became known outside the group could antagonise people who might otherwise have been won over to support C.N.D. Myra had disagreed, had said that there were many ex-members, and current members too, of the C.P. who were very active in C.N.D., and that anyone was welcome in it regardless of his or her political colour provided he or she was willing to support its aims, and that there was no danger of its being thought to be dominated by the C.P. — because the C.P. leaders had been completely opposed to it at the start, calling it an organisation of 'divisive maximalists', and had recently ceased to oppose it openly only because so many of their rank-and-file members were in favour of it. I hadn't been able to dispute these points Myra had put to us, and Elsie had fully agreed with her, yet I made it clear that I would still be reluctant to take anything but a minor part in the local group. I didn't recognise the true reason for my reluctance till half-way through the meeting yesterday evening as I sat silent in Dan and Myra's room.

I was inhibited, I became aware then, not because I was afraid that my former membership of the C.P. might scare off potential recruits to the local C.N.D. group but because during the past few years I had allowed my disillusionment with the Party to numb my will for political activity of any kind. The disillusionment had been cumulative: first I had discovered that the leaders of the British C.P. had degenerated into non-revolutionaries who believed or pretended to believe in the possibility of attaining socialism mainly by means of parliamentary elections, and then that the Soviet C.P. had become just as revisionist as the British and had approvingly published in *Pravda* in 1951 the whole of the British C.P's lengthy reformist policy statement, *The British Road to Socialism*; and finally I had come, culpably late, to recognise that propagandists against Stalin, whatever reactionary political sympathies some of them had been motivated by, had not been spreading lies about him when they had accused him of being responsible for the imprisonment of very large numbers of people who had broken no laws and were not counter-revolutionaries at all (though the propagandists often failed to admit the probability that at least some indigenous enemies of socialism and also some foreign agents did commit acts of sabotage in the Soviet Union) and for the use of torture as a method of extracting confessions of guilt, and for the execution of many genuine Leninists. However, nothing that had happened in the Soviet Union or in the British C.P. could justify the political inactivity I had sunk into during the years since I had ceased to be a Party member. The poems I had become able to write after leaving the Party had, it was true, been indirectly political, but hardly anything else I had done had been much at variance with what the imperialists and their agents wanted from all those ex-C.P. intellectuals whom they couldn't bribe to serve them actively. Now, in Dan and Myra's room among these boys and girls who not having had the wounding that Elsie and I had had in the Party were wholly free from any taint of defeatism — and were perhaps almost too optimistic, expecting the walls of the nuclear Jericho to fall at the first blast of the C.N.D. trumpet — I still could not recover enough political confidence to take part in their discussion about the coming demonstration. But I already knew they would help me to overcome my inertia soon, possibly at the very next meeting of the group.

At the end of yesterday's meeting, when Elsie and I were standing up ready to leave, I did at last say something: I asked whether there was anyone who was going our way and would like a lift in our car. A tall fair-haired girl said she would. When she was in the car with us she told us her name was Denise Dobson. She was very self-possessed and talked with assurance. I thought her age might be twenty-two or twenty-three. She talked about the parents of a friend of hers, who she said were very anti-C.N.D., and she referred to the friend's mother as 'Ann's poor dear mama'. She said that her own home was in the same road as the vicarage but that the vicar had never called on her parents. I couldn't help feeling that in these days when many households would not be particularly keen on having a visit from a vicar he was hardly to be blamed for not calling. She spoke familiarly of a local school. I, unable to be sure whether she was a pupil or a teacher there, asked if she was a teacher, thinking that if she wasn't I would be making less of a bloomer than if she was and I assumed her to be a pupil. She said she was a 'student', and I knew she did not mean she was a student teacher: she was using a word by which pupils recently, perhaps as a counter to being referred to officially as 'school children', had begun to prefer to describe themselves. I soon realised, when she told us what exam she was working for, that she was not even in the Sixth Form but still in the Fifth. I felt that my mistake must have made me seem slightly ridiculous to her; and later on, just before we arrived at the road in which her home was, she told us with undisguised scorn how the vicar had shown in conversation with her the other morning at the bus stop that he thought she was a teacher. Seemingly she had no intention of getting at me when she recounted this incident but had been reminded of it by my mistake, and possibly what roused her scorn for the vicar's mistake was that unlike me he lived in the same road as she did and she considered he ought to have known more about her. Nevertheless, even after she had got out of the car and we had said good-night to her and I had driven on again, I still felt rather foolish; so yet another new element was added to the accumulation of uncustomary emotions which had been building up in me during the evening. When Elsie and I were alone together once more, and as we talked on and on about the meeting we had attended and about everyone we had seen there, our excitement at having taken the first step towards breaking out of our long political isolation became increasingly strong. After we'd gone to bed we could not get to sleep for hours. I was unable to become calmer even though I warned myself that if I went on like this my writing would be bound to suffer next morning.

It did not suffer. I've seldom managed to start work with less delay after breakfast than I did to-day, and I added more to my poem than on any other morning since I retired here. Yes, but how do I feel about the quality of what I added? I suspect now that one reason why I have been thinking about yesterday evening instead of about my childhood imaginings as I intended when I started out on this walk is that those would have forced me to admit to myself how bleak and bare in comparison what I wrote this morning is. It may not be bleak to the point of lifelessness like the beginnings of the poems I tried and failed to write during my later years as a still loyal member of the Party, but its being so bitterly political could soon cause it to become poetically lifeless even though its theme is the need for the poet to break with an increasingly revisionist Party whose hold on him has been hindering him more and more from writing poetry. My present poem is going to be a long one, and I ought to know that although remembrance of my childhood imaginings may make it seem in comparison bleaker than it really is they can help me better than anything else to keep it poetically alive as I continue it. Let me begin to remember them now, as I intended. I have time before tea to walk on for two or three more miles, and though there is a stationary wave-cloud attached like an ensign to the highest point of the down ahead of me I am sure the sky generally is becoming brighter than it was and there will be no more rain this afternoon.

The country surrounding the market town in Essex where I lived when I was a child had no hills as conspicuous as these downs, but except towards the south where the sewage farm was — which I found scarcely less interesting than hills — it was undulating rather than flat. I remember best a long straight lane, straight as a Roman road, branching off at right angles from the main road about two miles to the north-east of the town and rising very gradually until, just before reaching the horizon, it suddenly steepened and took a rightward turn out of sight behind a farm house and a few tall trees. Beside the outer bend of the lane, and opposite the farmhouse which was beside the inner bend, I used to like to see when we got there — and how did we get there? Presumably in the one-cylinder de Dion motorcar driven by our chauffeur Frederick on an afternoon when my father was not using it to visit his patients — I used to like to see a pond whose surface was covered with fine green scum, duck-weed no doubt. Although I don't think I ever saw ducks on it I did once see in the middle of it a weedless black spiral whorl of pond-water surrounded by weeds, and I wondered with excitement how a duck could have caused this and then have swum to the bank of the pond without leaving a black path between the whorl and the bank. But I am faking this memory. There wasn't a pond or a farmhouse at the top of the straight lane, though the lane and the de Dion (which had to zigzag from side to side of it to get up the steep bit) were real enough, and so was Frederick whose face with the port-wine stain birth-mark covering its left temple looked perpetually cheerful and who was always willing to respond to my curiosity about the mechanism of the car — not only when I was sitting beside him as he drove it, or when he was busy on such minor jobs as lubricating the clutch flywheel by means of a long feather soaked in castor oil, but even when he was engaged in something difficult such as trying to put right the differential which often went wrong. Why have I been pretending to myself that at the top of the straight lane there was a pond with a black whorl in the middle of its green surface? I suspect the reason may be that this seems more poetic to me than many of my actual imaginative impressions in early childhood, some of which were of a crude kind that only Freudians might consider very significant. But if I am to realise my aim of using past imaginings to stimulate myself poetically in the present I need to remember those I actually had and not to indulge in fabrications.

The earliest incident which made any impression on my imagination — and I am sure my memory of it must be first-hand because it is something my mother would never have told me about later on — was my being lifted up half naked by her and being rushed into the bathroom to be held out at arms' length over the bath into which there dropped instantly from me a long slim slip of bright yellow excrement, and the feeling I had towards it was not of Freudian possessiveness but of astonishment at the contrast between its yellowness and the bath's whiteness. Astonishment was also the feeling caused in me by another very early, though not at all scatological, incident that I remember at first hand: I was being held on someone's lap, not my mother's but a nurse's I think, while a man who was a visitor to our house took down the Swiss cow-bell which used to hang by its leather collar from a hook on the wall near the front door, and rang it close to my face. Freud would no doubt have been more interested in the imaginative wish I used to have, which I don't directly remember but which my parents told me later that I had expressed to them when I was three or four years old, to hang upside down in the butcher's shop like the carcases of sheep and pigs I had seen there. My parents, knowing little or nothing of psychoanalysis, laughed about this when they told me of it, and my subsequent life seems to show they were right to make light of it, as I have not grown up to get sexual pleasure out of being physically hurt — nor to visit specialist brothels on the Continent. They would not have laughed about the sensual fantasies — if they had known of them — which the sight of large-uddered cows, roped by the neck to the dark red iron railing in the market-place and being milked into buckets, suggested to me at the age of six or seven. I did not 'identify', as the psychological cliché goes, with animals; I may have wanted to hang naked upside down with my legs apart like the carcases in the shop but I am sure I did not want to be dead like them. The knacker's cart drawn by a smartly trotting horse up the road past our house and returning half an hour or so later at an equally smart pace (because although this time it was fully loaded it was going downhill into the town) and with four hoofs and shaggy fetlocks protruding from under a tarpaulin on a sloping platform at the back of it, impressed me yet did not make me sad about the slaughtered horse. The first death to arouse imaginative sympathy in me was of a bumble bee: I had seen it crawl with extraordinary slowness along the inner ledge of a window and then stop, and my father — fearing perhaps that I was going to get myself stung — came up to investigate, and said, 'It is dying.' Perhaps its smallness made its death comprehensible to me and, for a moment, infinitely pathetic. I must have killed many insects later on in my childhood without a qualm and with hardly a thought. Imaginativeness of a cruder kind caused me, as I was sitting on my chamber-pot in the bathroom one morning, to become angry with the thick cork bath-mat on the floor there — it may have got in my way while I was playing a game of wriggling forward on the pot across the floor — and to make a promise to myself that if ever when I was older I was given a box of tools for a birthday or Christmas present I would use the saw from it to cut that bath-mat in half; and quite a long time later, several years later perhaps, I did get a present of a box of tools and in a spirit of obligation to perform the act I had formerly imagined I did saw the mat in half, with considerable difficulty. Another type of early imagining produced, or was produced by, fear in me: for instance when, as a result of reiterated warnings from my mother that if I cut my hand in the garden and did not immediately wash it I might get lockjaw, I once for a week or more was frequently and apprehensively opening and shutting my jaws to test whether they were beginning to show signs of stiffness; and earlier, at the age probably of between two and three, when I was being taken in a slow train by my mother to be shown to an old aunt of hers who had brought her up after her parents had died, I saw in a siding a derelict railway-engine, a small one, covered all over with bright yellow-brown rust, and the fear which the sight of it strangely caused in me increased during our visit to the aunt and became almost terror when we started on our return journey, but to my relief I did not see the engine this time because darkness had fallen before the train passed the siding again.

A recurring nightmare which I used to have when I was a few years older had something about it resembling the process of conscious imaginative creation: I used to dream I was downstairs in our house when the frightening events of the nightmare started — they took various forms, but I especially remember dreaming I was alone in our dining-room in front of the fire which gave out the only light there was in the room, and gradually I was aware of three huge man-shaped shadows joined together like God the Father, the Son and the Holy Ghost rising slowly up the wall behind me and beginning to encroach upon the ceiling above my head — I would then rush terrified out of the room towards the staircase in the hall and run desperately up the stairs to the first landing, but no safety was there and I raced on up the second flight of stairs to the top landing where without an instant's delay I forced myself to sink through the floor, and as soon as I had sunk through I woke up in my bed and was blissfully freed from whatever monster had been pursuing me. I think my use of this escape-device is at least comparable though far from identical with the deliberate control which a poet or an artist of any kind exercises over his imaginings and which distinguishes a work of art from mere dreaming. I told Hugh about the device, with the extraordinary result that he found he could use it as a means of escaping from his own nightmares. However, after a while I became too confident in it, and one night after running upstairs in my dream and then sinking easily through the floor of the top landing I seemed to wake up as usual but very soon a tall white phantom rose at the foot of my bed, and it remained there till I was genuinely woken by my own real screaming.

There were perhaps signs of incipient poetic imaginativeness in an infantile soliloquy of mine which my parents overheard as I was looking out of the nursery window one night and told me about with fond amusement when I was older, and of which I, indirectly, remember only the words, 'Yes, it's the moon. But it's a bwoken moon.' Certainly there was poetic appeal for me in two sentences I can directly remember being spoken to me at different times by a nursemaid whom I would have wholly forgotten but for them: the first was about a man she pointed out to me from the nursery window who was walking along the pavement rather briskly and very erect with his waistcoated belly bulging out into a tight curve in front of him — 'There goes Mr. Pomposity,' she said, and though I did not know the meaning of this abstract word its alliterative plosiveness combining in my mind with my visual impression of the walking man ignited in me an amusement so intense as to be akin to poetic joy, and I laughed till tears wetted my face; the other sentence was one that she read out from a nursery-rhyme book, 'Froggie would a-wooing go', and she spoke the long vowel of the word 'a-wooing' in such a way — possibly because she herself was without a wooer and longed for one — that the word, whose meaning I couldn't have understood, was for me the most beautiful I had ever heard, comparable to the sound of a humming-top spinning at highest speed though with a mysteriousness which that sound never had. Often, unlike these two experiences, my early imaginings were accompanied and helped by physical activity on my part: as when I ran excitedly up and down the lawn picturing in my mind every detail of the toy watering-cart — particularly the sprinklers on either side of it and the lever beside the driver's seat for turning the water on and off — that I would have liked to be given for my birthday; or when during a hot afternoon Hugh and I and some other children were allowed into a field for haymaking, and action gave the lead to imagination as after flinging ourselves about with abandon on the hay we began a hay-battle which had none of the anti-imaginative discomforts of battles with snow or water or stones and in the course of which we built seemingly huge fortifications not much less quickly than we were able to conceive them; and my extreme physical delight then had something resembling poetic feeling in it, just as later on I was able to feel something like physical delight in reading or composing poetry. Bodily activity was an almost essential accompaniment also to the stories I used to tell myself each afternoon when I was sent upstairs for an hour's 'rest' as it was called, in my bedroom — I seldom broke the rules to the extent of getting off the bed but I bounded up and down upon it — stories that were based on others I had listened to in the stillness of complete absorption when they had been read to me by my father who somehow made the time (he may have been less busy at this period than later because he was still only slowly building up his independent practice in an atmosphere of some hostility from the already established doctors of the town) to read to me on most days during the hour between the ending of his afternoon round of visits to patients and the beginning of his evening surgery.

My imagination was stimulated too by my mother's stories, though hers were seldom if ever fairy stories but were about actual events in her life. She told us about the travels she had set out on by herself before she was married: about seeing the midnight sun while drinking Swedish punch; about how she hadn't been able to restrain herself from smiling when one of two young Italian army officers sitting opposite to her in a train had commented to the other 'Una faccia simpatica', and how they had then simultaneously sprung to their feet, clicked their heels and bowed to her; about being frighteningly followed by a staring-eyed white-robed Arab in Cairo; about being on a liner adrift with a broken rudder in mid-Atlantic; about meeting the man in Constantinople who had since become Hugh's godfather; about her visit to Palestine where she had bought the flask of Jordan water which I was afterwards christened with (she did not know that my father in his efforts to loosen the cork in the flask before taking the Jordan water to the church, as he told me many years later, spilt much of the water accidentally into the kitchen sink and made the loss good by topping the flask up from the tap). But the story which impressed itself more vividly on my imagination than any other of hers, possibly because she was emotionally impelled to tell it more often than her other stories but also because I myself had witnessed some of the events she described in it, was about one of our nursemaids, Miss Bermondsey.

I doubt whether I ever knew Miss Bermondsey's Christian name (I assume she was a Christian). The fact that we never called her by it indicated that her status in the household was higher than that of the housemaid or the cook whom we never called by anything but their Christian names and whose surnames I never knew. The social origin of most nursemaids at this period was probably lower than that of most governesses — though I don't think any of the governesses we had later came from a family of professional status or was a vicar's daughter like Anne Brontë — but Miss Bermondsey was petit bourgeois rather than working-class. She had very dark hair and a pale face, and she must have been unusually short and small-made because she appeared so even to me who saw adults in general almost as giants. She resembled a child, though an older child than Hugh and myself, in other ways too — especially in the way she could join in our games with as much enthusiasm (and it seems as I look back on it to have been entirely genuine) as if she had been one of us. When she took us out walking, to the near-by public park for instance, she would talk to us, unlike our previous nursemaid who used to find some other nursemaid to join up with and to talk with always about the same subject of 'fellows', ignoring us as far as was safely practicable — though on one of the occasions when this nursemaid met another who was in charge of a little girl called Elizabeth they became very interested in trying to get me to ask her to marry me. I did, after showing some shy reluctance, at last ask her, not seeing the point of it but feeling it must be all right because they were so insistent about it, and as soon as I'd said the words that they had been urging me to say, 'Elizabeth, will you marry me?' they burst out into screams of laughter which I realised with shock were at my expense. Several times when Miss Bermondsey took us to the park she carried with her the football I had been given for a birthday present — a proper though small football made of leather and having a rubber bladder inside it — for the three of us to play with on the grass. One morning it rolled off the grass and across a path and into the lake where the swans and mallards and moorhens and the Chinese goose were. The sight of that lake in my mind now — we used to call it 'the pond', though it must have been almost a quarter of a mile long and at least a hundred yards broad — fills me with the keenest nostalgia. At one end of the pond there was a red-brick bridge, not quite hump-backed but with its parapet curving up from either side towards the middle, and below the parapet were four arches, three of them dummies bricked-up somewhere underneath and the fourth open right through to allow water from the pond to flow into a stream which eventually reached the river Thames. It was this bridge which, when my father first read the story of Great Claus and Little Claus to me, I saw in my imagination as the one over whose parapet the bully Great Claus at his own demand had been dropped by the wily Little Claus into the river in a sack weighted with stones. The scenic background for many of the stories read to me at this time was provided by various other features of the park: such as the long tree-covered island in the middle of the pond; or the two ivy-covered lodge buildings, on either side of the park entrance, one of which had been converted into a public shelter and was attractive to Hugh and me because of the echo it gave when we shouted inside it but was also alarming to us because of its insanitary smell; or above all at the far end of the lake, the sloping wood with the narrow path through the middle of it and the stream running along its lower edge to pass through a weed-clogged grating into the pond. But the small football floating on the pond just out of reach from the path never became a background feature for me in any story that was read to me or that I invented for myself during my afternoon rests, because it — together with later events in which Miss Bermondsey was involved — was in itself a story and occupied the foreground of my imagination whenever I thought of it.

I am fairly sure Miss Bermondsey and not Hugh or I gave the ball the kick that sent it across the path into the pond. I felt hardly any distress at the happening, probably because she herself showed such active concern about it, running immediately to the water's edge, going down on her knees in spite of the sharp gravel and stretching her arm so far that she seemed almost about to overbalance and managing to touch the ball with the tips of her fingers but unfortunately pushing it farther out on to the water, then hurriedly getting up and looking round and running towards some nearby trees under which after a while she found a piece of broken branch, though when she got back with this to the water it was just not long enough even to touch the ball which had drifted still farther out. She began picking up handfuls of small stones from the path and throwing them overhand with impressive accuracy so that they fell on the far side of the ball to create ripples which for a while seemed at least to halt if not to reverse its outward drift, but her final throw hit the ball itself on its near side and undid all the good her previous throws had done. We stood movelessly watching it float slowly towards the middle of the pond until she, sensing my despair which was all the keener because of the hopes temporarily raised in me by her confident attempts at rescue, said, 'It won't be lost. I'll fetch it when it reaches the other side of the pond'. I couldn't imagine how she would be able to do this, because even if the ball did travel right across there was a field on the other side which didn't belong to the park and there was a low wire-mesh fence in the water at the edge of the pond to prevent the ducks getting out on the field. I wasn't capable of wondering why she didn't go to the park-keeper's lodge to ask if he could help us. And on our way back home she couldn't find a gate into the field. But as soon as she had got us home she went out again, by herself, and after perhaps an hour she returned with the ball, having climbed a wall to get into the field, as she told us, and having stepped knee deep into the water to lift the ball from where it had come to a stop against the wire-mesh fence.

Other exciting things soon began happening during the period when she was our nursemaid. One night there was a burglary in the house, before my mother and father had come upstairs but while Hugh and I were already in bed. Miss Bermondsey made the discovery that all the drawers in the spare bedroom had been pulled out and emptied on to the floor. The police were called, and they searched the house, one of them shining his torch under my bed. No burglar was found, nor did anything seem to have been stolen, but after that night thefts began to occur regularly in the house. Money was stolen from most members of the household including even myself as well as the cook and the housemaid and Miss Bermondsey. She used to talk, excitedly, to Hugh and me about the mystery of the thefts, and her theory was that they must have been committed by the same burglar who had been interrupted while pulling out the drawers in the spare bedroom. I wasn't absolutely certain that some of the pennies had been taken from the little black money-box in which I kept them on a shelf in the toy-cupboard — my awareness of loss was not much clearer than a bird's might be from whose nest two eggs at most have been stolen out of a clutch of five or six — but I moved the money-box from the toy-cupboard and put it at the back of a wardrobe in our bedroom. After this I was quite sure that for some while none of my pennies disappeared. One evening while Miss Bermondsey was talking with Hugh and me about the thefts that were still going on in the house I proudly let her know how I had outwitted the thief by changing the place where I kept my money-box, and she asked me where I had put it and I told her, and next day when I went to look again I saw there were fewer pennies in the box than before. I don't think I suspected yet for an instant that she, who was so nice to Hugh and me, could be the thief.

The most sensational of all her thefts was committed while there were about fifteen people in the drawing-room whom my mother had invited for an evening of music. Miss Bermondsey had a brother who could play the violin, and she convinced my mother — who hadn't heard him play — that he was a very gifted musician. The local middle-class acquaintances my mother had invited to hear him may none of them have been really musical, but they were able without difficulty to recognise that Miss Bermondsey's brother, in spite of his black cravat and long hair, was an atrocious player. After the performance, when they went to get their coats from the hall before going home again, those of them who had left money or anything else of value in their pockets discovered that it was missing, though they were too polite to make a scene or even to mention their losses at the time. My mother, on hearing later what had happened, did not think it at all comic, and she was desperate until she had the idea of consulting her old friend Margie, my godmother, who was matron of a large hospital in a northern town and who had had experience of dealing with thieving among her nurses. Margie sent her a box containing a colourless powder which if it got on to anyone's hands would stain them indelibly blue. My mother put money as a bait in several not too conspicuous places about the house and sprinkled the powder on it. One morning she found Miss Bermondsey scrubbing her hands vigorously over the basin in the bathroom, and when my mother asked her what had happened she explained that she had spilt some ink, and she pointed for proof at a big ink stain across the pocket of the cotton pinafore she was wearing and also at a half-empty ink bottle standing on the ledge at the back of the basin. The detective who came to the house after my mother had telephoned the police-station said there would be no difficulty in obtaining a conviction, but my mother was unwilling to take legal action for fear of being dragged through the mud by the questions that defending counsel might put to her in the witness box. Miss Bermondsey went home the same day — leaving behind her, so my mother was to feel, a defilement, a horrible pollution, which lingered on in the house for many weeks if not months. Nevertheless my mother was able to smile when three days later after receiving a visit from Miss Bermondsey's parents she described to us how the father, a very portly man, announced that they were Mr and Mrs Berman — he was unaware apparently that his daughter had added 'dsey' to her name when applying for the post of nursemaid — and how he had protested that his daughter could not be a thief because he and her mother were people of substance in the world, and to prove it he drew out from his pocket a large round cream-coloured object which he said was an ivory chronometer, an heirloom worth at least a thousand pounds. I could not share my mother's horror at the thefts, but neither could I feel a liking for Miss Bermondsey any longer, and certainly I was incapable of recognising her thieving as a sign of a spiritedness in her nature and of a desire to put colour and excitement into her restricted life. Yet she became for me a more impressive person than she had been before, and during my afternoon rests I used sometimes to think about the things she had done while she had been with us, and these came to have almost the same kind of interest for me as the imaginary happenings in stories that were of my own invention.

Equally impressive, and even better than Miss Bermondsey at playing games with us like another child, was Uncle Edmund, though he was a writer of books, not a burglar. We called him Uncle Edmund but really he was my father's cousin. He was a small man with a pointed beard and he used to come roaring up the stairs on all fours pretending to be a lion. He was fond of playing funny tricks. Once when he was having Christmas dinner with us and we were discovering in our helpings of Christmas pudding the sixpences and shillings that had been put into it when it had been made, he found a gold sovereign in his helping and soon afterwards he pulled out from under the brandy-sauce-covered heap of pudding on his plate a gold watch, which however I saw to be connected by a gold chain to his waistcoat pocket. He also produced a hard gold sovereign from behind the lobe of one of my ears, quite painfully for me. At another time when I was with him on the platform of a railway station he pointed to a Lifeboat Society collecting-box there which was in the shape of a model lifeboat and he gave me a shilling and said 'Put it into the slot and a model life-boat just like that one will come out for you.' I can't be sure whether his motive was to get amusement from any disappointment I might show after putting the shilling in, or to teach me a moral lesson, or to excite my imagination: I think that he himself may possibly have half-hoped that a model life-boat might come out of the collecting-box for me if he wished hard enough that it should. One of my father's stories about him was that he had been invited once to take the place of a goalkeeper who had failed to turn up for a water-polo game in the sea beside the pier, and that during the first part of the game he had performed only moderately badly but after the change-over at half-time he was out of his depth and was soon seen to be clinging to one of the goal posts: he had explained afterwards that though he couldn't swim he had believed that he could will himself to do so for the occasion. On the railway-station platform when he gave me the shilling I couldn't think what part of the lifeboat-shaped collecting-box a model lifeboat could come out of, yet I didn't quite disbelieve him. After I had put the shilling into the slot and nothing happened he did not laugh or even smile, nor did his expression of face give any sign that he had ever told me a model lifeboat would come out, but I felt bewildered rather than resentful, and my admiration for him was not lessened. It increased as I grew older. When I was sixteen and had begun to write poetry he advised me to take warning from his own experience and never want to earn my living by writing: he himself had made money out of it to start with, had sailed his own yacht on the Solent and had bought his suits from the very best tailors, but he had had to give too much of his energy to producing sensational novels instead of poems and philosophical books which could bring him no money though they alone gave him any real satisfaction to write. I was impressed by his advice; and it did not weaken my determination to make poetry my main aim in life, no matter what unpoetic job I would have to do for a living.

When I was six or perhaps seven an episode in which Uncle Edmund played no part had probably a greater influence than he was to have on the direction my future imaginative development took. I was sitting in the dining-room facing the fireplace and the flickering coal fire, just as I had seemed to sit when I had had the nightmare about the three shadows, though now in actuality the room was illuminated not solely by the fire but much more by the whiter light of a glass-shaded mantle on an ornamental iron bracket attached to the wall. My father was sitting at one side of the fireplace and my mother at the other. Neither of my brothers, nor my sister, was in the room; probably they were already in bed upstairs. My mother and father were talking; I can't remember what they were saying but I am certain it was not about me. They paused; and, to my surprise almost as much as to theirs, I burst out into a fit of the bitterest weeping. They were greatly concerned and they lovingly asked me what was the matter, but I could not tell them — because I did not know. They asked me if I didn't like the kindergarten I went to. I said I liked it. (This was true. The kindergarten, run for a hobby before marriage by the pleasant daughter of a deep-voiced florid-faced stockbroker who was a patient of my father's, was the only school I have ever — either as a pupil or as a teacher — longed for during the holidays.) I did my best, as I became less tearful, to help my parents to discover the cause of my grief, but when I went up to bed the mystery was still unexplained. I'm not sure I know the cause even now. Did I feel they were ignoring me as they sat at opposite sides of the fireplace talking across to each other, or could there have been something in their tone foreshadowing the mutual hostility which was to develop between them in later years? I don't remember any hint of quarrelsomeness in their talk: on the contrary I think they seemed at ease and happy before I burst out crying. Perhaps their very contentment

64

helped to upset me. I may have felt I was excluded from it not by them but by some fault in myself, by an oddness which I was becoming conscious of for the first time. They fondly tried to calm and cheer me, and soon I stopped crying and went up to bed. Hugh, who shared the bedroom with me and whose bed was close to mine, was already asleep. I remained awake, hearing the sound though not the words of serious talk continuing for a long while between my mother and father downstairs, and I guessed they must still be talking about me. At last I heard my father stepping up the stairs, and then more quietly along the landing towards Hugh's and my bedroom, and then more quietly still into the room and towards my bed. He stood beside my bed in the dark, uncertain perhaps whether I was awake until I moved my head on the pillow to show him that I was. He bent his head down towards mine and he whispered to me, 'You are my eldest boy and you are my best boy.' My first feeling was of alarm lest Hugh might be awake too now and might overhear these whispered words. I loved him and I sensed how they could hurt him if he heard them. I believe he was asleep, but even this afternoon more than fifty years later the thought that he might have heard them makes me uncomfortable, as does the thought of how they might affect him if I were to tell him of them at any time in future. My second feeling was of reassurance and gladness. I think my father became aware of this. He rubbed his face against mine, and then stood up and quietly went out of the room.

I did not know why my being his eldest boy should make me his best boy, but these words he'd whispered to me had the effect both of confirming my new belief that there was something odd about me and of convincing me that he didn't disapprove of my oddness and even loved me for it. The influence on him of the feudal idea of primogeniture, unlike the influence of another equally anachronistic idea according to which a man ought to be master in his own house and which was an important cause of later

65

quarrelling between him and my mother, did hardly any less harm to me than to him. I began to see myself as someone out of the ordinary, from whom much was expected; and this was to result many times in wretchedness for me when I grew older.

But also it was to result in a strengthening of the wish to be a poet which first came to me when I was fifteen. And the memory of my feelings after my father's whisper to me can strengthen me as a poet now. I needed to think of my childhood during this afternoon's walk not solely in order to bring into the poem I'm writing at present something of the same kind of warmth my early imaginings had but also in order to restore to the act of poetic creation the drive of a conviction that I was 'born to be' a poet. There can be no danger that this conviction might lead me once again towards a disastrous failure such as it led me into years ago: that happened because poetry was all in all to me then and my poems were consequently devoid of significant content and I had to recognise at last that they were worthless. The content of my poems now will be overtly or implicitly political, and my life won't be all for poetry but will include political activity. Yet I must never forget that I need to be a poetic creator primarily, and a political activist only secondarily. My work for C.N.D. must never be allowed to become dominant, or else it could put a stop to my poetry once again just as my dedication to the Party put a stop to it in the nineteen thirties. I must live not the old poetic life, nor the old political life, but the new poetic life.

I needed to re-affirm this. I am glad I walked on farther today along the cliff path than I at first intended.

4

After a morning of quite good progress with my poem why am I suddenly in such a mood of unpoetic despondency as I turn into Prince Consort Street to go down to the esplanade? I make a note mentally that on this cloudless spring afternoon the sea rising like a low hill in front of me with a very slight white haze, almost invisible, over its surface, has a colour that could be called powder-blue, yet the sight of it instead of exalting me at all only emphasises and deepens the dreariness in me. The especially menacing thing about this attack of negative feeling is that it seems on the point of becoming physical, as though it had already driven down through the areas of consciousness which my will can control and was trying to root itself in the nerves. I've had other attacks similar to this one several times during the past few weeks, and I'd better recognise that unless I'm able to discover their cause and prevent them from recurring they could worsen and become more frequent — not that they would be likely to develop into the kind of neurotic illness I had some years ago while I was still in the process of freeing myself from the Party, but they could make poetry much more difficult for me to write. Might their cause be that the C.N.D. activities Elsie and I have been taking part in have put a greater strain on me than I've been aware?

Hardly, since at most we've probably never attended more than two C.N.D. meetings in any one week. And far from depressing me these have stimulated and heartened me both at the time and on the mornings following them when I've always found I've been able to work better than usual on my poem. It's true that for several hours before last week's demonstration I couldn't overcome a slight apprehensiveness, but this passed as soon as we were heading the procession in our mini-minor car with those large ban-the-bomb posters stuck across its sides. The stimulation was all the stronger because I was conscious that it was felt not just by myself and Elsie and the young marchers behind us but also by more than a few of the people along the pavements on either side of us, even though only one or two of them clearly showed approval. There were conspicuous disapprovers as well: the three oldish-looking men who shouted indistinct jibes from inside the open door of a pub that we passed, and the man who stepped off the pavement almost directly in front of our car pretending he had not seen us or the procession and who then leapt back with his head jerking from side to side and with fury on his face as if we had been trying to run him over. But soon afterwards a middle-aged woman put down her shopping bag and stood on the kerb clapping her hands as she watched us go by. And whether most of those who saw the demonstration disapproved or approved of it I knew it was making its mark, was showing even the most unpolitical among them that not absolutely everyone believes nuclear weapons make Britain a safer place than it would be without them, and that to believe they don't is at least not an impossibility. If I were to cut down on my C.N.D. activities, or to stop them altogether, with the idea that I could thereby prevent future attacks of anti-poetic dejection, I should be withdrawing my support from a movement which can help to bring human liberation nearer and which has already begun to have its effect on the world; and the attacks would be strengthened not prevented, because they have been brought on at least partly by a helpless passivity in face of the external menace that C.N.D. has started to combat. But mainly they are due to my not having learnt yet how to live the new poetic life successfully, and I ought to know by now that the way to learn this is by remembering my past poetic life. For the last ten days or more I have been neglecting to remember, and the fact that on several afternoons I was walking with Elsie is no excuse because on the other afternoons when I could have been remembering I allowed myself to think of politics or of the writing I had been doing in the morning. Let me go back immediately out of this despondency to a time when my imagination was fully alive.

I will not try any more to go back to this town as it used to seem to me. Its actuality during the months since my retirement began has increasingly been supplanting its past in my mind, and I would be less easily able to resurrect what I formerly felt here than I would have been if I had retired elsewhere. I will not try either to think any more yet about my childhood in my Essex home, because I was usually happy there and a better cure for my present dejection might be to make myself remember a time when my imagination had less favourable conditions to develop in than it had at home. Let me think of my Preparatory school years at Marchfield.

It wasn't till the end of the first week of my first term that I was able to begin to get any comfort from imagination there, though my wretchedness was due less to anything threatening I had so far discovered at the school than to the loss of the surroundings I had been used to at home. It's true that on my third day Simon Padley, an older boy with a sneering face, briefly twisted my arm, and his brother Nigel whose face was nicer winded me by unaccidentally barging into me in the corridor, but they left me alone afterwards and I hoped that if I tried to keep out of their way they would not deliberately seek me out. And a new boy named Houghton was timidly friendly towards me at tea on the first day, showing me various presents he had been given during his last week at home, saying 'I've got a watch. I've got a purse. I've got a half-a-crown', and I in turn showed him the pocket-knife my godmother Margie had given me.

My new environment, while it did not seem very alarming, nevertheless had an unpleasantly enigmatic quality for me during my first few days there, as if it held within it the potentiality of becoming hurtful later on in the term. This quality seemed present everywhere: in the glass-roofed main corridor known as the Red Lane with its chequered floor of worn red and grey tiles; in the smell of Jeyes' Fluid disinfectant pervading the interior of the laurel-screened lavatory building on the far side of the asphalt quad; in the dark-grey pumice-like material of which the urinals were made and which also formed a surrounding surface for the changing-room wash basins and could be used there for rubbing ink stains from fingers; in the strange fact that my locker and clothes-hook there were numbered 39 but that the numbers between this and 29 — except for 38 which was Hugh's — had not been allotted to other boys, nor had any of the numbers above 39, so that Hugh and I seemed to be set apart from the others. I didn't realise then that there were only twenty-seven boys in the school, and that there had once been more, and that the school was in decline. Nor had my parents discovered this when they sent us to this school; what made my mother decide in favour of it was that her old friend Sophie Draper had a son Donald already there who liked it and who thought Mr Radnage was a decent headmaster, and when Donald was invited over to see us at our home he not only went to wash his hands before lunch but even took off his jacket and rolled up his shirt sleeves in order to do so; and my father decided in favour after asking to examine the drains at the school and after noting that though all the sewage flowed into a cesspit in the grounds this was far enough away from the buildings not to be unhealthy. He also inquired about the academic qualification of the staff, and was told that only Oxford or Cambridge graduates were employed. He was pleased with the nine-hole golf course which Mr Radnage had made in two nearby fields, and my mother may have found the buildings attractive because rather than in spite of their being of various ages and in various architectural styles with a Swiss chalet-like annexe at one end and with an eighteenth-century inn — which according to Mr Radnage had once been frequented by Dick Turpin the highwayman — as a nucleus. At the opposite end from the chalet was Mr and Mrs Radnage's private section, separated from the rest of the school by two doors, the inner one covered with red baize, and the big lawn outside Mrs Radnage's drawing-room window was flanked by sycamores and cedars. From a distance this part of the school looked like a gentleman's country house, my mother said. In it, at the top of a broad staircase which had a central well and a dome-shaped frosted-glass skylight, was the new boys' dormitory. Lying in bed there I was able every night during my first week to give up the struggle to prevent myself from weeping.

I tried to stifle the sound by pressing my mouth into the pillow and pulling the bedclothes up over my head; but the precaution was unnecessary because some of the other boys in the dormitory — and certainly poor Hugh who being only seven was the youngest there and had already been weeping unrestrainedly during the daytime as the others hadn't — were giving way to their homesickness too, and not even those who weren't would have despised me if they'd heard me. As I wept I wished that my mother or my father before kissing me goodbye had said something to me which I could use against the misery I was feeling. Oh if only they had spoken just a few words that had shown they knew what homesickness was like and that I could repeat to myself in order to lessen it. Even if they'd said nothing more than 'Be brave', those two words would have been enough; but I wasn't helped by trying to imagine my mother or my father saying those or any other courage-giving words to me as I lay with my head under the bed-clothes on my black iron school bedstead. The only thing that did help me was that I was always able to fall asleep before long.

I did not get over the worst of my homesickness till the end of my first week at the school. The loss of home became suddenly more bearable to me on the same day that Hugh stopped crying publicly in the daytime. During that first week I had tried to comfort him whenever we were able to be together away from other boys, though usually the result had been that I had come nearer to bursting into tears myself than to making him stop his, and once I had tried unsuccessfully to comfort him in front of other boys after he had been crying continuously through twenty minutes or more of a lesson with our form-mistress Miss Cairns who had asked me whether I couldn't do something to cheer him up. For the whole of our first term Hugh and I spent as much time together as we could. We did not talk often about home, at least not until three weeks before the beginning of the holidays, perhaps in order to avoid the risk of becoming homesick again, but we were able at times to find things to do which gave us a little of the same kind of pleasure as if we had not been at school. Some of these we had not known of at home, and we got the idea for them from other boys at the school: as for instance the making of paper darts and gliders, and better still the pen-nib game in which each player tried with one forefinger on the desk surface to push or swivel either the pointed or the blunt end of his own nib under one of the ends of his opponent's nib so as to be able to toss it over on its back by pressing down the free end of his own. We were soon playing this game with other boys too. There were several variations of it — nib football and nib cricket were two of them — and there were several different kinds of nib, the best attacker being the Waverley, or 'Devil' as the boys always called it, with a pointed end lower than that of any other nib though with an exceptionally high rear end which made it very vulnerable to counter-attack. Hugh and I began to collect nibs, and we used to examine and discuss each individual nib almost as keenly as we had examined and discussed individual toy soldiers of ours at home.

But there were many things at this school that my imagination could not often help me to take pleasure in. The food was one of these. My mother had been more anxious about how well Hugh and I would be fed here than about almost anything else the school would do to us, and she had arranged with us that in our first letters home — which she expected Mr Radnage would read, as in fact he did, before they were sent off — we should put three crosses for kisses if the food was good, but only one cross if it was bad. Both of us when we wrote home on the first Sunday put three crosses at the end of our letters; probably we were trying to make ourselves feel a little less homesick than we would have felt if we had put only one cross and had thereby admitted to ourselves that the beef we had had for lunch on our first two days here had been even less nice when it had been served warm with strange-flavoured dark brown gravy covering it than when on the second day it had been served cold and had not had so much taste to it, and that we had hardly been able to prevent ourselves from retching over the stickily thick tapioca pudding smelling of condensed milk — we had heard it called frogspawn afterwards by an older boy — which we had been given on the fourth day. Later on in the term I learnt to hold my breath while putting each spoonful of it into my mouth and to wash it down quickly with gulps of water, an expedient which I found worse than useless however with the marmalade pudding that we had every Friday and that tasted all the more bitter if chased down the throat by cold water. (During my second term when I no longer had fears of making myself homesick I reported in a letter to my parents that most of the boys had become ill on the previous Friday after eating marmalade pudding and had been allowed to stay in bed late the next morning, so perhaps the detestation we all felt for it was not due just to juvenile faddiness, powerful though the effects of this can be.)

Compared with the marmalade and tapioca puddings, the daily and even the Sunday services we had to attend in the little corrugated iron chapel in the school grounds were slightly less difficult for my imagination to make tolerable. I could daydream even while I sang the hymns and recited the prayers, although on Sundays the service was so long that boredom often won and I was reduced to staring up at the wall near the pulpit where the hymn numbers were displayed in a wooden frame and to drawing an imaginary thick black line through each of these in turn as we finished singing the hymn it indicated. After three or four terms I took to crossing my fingers secretly while I recited the Creed aloud with the other boys, asserting to myself a disbelief which I might not have thought of having if I hadn't guessed that my father, in spite of his attempts to hide the fact from his children as he had promised my churchgoing mother he would when he had married her, was a disbeliever. Rags (this, and not Radders as Donald Draper had incorrectly told my mother, was the nickname by which the boys usually referred among themselves to Mr Radnage) on the other hand was a believer to the point of being a fanatic, and perhaps the more the school declined the nearer he came to being so. The boys knew that if he were to overhear them using exclamations like 'oh Lord' or, worse 'my God' he would submit the offenders to almost as severe and lengthy a pi-jaw as if they had used the word 'damn', though he would have been unlikely to hear this word because there was a half-believed legend among us that a boy had been expelled a few years before for writing it in pencil on the wall of the cricket pavilion. His piety could control our conduct more directly and inescapably however when he made us learn by heart from the Prayer Book, every Sunday in bed before breakfast, the Collect for the day. Not much daydreaming was possible for me then because within half an hour, after he or at least the domestic and the assistant teaching staff had been able to enjoy their extra Sunday morning lie-in, he would return in his dressing-gown to the dormitory to hear each of us repeat the mostly unintelligible words we had learnt, and if we didn't know them properly we had to learn them again. After breakfast and before chapel we had some more and worse learning-by-heart to do, this time of a longish passage from the Bible — it was always known as Fawcett, the name of a woman relative of Rags's who was suspected of being still more pi than he was and who gave a yearly prize to the boy with the highest marks for learning Fawcett — and this passage besides being longer often had less rhythm in it than the Collect and was therefore harder to learn. Nevertheless I did get some pleasure sometimes from the words of the Bible, which I seldom got from those of the Prayer Book.

The games of cricket I took part in during my first summer term were rather less restricting to my thoughts than chapel services or Fawcett and the Collect were. Batting, which required some concentration, I didn't do much of because not being good at it I was soon bowled out and also because we used to go in to bat in alphabetical order and every so often the master in charge would not know who had batted last on the previous day and would start from the beginning again, with the result that Hugh and I whose surname came near the end of the alphabet would both of us lose our innings. I was seldom put on to bowl, so during most of each long' cricketing afternoon I was a fielder, often in the deep field near the long grass where I could think of other things than the game I was supposed to be taking part in and could pull up stalks of thirst-quenching sorrel to chew or could sometimes catch a grasshopper which had been stridulating near me and put it in my pocket. I liked the smell of the summer grass, and also of the linseed oil on the cricket bats in the pavilion, though there was something of apprehensiveness in the feeling that the oil smell gave me, no doubt because I associated it with having to go out to the wicket and to face the bowling. I was fascinated by Daddy le Marchant, a rich man living in a big house not far from the school who was paralysed and was brought into the school grounds in a wheel-chair by his male nurse on fine afternoons to be among the boys. He would sit smiling beneath the oak tree which was between the upper and lower cricket fields, a very thin thread of spittle descending sometimes from the corner of his mouth while sometimes a small green caterpillar would simultaneously descend on a still finer thread towards his hatless head from the oak leaves above him. I watched him and heard his voice, slow and slurred, though I never went near enough to get into conversation with him as many of the other boys did, whom he rewarded generously now and again with presents of toy howitzers and of blue-painted boomerangs.

Football in the winter gave me less leisure for forming interesting impressions, but the actual game — which I was better at than at cricket and which anyway did not take up so much time — often gave me a more than physical satisfaction. I did not like having to play in matches against other schools — as I had to later on when I was put into the first eleven — because in these the game ceased to be a game and became, for Rags on the touchline at least, a serious struggle to beat the other side, and the conspicuous deterioration that this always caused in my play was made still worse by the anger that Rags showed at what he obviously regarded as wilful perversity on my part. The appeal of football for me already at the age of eleven was aesthetic rather than competitive. A neat bit of dodging followed by an accurately kicked pass that was not taken advantage of by the player to whom I had kicked it, or a quick strong shot that travelled with a low trajectory towards the corner of the goal but was saved at the last moment by the opposing goalkeeper, would gratify me more than any goal I might score as a result of muddling on the part of our opponents. The only seriously competitive games of football I did enjoy at this school were House matches between the Reds and the Blues (the school hadn't enough boys for more than two Houses) and the reason why I enjoyed them was that I was not playing against strangers whose reactions to victory or defeat were of no interest to me. But I always liked best those non-competitive games that allowed me whenever I succeeded in doing anything at all skilful to pause and dwell on it for a moment or two. I got pleasure also from seeing skilful play by other boys, whether they were on the same side as me or not.

Lessons in class did not put a stop to imaginative activity in me altogether. Sometimes they directly helped it, when the subject I was being taught was one I liked; and sometimes they hardly hindered it at all, when though the subject was dull the master or mistress seemed unaware that I wasn't really listening. My thoughts seldom wandered during the lessons taken by Mr Watkin. He was a fresh-faced forceful young man just down from Oxford who owned a trembling golden Retriever puppy which he called Beppo and which he often brought into the formroom with him, setting it down on the master's desk in front of him and combing it, and whenever it struggled at all or even winced he would reprimand it with a fierceness that I and the other boys felt, and were meant to feel, he would transfer to any of us whom he might decide to catch watching him instead of getting on with the work he had set us to do. But when, more than half way through a lesson, he called us out one by one to test us on what we had been learning, usually poetry, he was extremely lenient with boys who had been members of the form for longer than a term and if they began to stumble in their recitation he would hold his own copy of the poetry book up to them so that they could read from it — though before holding it up he would order the rest of the form to keep their eyes on their books and would specifically warn boys who were new to the form that in previous terms one or two who had been rash enough to raise their eyes after being told not to had been sent down to the school cellars from which they had never again emerged. He would then appeal to the rest of the form to confirm that he was telling the truth, and they would all call out 'Yes sir'. When the boys who were new to the form came up to him to recite what they had learnt he didn't show them his book if they faltered but was severe with them and sent them back to their desks to learn the piece again. This game of his didn't worry me during my first term in the form as I found the poetry fairly easy to learn, but during my second term he used to hold his book up to me even though I hadn't faltered, and I wasn't happy about this because I wanted to show that I had done the work he had set and perhaps because the poem I was reciting appealed to me and he made me feel he didn't care about it. Poetry and the learning of poems by heart were associated for me with home — my father had at one time given me sixpence for every poem I had recited to him, an encouragement that he too as a child had had from his father — and my liking for poetry was one of the home feelings I hoped to be able to continue indulging in without much hindrance at school.

Though Mr Watkin's lessons did not frighten me I couldn't succeed in making myself imagine I liked them, and there were things at this school which my imagination not only failed to find any pleasure in but was dominated and distorted by and saw as even more menacing than they actually were. I had been here for almost a whole school year before I first heard anyone mention black hypo. A boy named Powys-Phillips told me about it. He had been at the school only a term longer than Hugh and myself but he seemed to know everything that went on here and all the conventions and customs — which he regarded with reverential approval — and he used to air his knowledge in an assertive and irritating way. However, apprehension and not irritation was my feeling when he told me he had heard that the fifth formers (the fifth form being the top form in the school) were going to start giving black hypo again, an old custom which had been forgotten for several years. There was less of the usual zest and more of awe in his voice as he explained what this meant; the fifth formers would pick on some of the younger boys and would take them one by one into the photographic dark room and would force them to swallow a drink made from the hypo which was used for developing photographs. He said that the drink was mostly water but that the hypo was a deadly poison and could kill you if too much of it got put into the water by mistake. I did not ask him whether any boy had died after being given this drink. He had implanted a dread in me which prevented any such rational question from entering my mind and which persisted for a day or two, though it diminished after a week had passed without any attempt by the fifth formers to give black hypo to anyone.

Except for Donald Draper, who had made a point of being nice to Hugh and me during our first few weeks at the school, most of the fifth-formers took little notice of us, though at the beginning of our second term three of them who had somehow discovered that we knew some German songs made us stand up together on the seat of a double-desk and sing one of these to a lot of boys in the fourth form room, which was the largest form room in the school. We sang a few lines of the song we knew best:

> Hänschen klein
> Geht allein
> In die weite Welt hinein
> Stock und Hut
> Steht ihm gut
> Und ist wohlgemut

Our hearers did not jeer at us, as I had feared they would. The three fifth-formers even clapped us when we finished, though the song was all double-Deutsch to them. (This was before the outbreak of the 1914 war with Germany, but I think their attitude to us would have been much the same if the war had been already on.) And there was an occasion too in my second term when a fifth-former named Henderson asked me in a quite friendly way 'Why are you always smiling?' I couldn't tell him I was doing it to keep my courage up and also to appease possible attackers, so I broadened my smile and said I didn't know. The fifth-formers, though I saw them all as being very tall, seemed less dangerous than the fourth-formers, some of whom were very aggressive. However there was one puzzling thing I had seen the fifth-formers doing which I didn't at first guess was bullying but later I realised it was torture of an appalling kind. There was a boy in the fifth form with the surname of Ralph whose jacket the others would take off and put over his head and they would hold his arms and run him along among them with his shoulders bowed forward so that he looked like the back part of a pantomime animal whose front legs had gone off somewhere else. I thought they were having a joke in which he was sharing, but once during a Sunday walk led by a master who didn't seem to notice what they were doing I saw the look on Ralph's face just before they covered his head with the jacket. They may never have been taught anything about claustrophobia, nor had I been, and like me they may not even have heard of that word, but they were aware of the extreme terror he felt and they relished it. In my third term at the school they had the idea of varying the torture by taking him into the dark room and uncovering his head when they'd got him inside there, and probably it was this variation that suggested to them the further idea of reviving the custom of giving black hypo to the younger boys.

One wet afternoon when cricket had been cancelled and I and a lot of others were playing about unsupervised in the gym, two fifth-formers, one of whom was Henderson, came in and led away a third-former named Hardwick whose face as he went with them looked more pallid than it normally did, and after five or ten minutes they came back without Hardwick and took Powys-Phillips, his large dark eyes wide open with fright in spite of all his reverence for school traditions, and I had no doubt that he was going to be given black hypo and wouldn't be seen in the gym again and that I might be the next to be taken. I was not the next nor the one after the next, but no hope began to arise in me that there would be insufficient time for all the third-formers to be taken and that I might be passed over. My fear grew so great that, when at last the two fifth-formers did come for me and caught hold of my arms to bring me along with them, it seemed almost to anaesthetise itself, or at any rate it was unable to become worse even after they had led me up the steps at the end of the Red Lane and round the corner and into the dark room itself. Did I really believe they were going to poison me? I don't think so, and yet if I had absolutely believed it I could hardly have felt more terrified. When Henderson shut the door of the room behind me I saw a dull red light, darker in colour than blood, coming from what seemed a small window in front of me, and a boy I could not recognise pushed the edge of a white developing-dish between my lips and tilted it quickly so that the liquid it contained went at least partly into my mouth though mostly down my chin. Then quite soon Henderson opened the door again, and after telling me that what I had drunk had really been nothing worse than pure water he took me along the corridor into the fifth form room where six or seven previous victims including Powys-Phillips were being held in order to prevent them from going back to the gym and revealing the truth to the others whose turn to be given black hypo was still to come.

My fear was over, and like a frightened sheep that has been let go at last by the shearer I soon forgot it. Nevertheless, I think it had its after-effects. Having been terrified I developed a taste for terrifying others. I began to take part in the general bullying by third-formers of

81

Houghton, the boy who had been timidly friendly towards me on my first day at the school but who afterwards had turned out to be rather simple and also to have a temper which could be very easily roused if he was baited. The peculiarly throaty cry of rage and woe that he let out when he was attacked was exquisitely pleasing to us, and I used to look forward with rising excitement in the evenings to the brief free time after supper when we would be able to go and make Houghton blub. One evening I followed him out alone on to the asphalt quad and caught up with him just as he went into the laurel-screened and not very well lit lavatory building. I told him he might see a ghost there. I pointed up at the grating high in the wall above the urinals and said it often came in through that at about this time. I explained it was a horizontal ghost (though I'm not sure I actually used this word) and when seen from outside the lavatories in the dusk it looked like a large model airship, but it wasn't a model airship — it was a man dressed in grey and without a head, and the extraordinary thing was how he got in through the grating; he went through it like meat through the holes of a mincing machine but the bits instead of falling to the ground became joined up again on the other side. At this point of the story, just when I was feeling I had been too extravagant to be convincing, Houghton gave the loudest and shrillest shriek I had ever heard from him. He ran out on to the quad, still shrieking, and I ran after him trying to tell him that there was no ghost really, trying to quieten him, fearing the consequences if he did not stop shrieking when he got inside the main school building. But I was not able to quieten him.

Within a quarter of an hour Rags got together all the third and fourth-formers, except Houghton, into the fourth form room. When he had made us sit down at the desks he stood silent in front of us for a moment and then very gravely asked which of us had told Houghton that there was a ghost in the lavatories. The terrible thought came to me that Houghton might have become ill from shock, might even have died. Rags repeated his question, this time in a less dramatic and more matter-of-fact way which made me feel that Houghton was not dead or ill, and I could almost have spoken if only there hadn't been so many boys in the room to hear me and also if I hadn't had a half-hope that Rags didn't know I was the culprit and that he might never find out. After a silence which grew longer and longer Rags said how important it was that a boy who had done wrong should be courageous and honourable enough to own up, and that not to own up could be worse than the offence he hoped to hide. I was by this time wholly incapable of speaking, and the silence seemed endless, till at last Rags asked me directly, 'Sebrill, were you the boy who told Houghton there was a ghost in the lavatories?' I didn't answer, not even in a whisper. Rags dismissed the rest of the boys from the form room, telling me to stay behind. He came up to me, and said, 'What would your mother and father think if they knew what you have done?' The only meaning that this question and the tone in which it was spoken conveyed to me was that he was not going to punish me further. He probably saw how wretched I already felt, and perhaps he wanted to avoid any action which might lead to revenge being taken against Houghton for sneaking. I still could not say anything, and Rags told me to go up to bed in the dormitory with the others.

Two days later his question had for the first time a further effect on me besides its immediate one of relieving my fear that he might be going to cane me. I was crossing the quad soon after lunch when the realisation came to me not only that my mother and father would have disliked what I had done to Houghton but also that I myself didn't like it. I felt that it was in some way a betrayal of my home, and that the school had caused me to do it. From this time on I was less often tempted to misuse my imagination for the purpose of frightening anyone — though in the 'Red

Brotherhood' which I and Hugh founded several terms later, after we had seen a cinema film during the holidays about a criminal gang who called themselves by that name and whose emblem was a clenched hand holding a dagger, there was an element at least of unfriendliness towards some other boys. Our Red Brotherhood had the same emblems as the gang in the film but unlike the gang we did not attack anyone: our main activity was writing notes to one another in 'Cat and Dog', a code invented by Hugh and myself which used conventionalised drawings of common objects and of animals to represent the letters of the alphabet and which everyone who wanted to join the R.B. (as we soon called it for short) had to pass an examination in before being accepted as a full member; however, the R.B. excluded boys I did not like — such as Powys-Phillips — and by flaunting our secret code in front of them we made sure that they felt their exclusion.

But there were things I was able to do at this school which were less distorting to my imaginative development than the R.B. or my participation in the bullying of Houghton. One of these was reading. There was a small school library, and Rags allowed and even encouraged the boys to take books from it into the dining-hall and read them during breakfast and tea, though not during lunch. My parents when they heard of this custom had misgivings lest the good we would gain from reading might be outweighed by the permanent harm that could be done to our table-manners, and possibly Rags's intention in allowing books at table was quite as much to prevent the dining-room from becoming too noisy during meal-times as to further the boys' education, but whatever the effect on my manners I read very much more in my five years at this school than I could have done if meal-time reading had not been allowed. I began with books like *The Great Aeroplane* and *Coral Island* and *The Gorilla Hunters*, then after three or four terms I started on Scott's novels. I skipped the general historical passages in these but persisted with the narrative, at first partly because I had been told that these novels were great literature and I prided myself on reading them, but soon they took hold of my imagination and became less and less of an effort for me. They prepared me to feel emotions which real life had not yet aroused in me, such as romantic love. The details of the scenery they described — as for instance the fountain trickling from the rock into a basin of roughly hollowed stone in front of the forest hermitage where the Black Knight and Friar Tuck shared a large pasty baked in a pewter platter — often gave me an even greater pleasure than the narrative itself, and taught me to see the real countryside in a new way. Scott helped to make me, by the age of twelve, a romantic, though I didn't know at the time that this was the word to describe me. Only one other imaginative excitement I was able to get while I was at this school was almost as pure and keen as any I got from reading — the excitement of the dancing-class that used to be held once a week during every Christmas term.

It was held in the evening, and before it began boys whose parents had paid for them to learn dancing (this was an extra) went up to the dormitories to change into clothes which we did not often have to wear at other times except always on Sundays — Eton jackets and large starched Eton collars — and which, not because I thought of these yet as snob clothes but mainly because of the difficulty of fitting the stiff collar to the bone stud at the back and worse still at the front of the shirt, I hated having to wear on Sundays, but I liked wearing them for the dancing class. Everything that was done in preparation for this helped to heighten my feeling of exhilarated expectation. We brushed green Brilliantine or brown Bay Rum into our hair to smarten and scent it, and we dusted and rubbed our already shiny patent leather dancing pumps. From the dining-hall downstairs where the class was to be held came the scraping and creaking sound, strangely distant it seemed to me, of

85

tables being removed and of benches ('forms' as we called them) being pushed up against the walls. Then I would hear a first brief far-away ramble of notes of music from the piano, stopping as abruptly as it started, full of the wildest promise. At last one of the older boys who had been helping to get the dining-room ready appeared at the top of the stairs to tell us we could go down now. We did not run, and as far as I was concerned this was not just because Rags had made a rule against running on the stairs but because the intensity of anticipation in me was almost like an awe. From the not very bright light of the electric bulb above the staircase we came down into the Red Lane and along it towards the wide open doorway of the dining-hall which seemed to shine with a glittering brilliance as from many chandeliers, and the music of the piano was loud now. Trying to remember at present how I used to feel after coming in through the doorway I think of two lines from Burns's poem to Mary Morison, which I did not know at that time — 'Yestreen when to the trembling string/The dance gaed thro' the lighted ha' ', though in the dining-hall there was no violinist but only Miss Cairns at the piano. And there was no Mary Morison for me, nor was there any boy towards whom I was romantically attracted at all. The dancing itself was the attraction. Mr Duval, the visiting dancing-master, stood waiting in the middle of the room for us, grey-haired and rather stiffly erect, wearing evening dress with tails and a white tie and white gloves. His pinkish face had an almost unchanging expression which combined a prim firmness with amiability, and on the skin at the back of his neck there were numerous small circular scars, some of them overlapping others: as I think of them now they seem to have resembled the small fossil shells cemented together in broken slabs of calcareous sandstone that I have been noticing recently on the beach. He carried an ivory fan which he seldom opened to fan himself with but sometimes used for beating time during the dancing. The dances he taught us were, first, the Barn dance — 'in front, behind, and one, two three' he would rhythmically call out to us as we danced it — and then Sir Roger de Coverley, which reminded me of the game of Oranges and Lemons at children's Christmas parties, and then some of the less complicated figures of the Lancers, and also several dances for pairs only such as the polka and, less easy, the waltz — though the music Miss Cairns played for this appealed to me more than the music for any other dance — and the gallop, always the final dance of the evening and the most exciting, surpassing even the polka, orgiastically superheating our emotions as it superheated our bodies in their Eton jackets and stiff collars. The only comparable excitement I had ever experienced had been during haymaking in my earlier childhood; though, unlike that, the excitement of the gallop had perhaps something feverish and even a little desperate in it towards the end, as if I could never quite lose my awareness of the normally anti-imaginative school routine I must return to after it was over.

Among the boys the one who chiefly embodied anti-imaginativeness for me was Powys-Phillips, my rival and enemy with whom I sometimes physically though more often verbally fought. I remember how, with his large protuberant brown eyes wide open, he was volubly enthusiastic during almost a whole lunch time about the Ashburton Shield, which was a trophy awarded for shooting and which he said was one of the greatest honours that a school could win. I had nothing against shooting — I quite liked it when we shot at targets with a B.S.A. airgun in the gym under the supervision of Sergeant Trewin — but Powys-Phillips's assertive fervour goaded me at last to say that I didn't think winning the Ashburton Shield would be much of an honour, and his face showed outrage as if I had spoken a monstrous blasphemy and he became wild with fury against me. Once, soon after the 1914 war had begun, he was talking on and on to me across the table during breakfast about how wonderful the British fleet was, till I suddenly told him — though I didn't really believe it — that the German fleet was better than the British. He didn't react with fury: he was appalled and even frightened. Immediately after breakfast he went to tell Rags what I had said. He must have felt very much in need of reassurance, otherwise his reverence for school conventions would have restrained him from breaking the taboo on sneaking. Rags soon sent for me. Surprisingly he did not seem angry. He told me with hardly any suggestion of reproof, as though he was correcting some pardonable grammatical error I had made in an English essay, that I was wrong and that in fact the British fleet was better than the German. But I felt he did not like me, and I continued to feel this throughout my time at Marchfield. Nor did he like Hugh, and perhaps he didn't like our mother either — whether or not he knew of her pre-war enthusiasm for Germany.

But there was a master who did like us, and whom we liked. He came to the school in the middle of our second or third term there, and on his first appearance at the staff table in the dining-hall there was a pleasing oddness about him that made the boys laugh. His dark red face, which seemed to have a hint of a grin on it, was shinily close shaven and tinged slightly with blue over the sides of his cheeks near his large ears, and he wore a clergyman's collar. We immediately began to invent nicknames for him, such as 'Friary Ale' — his looks reminded one of us of a picture of a monk in an advertisement for this ale — and eventually we called him Grundy, because someone suggested he was like Mrs Grundy and we all thought this sounded absolutely right for him, though none of us had any idea who Mrs Grundy was. Grundy, as we soon discovered, had been the vicar of a parish in Suffolk, and there were rumours that he was a distant relative of Rags's and that he had had a sort of breakdown in health which made him need a change from his work as a vicar, so Rags had invited him to do some teaching at Marchfield — where he lived in a small cottage at the bottom of the school grounds with his tall Scottish wife who seldom came up to the school and, although he told us she was a wonderful woman, we never saw her smile or heard her speak a single word. He wasn't strict in class, and I and the others sometimes played about when he was trying to teach us, but often his lessons were very interesting. He had two fountain pens, identical to look at and both rather small, one for red ink and the other for blue, and he used to copy out poems alternately in red and blue into a thick notebook which had a shiny cover. His handwriting was marvellously clear and the red ink was beautifully translucent, almost transparent, as it came from the tip of the gold nib of his red-ink pen. His favourite poets were Scott and Jean Ingelow. He read us most of the canto about the combat in *The Lady of the Lake* and I learnt by heart the passage which began, 'Fitz James was bold though to his heart/The life blood thrilled with sudden start.' He also liked to tell us or read us gruesome stories which I listened to eagerly, and one of which caused Martin, the strongest boy in the school and the best at games, to show signs of feeling faint (he was a boy who had less cruelty in his nature than almost any other I have known, but was to spend much of his adult life supervising black labour in a British colony), and I was proud when Grundy asked me to take Martin into the changing-room and give him a drink of water. Grundy's stories were often real-life ones about things that had happened in his parish: the one that upset Martin was about a woman with a diseased leg who had had it amputated at home and it had been wrapped up afterwards in brown paper but the surgeon had left it behind by mistake when he had gone out of the house. Whether or not such stories gave a decadent turn to my imaginative development, I have no doubt that his love of poetry helped to increase mine, and soon after I left Marchfield I too began copying out poems into a thick notebook, and my doing so was probably one of the things that led me on to writing down poems of my own.

Another master who did not dislike me or Hugh was Mr Snell, — but we feared him, as all the boys did, and his influence on my imagination was restrictive rather than expansive. He too was a clergyman, though not a vicar, nor was he married. He had a Cambridge degree in classics and he was a rugger blue, besides being an efficient teacher: it never occurred to the boys, or possibly to any of their parents either, to wonder why with these qualifications he chose to teach in a small Prep school like Marchfield instead of in some well-known Public school where he would have had better pay and prospects. When he came to Marchfield — a term or two after Grundy — I wrote in one of my Sunday letters to my parents that he was very strict in the classroom but awfully sporting out of it. I didn't mention in any of my letters home the strange humorous stories I listened to from him later on during lunch sometimes when he was at the head of the table and I was sitting near him — strange because they were not the kind of stories to be expected from a master. One of them was about a man who had chronic attacks of vomiting which were so severe that he was terribly afraid he might sooner or later bring up his entrails: while he was asleep one night his friends played the trick of putting a sheep's internal organs into the basin he always kept by his bedside, and in the morning when they asked him what sort of night he'd had he said that the worst had happened at last but that after bringing up all his intestines he'd managed by great good luck and with the aid of a rusty nail and an old toothpick to get the lot of them back again. Then there was the story of the visitor staying for the weekend in a large country house who also woke feeling very sick in the night — the word 'sick', however, was spoken by Snell this time in a way that suggested he really meant something else which he didn't think quite fit for us to hear him say — and this visitor after wandering down various corridors vainly looking for a lavatory was at last in a state of being unable to hold out a moment longer when he saw a sheet of newspaper lying on the floorboards and was sick into that, but when he bent down to pick it up he found it was only moonlight reflected on the floor from a nearby window. These stories seemed intended by Snell to make the boys feel he was one of us, and I was so much at ease with him after hearing the story about the moonlight that I had the nerve to say to him, 'I wonder what Mr Radnage would think if he found out you were telling us stories like this.' Snell answered very sharply, 'You know quite well that among yourselves in the dormitories you tell much worse ones than that.' Like Grundy, he used to tell us real-life stories as well as made-up ones, but his real-life ones were more about himself than Grundy's were, and Snell talked a lot to us about himself. I remember him saying he always cleaned his teeth with soap not toothpaste, and I looked at them as he was speaking and saw how large and how yellow they were, rather like a horse's teeth; and I actually laughed, yet he took no offence. Another time he said that the clerical collars he wore were celluloid and could be thrown away instead of having to be sent to the laundry, and I looked not so much at his collar as just above it at his very prominent adam's apple over which the shaved skin seemed like the skin over the breastbone of a plucked chicken, though on this occasion I did not actually laugh. He liked talking to us about his two elderly maiden aunts whom he said he was very fond of: he told us once how they'd considered the idea of making themselves independent of the milkman by keeping a cow in their back garden all the year round, and he added with a suggestive smile whose meaning I didn't understand, 'They didn't realise why their plan couldn't have worked in practice.' One day he quoted with a sympathetic laugh a sentence from a letter written to him by a friend who, as Snell had more than once previously told us, did voluntary work in a club in the East End of London: 'Oh dear, I've fallen hopelessly in love once again'; and he was obviously pleased when I without quite knowing why laughed too. Snell himself was very much interested in the East End, and he often said to us that his favourite book was *Froggie's Little Brother,* a novel about a boy whose home was in a slum, and that every time he read it he wept over it. He also told us how, when he had been a chaplain on a training ship for boys, he had caught a boy in the act of stealing money from his cabin and had given him the choice either of being reported to the captain, who would certainly have expelled him, or of being privately thrashed there and then over the bunk in the cabin, in which case nothing more would ever be said about the theft. The boy had been brave enough, as Snell appreciatively put it when describing the incident to us, to choose the thrashing and Snell had taken a thick cane and given him twelve strokes, laying into him as hard as possible. My imagination was certainly impressed by this real-life story, but it was passively impressed, as though an ugly lesion had been made in it. However, sometimes Snell told us things which had a positive imaginative appeal for me, as when at the beginning of one term he said he proposed to start a Scout troop at the school and he described various activities we should be able to take part in in if we became Scouts.

The idea I formed of these activities as he talked about them at lunch-time was very exciting to me, though when I asked him whether we should be able to have real Scout uniforms with Scout hats and scarves he answered rather chillingly, 'My favourite maxim has always been "If a thing is worth doing at all it is worth doing well" '. And later on when I actually experienced some of the activities I found them unenchanting, except for the eating of a mutton chop which I cooked over a twig fire in the open air to pass the test for my cookery badge: this chop, perhaps mainly because it was so different from the meat I had been used to at school, tasted more delicious than any other I had ever eaten, even at home. But although Snell did not get much control over my mind through Scouting he was able to influence my imaginative development effectively in another way: he re-converted me to a belief in God, whose existence I became more strongly and more emotionally convinced of than I had been as a small child. I stopped crossing my fingers during the Creed in chapel, and in the dormitory at night when all the boys knelt down from habit beside their beds to say their private prayers I said mine very earnestly. And as a result of a sudden discovery by Mr Hitchcock, our visiting music teacher, that I had a fairly good treble voice, I was chosen to sing a short solo on my knees at the end of a chapel service, and sang it rather badly because I was nervous and also because I had been taught too little about singing — so little that I did not know what Grundy meant when he told me afterwards that some of my notes had been flat. I was not conscious that Snell's religious influence over me was hurtful and had a narrowing effect on my imagination, and I didn't break free from it or resist it at all until after I left Marchfield and went to Rugtonstead. But I did at least once dare to escape from doing what he wanted from me as a Scout.

Soon after the beginning of one summer term he said that he was going to have a Scout camp during the first week of the holidays and that I was one of the boys who would be old enough to go to it. The idea, not so much of the camp itself as of having to lose seven days which I would otherwise have been able to spend at home, was instantly unwelcome to me; however the fear of angering Snell if I said I didn't want to go and the thought that the end of term was a long way off and something could very well happen before then to get me out of going, made me tell him I would go. But as the term continued my hope of escape became less and less, and the prospect of camp became increasingly unbearable to me. During a school walk conducted by Grundy on the afternoon of Unbutton Sunday, when every boy wore the top as well as the bottom button of his Eton waistcoat undone and when there were only two more Sundays — Brush-hair Sunday and Cock-hat Sunday — still to come before the holidays began, I was in such a state of unhappiness that my friend Tilford with whom I was walking noticed it though I had said nothing to him about it. The walk was across a heath towards some pine woods, and Tilford and I had been lagging behind the other boys. The path we were following them along led to a small footbridge over a railway cutting and he and I stood still on this bridge to look along the line which curved to the right within two or three hundred yards of us and became hidden by the right-hand side of the cutting. When I had been here during previous walks I had wished that while I was on the bridge a train would come suddenly round the curve, moving very fast, its engine swaying slightly and with steam spurting alternately from each of the two external cylinders, that it would rush straight at me so as to test to the utmost my resolution not to run away off the bridge or even to flinch, then would pass immediately beneath me sending a blast of warm funnel smoke violently up through the gaps between the wooden planks of the footway I was standing on. Tilford, whom I must at some time have told about this wish of mine, suggested we should wait for a bit in case a train might come, but I said I didn't think there were any trains along this line on Sundays; and he, sensing my lack of interest, asked almost without irritation and with something like sympathetic concern: 'Is anything the matter?' I didn't answer him. His concern instead of improving my mood made me sorrier for myself than before and even less disposed to hear the praises of camping I would be likely to get from him if I confided in him how much I hated the prospect of it. He said nothing more to me until we came to a clearing among the pine trees where we saw most of the other boys sitting grouped together semi-circularly in front of Grundy who had begun to read to them from a book. I was about to sit down at the back of the group, with the intention not so much of trying to listen to the reading as of making my untalkativeness less noticeable to Tilford than it must have been while we had been walking together, but he warned me quickly that there was an ant-heap just where I was going to sit, and we moved a few yards away from it before we both sat down. Normally an ant-heap like this, constructed of dead pine needles and with big red ants moving about in it, would have been interesting to me, yet now I didn't give it a second look. But I did look at Grundy; and the sight of his dark red face, so different from the whitish face of Snell, brought me a kind of relief. The story he had begun to read — perhaps it was from Harrison Ainsworth's *Tower of London* — gave promise of being horrific, yet I didn't listen to it for long. I was still too much troubled about camp, and also I had difficulty in listening in the open air with various small distractions interposing between me and Grundy, such as the movement of a slight breeze and the strong smell of pine resin and noises coming from somewhere else in the woods. And suddenly there was a very startling interruption.

A boy came rushing out from among the trees to the left of us shouting 'Fire'. He was Whitworth, who might be trying to be funny. Grundy went on reading for half a moment. Then we all heard the crackling of the fire and everyone including Grundy got up and we began running in among the trees towards the crackling. The fire was in a clearing like the one where we had just been sitting. No trees were burning yet. I saw a line several yards long of low flames on the ground among the dead pine needles and fallen twigs and cones. There may have been some heather alight there too. The line of flames was visibly moving forward and also was quickly extending at both its ends. Grundy ran towards the middle of it and began stamping on the flames and we all came up on either side of him and did the same. His face had a peculiarly grim look which I had seen on it once before — in the classroom one afternoon when he had taken up his mark-book and gone to attack a hornet that had flown in through the open window. The specially large-soled boots with broad and supple uppers that he always wore because of the bunions he suffered from seemed very well suited to the stamping he was so heavily and vigorously doing, but his efforts and ours had little effect on the fire, and soon I and others found it too hot to stamp on and we rushed off to find sticks to beat it with. These weren't effective either. The almost pleasant excitement I had at first got from attacking the fire did not last long. As I stood still for a moment to relieve the ache which my beating the flames with a stick had caused in my arms, I saw the fire reach a small and solitary sapling only two or three feet high which instantly blazed up from bottom to top and was stripped of all its needles, and though for a while after this it was free of flame, as if the fire was now going to leave it alone, I knew the rest of it must be rapidly getting hotter and would be burnt up totally at any moment. And I knew that the fire was steadily getting nearer to the other trees, the full-size trees. I felt fear. Then a boy behind me whose voice I couldn't quite recognise, and whom I didn't turn to look at, said to me, 'You know it was your bro. and Whitworth who started this.' The reason why I didn't look at the boy who spoke to me was that I was looking at Hugh. He was at the end of the line and was beating quite frantically at the flames with a small branching bit of pine bough he had picked up. Before I had time to feel fully what I had just been told, Grundy called out, 'One of you go and fetch the woodman.' I at once said I would go. I started running towards a path I saw at the far end of the clearing but I wasn't really sure that it would lead towards the woodman's cottage, though I had seen where this was during previous Sunday walks to these woods. My main purpose for the moment was to get away from the fire. Fortunately Tilford, who had a better idea than I had of the whereabouts of the cottage, followed me and caught up with me.

He ran ahead of me along the path, which was a narrow one. He ran fast, and from the sight of his back I could sense that he too felt fear of the fire. He had always been a better runner than I was, yet now I was able to keep up close behind him. As we got farther away from the fire my fear became greater instead of less; it grew into a fear of the consequences that might follow from the fire as well as of the fire itself. The damage might be so bad that Hugh would be expelled from the school. But there might be a still more serious consequence even than this. Suppose the whole wood was burnt down. My father and mother would have to pay the owner. It might cost thousands and thousands of pounds, far more than all they had. They would be ruined, made bankrupt. Our house would have to be sold. There would be nowhere for Hugh and me to go home to any more. It would be like death. As I ran on I felt that nothing more dreadful than this fire had ever happened in my life before. It was much worse than when I had nearly drowned a year ago in the lake among pine trees which Rags took us to for early morning bathes during summer terms. The memory of that incident came to me in my fear now just as memories of a person's past life are supposed to come to him while he is drowning, though actually they hadn't come to me when I had nearly drowned a year ago. I had been in my depth near the shore and had reached out to an overhanging bough which another boy, who unlike me had already learnt to swim, had been holding on to, and when he had let go of it and swum away it had swung me a little farther from the shore, less than a yard farther perhaps though enough to take me out of my depth, and after a while I too had let go of it and had sunk under the water again and again — certainly more than three times — without anyone noticing until at last Powys-Phillips, my enemy, saw me and swam to push me into my depth once again. I had felt bad as I had staggered out of the water on to the shore, but I had not felt bad while I had been repeatedly going under, though my lungs must have been even shorter of breath than they were now as I desperately ran on behind Tilford towards the woodman's cottage. The path we were running along went downhill and was a narrow and sunken one, with a kind of meandering rut in it caused by water which was no longer there now during the dry weather. I was aware of the risk of tripping up and falling, but my awareness could not increase my already extreme anxiety, and I arrived behind Tilford at the gate of the cottage garden without having stumbled once throughout our run.

When the woodman opened the door of his cottage and one of us, probably Tilford, told him there was a fire in the woods, he said nothing but went round to the back of the cottage where there was a small shed from which he fetched out a long-handled axe. Tilford tried to tell him just where the fire was. The woodman nodded but still said nothing. It seemed to me in my anxiety that he was in no great hurry as he set out with us along the path uphill into the woods. He was certainly not going to run. I did begin to run. I felt that even if my running wouldn't make him walk any faster my getting back to the others before he arrived and telling them he was on his way would somehow be of help. Tilford soon joined me. When we reached the clearing again I saw immediately that the fire was out. I was hardly able to believe it could be out; it had been so obstinately fierce and the small bit of it I had tried to stamp out had, after the shortest of pauses, glowed up more redly than ever. Grundy and the boys with him had somehow got the better of it. There was not even much smoke about, though the smell of the burnt pine needles was still strong, and still frightening. Tilford went to tell Grundy the woodman was coming. I saw Hugh standing by himself and I ran to him and spoke to him. 'How did they put it out?'

'We went on beating it with sticks,' he said.

I looked round to make sure Grundy was not near enough to hear before I asked:

'Did you start it?'

'Whitworth had some matches and we made a pile of pine needles and I lit it. We only meant to have a small bonfire. Grundy knows, but all he said was "don't do that again." '

Only when I knew there was no likelihood of Hugh's being punished was I able to realise to the full that the dreadful fears I had had while running to the woodman's cottage were now proved false, and that our parents would not be ruined nor would we lose our home. I wanted to tell Hugh about the relief I felt, but I did not know how to; and perhaps there was no need for me to try to, because he probably felt just the same as I did. We stood silent, watching the one or two boys who were walking round and stamping on parts of the ground from which smoke was still very faintly rising. I watched almost without seeing, because home was in my mind. Or, rather, it was in my feelings, mistily and intensely. It had never seemed more beautiful. Then the woodman at last arrived, carrying his axe. All the boys were quiet as Grundy went up to him and apologised for having sent for him unnecessarily, and on his day of rest too. Grundy said the boys had done well to put the fire out so quickly. He told no lies, perhaps because the woodman asked no questions.

When Tilford and I were walking back with the others towards the school — not lagging behind this time — I was less untalkative than I had been on our way to the woods, because everything Tilford said about the fire interested me and because I needed to work off the unpleasant feelings that lingered on in me about it; nevertheless, even while we were talking my thoughts were partly of home, and as we crossed the footbridge over the railway and I looked down at the curving track I decided that to-morrow whatever happened I would speak to Snell and tell him I would not be able to go to camp. I wondered what reason I would give him for not being able to go. I might say that my mother wanted me back because an old friend of our family who lived in China would be coming to stay with us for a week just at the time of the camp. After all, my mother did have a friend, Agnes Dangerfield, who lived in China, and she was coming over here sometime soon. However, Snell would be quite likely to discover later on that I had been lying, even if he didn't see it in my face immediately, as he would be almost bound to do. An absolute lie would be no good; I would have to think of some reason that would be very nearly true. I would have to think of it before to-morrow. But suppose I couldn't? I would have to rely on having an inspiration at the very last moment just as I began speaking to him. The one certain thing was that I would speak to him, and no matter how angry he might become I would not let him make me change my mind.

I felt completely sure of this not only as I was crossing the footbridge but afterwards also when I got back to the school, and during all the rest of the day, and in the evening when I went to bed in the dormitory. Next morning just before breakfast I came upon Snell in the corridor outside the fourth form room. I felt horribly afraid as I spoke to him. I hardly knew what I was saying and I had no last minute inspiration, but he understood me at once. His look was not so much angry as sulky and hurt. He said he didn't want to take anyone to camp who didn't want to go. Then he walked on down the corridor while I stood where I was, not even daring for a moment or two to let myself feel glad. But when I moved again a happiness arose in me as though the last day of term had already come.

Yet seventeen days later as I lay in bed at home on the first evening of the holidays such a misery came over me that I half-wished I could be back at school. The feeling began almost as soon as I got into bed after standing with

Hugh at the window of our bedroom looking out, though without coming so close to the window as to be seen to be looking, across the road at green-baize-aproned Mr Holt the furniture remover whom often before we had been fascinated by when on fine summer evenings he had stood in his open gateway as now with two large women talking and laughing one on each side of him while all three of them watched the traffic go by. Behind them the gravel drive curved back towards a gabled chalet-like building which had always appeared mysterious when the summer trees half hid it. This evening the broader of the two women, whom because of the big prominences of her bosom we had long ago given the mimetically-doubled name of Woomany-Wommany, abruptly stopped laughing and seemed to be staring towards something farther along the road past the front of our house and invisible to Hugh and me. Immediately afterwards Mr Holt and the other woman stared too, and then Mr Holt began to walk quickly though heavily in the direction of what he had seen. Soon our view of him was cut off by the corner of our house. The two women started to follow him, stopped, consulted with each other for half a minute, stared up the road again, consulted again, separated, Woomany-Wommany hurrying back towards the gateway and through it towards the gabled building while the other woman walked on almost as hurriedly after Mr Holt and was lost to view as he had been. We waited for them to reappear soon but they didn't, and after a while our interest in them lessened. Just before we got into our beds I heard the voice of our housemaid Ethel downstairs saying, 'There's been an accident.' Hugh may have heard her too, but neither of us said anything to the other about it as we got into bed. Perhaps — though I think this is unlikely — he was inhibited from speaking by the same sort of misery that came over me, a feeling as if this house was not my home any more, as if it was totally changed and strange to me.

The misery was not caused by the accident. There had been road accidents near our house before during my holidays at home, and I had been proud when my father had been called out to attend to the injured. Unhappiness had been latent in me to-day ever since I had arrived back home at tea-time with my mother and Hugh in the taxi from the station, and this present accident had merely helped to activate the feeling. Nor was it due to my father's being away from home now in the Royal Army Medical Corps which he had joined in the first year of the war: he had been away during previous holidays without my being miserable because of that, and he hadn't yet been sent abroad and would be coming back on leave from Norfolk in a week's time. As I lay unmoving in my bed I before long realised that the heartbreaking strangeness I was aware of was not caused by any change in the house here but by a change in me: it was I who had become estranged from what I had longed for, and school had made me become so. There had been earlier occasions when I had been upset on the day of my arrival home for the holidays — in the taxi from Waterloo to Liverpool Street I had so regularly felt sick from overexcitement that my mother always took the precaution of bringing a newspaper for me to vomit into if I had to — but there was something new and much worse than before about what I felt this evening. There was something in me which seemed like a half-wish to be back at school again, and as I recognised the existence of this unnatural wish my unhappiness became so great that only my awareness of Hugh lying awake in his bed beside mine prevented me from sobbing aloud.

I succeeded in destroying the horrible wish by forcing myself to remember what Marchfield had really been like. I thought of Snell. And before long the bedroom in which I was began to appear less alien. Something about the look of the wall near the foot of Hugh's bed opposite the windows was soothing to me. The sun going down behind Mr Holt's house across the road was not shining directly into the room any more, and its mild and mellow light on the wall seemed like a smile on a drowsy contented face. Other parts of the room became comforting too in the weakening brightness. I noticed on the dark green tiles of the mantelpiece a vermilion gleam, more sharply bright than the light on the wall because the tiles were glazed, and this gleam reminded me of the sea-serpent with glowing eyes at the bottom of the sea in a picture book I had had as a child before I could read. But am I beginning to invent impressions which I did not actually have while I lay in bed at home that evening? Is it true, as I would like to think it is, that the sequence in which I looked at objects in the room — first the green tiles, then the gas-bracket with its white glass globe on whose surface the windows were reflected as a small curving rectangle, then the bright tall mirror of the wardrobe to the left of the door — had the effect of seeming to reverse the process of sunset and to make the room become lighter, until after looking at the mirror I turned my head, and saw how much darker the chest-of-drawers against the wall near my bed was than it had been five minutes before? I don't doubt that I felt a happiness which seemed to arise from my seeing the evening light on objects in the room. And the happiness remained until I fell asleep, and it continued after I woke the next morning.

How different that happiness was from my feeling now as I walk along the cliff path and stare towards the curving white edge of the powder-blue sea in the bay. And yet, was that so utterly different? The anti-poetic despondency which came over me earlier this afternoon has been dispelled, even if not quite as quickly as my much more intense unhappiness was dispelled during my first evening home from Marchfield at the beginning of my third summer holidays. I see the gulls floating on the calm water not far out from the shore; there are twenty or thirty of them, in a configuration like one of the more complicated constellations — Draco or Hercules or Pisces — and my observing this likeness gives me something of the same kind of pleasure as I got from looking imaginatively at the evening light on objects in the bedroom of my Essex home fifty years ago. If I'm to live for poetry what I need isn't to do less work for C.N.D. but to continue more regularly the practice of making myself remember my past imaginings. I must be active for C.N.D. because I can find no other way yet of opposing the external menace which is the root cause of my despondent moods and which nothing can prevent from causing them except my actively opposing it. The truth is I need to do more not less work for C.N.D. I need to do more because the external menace has become greater now that the Soviet government, after breaking its own unilateral moratorium on nuclear tests a year ago and thereby giving the American imperialists a pretext for resuming their tests, is soon going to carry out further tests that will be followed by further American tests. I must do more not less to support the fight for the abolition of all tests and of all nuclear weapons if I am to be able to keep my mind poetically alive, as it is once again at the present moment.

I look inland at gulls on an undulating field with elms and a big thatched barn beyond it — the thatch in disrepair and uneven like mange on the grey back of a large prehistoric animal — and the gulls suddenly and simultaneously rise, at least a hundred of them, far more than those I saw just now in a configuration on the sea. They give the impression of carrying up with them into the air a wavy diaphanous fabric in which each individual gull is a unit of a repetitive pattern, and my spirits rise in me like the imagined fabric, and I am eager at the prospect of being able to work on my poem again to-morrow morning.

5

Why do I feel such a joy, such a calm and immutable-seeming exaltation, this afternoon as I walk up the High Street to pay bills at the newsagent's and the Gas Board showrooms before I go down to the shore? The look of the sky widening above the roofs of the buildings ahead is not the cause, any more than the look of the sea was the cause of my anti-poetic despondency a fortnight ago: I have not become so perverse that the sky elates me when it is overcast with evenly grey-white cloud and the sea depresses me when its colour is powder-blue. If I am to succeed in holding this joy for more than half an hour and in reviving it on other afternoons I need to discover its cause. The look of the street has nothing to do with what I feel: I am no less aware now than usual of things that have changed for the worse here since I was a boy — chiefly the motor-traffic which is already almost continuous to-day more than a month before the start of the holiday season; and I think I shall never be unaware of the disappearance of the bookshop at the corner of the road leading down to the War Memorial and its replacement by a shop selling fancy-goods and souvenirs. I admit that the squat white-painted balusters of the balustrade topping the façade of the Royal Marine Hotel are almost more beautiful to me this afternoon than they were fifty years ago, but it is my joy that makes them beautiful and not their beauty that causes my joy. Nor is the cause to be found in the work I did on my poem this morning or yesterday morning: both times I wrote less than usual, and what I wrote seemed bleak. No, I think my joy can only be explained as an after-effect of the C.N.D. vigil I took part in the day before yesterday, at the

War Memorial, to protest against the new series of nuclear tests that the Soviet government has begun.

But previous public C.N.D. activities which I have taken part in have never had quite such an euphoric effect on me afterwards — though it's true that, unlike the vigil, they have often helped me or seemed to help me to get on better with my poem the next morning. What was there especially about the vigil to make me so glad now? In one way it was less successful than several of our other public activities have been. I think it aroused more hostility; possibly our holding it at the War Memorial was regarded almost as sacrilegious by some people. There appeared to be at least half a dozen car drivers who sounded their horns at us as they drove past, in the manner of French rightwingers and neo-fascists demonstrating along the Champs Elysées, but there may have been fewer than half a dozen — I suspect that one or two of them may have driven past more than once purposely in order to sound their horns. Then there was the small crowd of children, who because it was a Saturday were off school and who, after staring for quite a while at us as we stood in silence and at the posters we were holding on poles and at the other posters we had leant up against the Memorial, became bold enough to climb on to the plinth behind us and to wander round it while we hesitated to order them off because of the undignified and perhaps antagonising impression this might have made on the public, particularly if the children had resisted. The arrival of the mad soldier half-way through the morning may have saved us from having them with us or near us for the rest of the day. I did not immediately know he was a soldier, as he was in civilian clothes and he said his home was on the Council estate just outside the town. His manner made me suppose at first that he was drunk but I soon decided he was more probably in the early stages of a mental illness, though I did have the passing thought that he might be some kind of provocateur. He kept on demanding, in a tone which seemed increasingly threatening, that we should give him one of our posters so that he could put it up in the window of his house on the estate, and he took no notice when we told him that we had no spare ones here but that if he would give us his address we would send him one by post. I felt that he might at any moment snatch the poster I was holding and walk off with it, or that he might push violently at some point through the single line we formed round the Memorial and might leap on to the plinth and seize one of the posters up there behind us. He did in fact notice a gap in our line and he moved towards it as if about to go up on to the plinth where several of the children had begun to chase one another round giggling quite loudly, but instead of going up he jerked forward his arms towards the children, his fingers curving like claws; and with his mouth wide open and his teeth bared he let out a tremendous roar which so effectively frightened them that they scuttled off immediately and did not return for the rest of the day. When they'd gone he came and asked me 'Why are you doing this? What is there in it for you?' I explained that I wasn't doing it for money nor as a cure for the varicose veins in my right leg (this rather risky bit of facetiousness luckily did not infuriate him) but because I had begun to doubt whether the Soviet government was any more fit to be trusted with nuclear weapons than the American and British governments were. He ignored my answer and asked the same question again and I gave much the same answer, though this time I stressed the huge destructiveness of these weapons, and he began to ask the same question a third time but abruptly stopped, changing the subject to some other weapon, perhaps napalm — his description of it was confused — which he had seen fired during army exercises and which he evidently regarded partly with horror as well as with some pride. His horror, I thought after he had walked away from us up into the High Street, was what had brought him to approach us at this vigil, and the hope came to me that as a result of his reading our posters and of remembering what I had said to him he might eventually join C.N.D., and/or better still might do anti-nuclear war propaganda in the army. However, it was not my conversation with the soldier, nor was it anything else that happened during the vigil, which has caused the joy I feel this afternoon. The real cause, I realise now, is that the vigil as a whole was an occasion when for the first time and at long last I protested publicly against something done by the Soviet government.

I did not feel this joy while I was actually at the War Memorial. My feeling then about protesting against the new series of Soviet nuclear tests still had something of guilt in it. Although for eight years the Soviet Union had no longer seemed to me, as it had during my sixteen years in the Communist Party and even for a while after I'd left the Party, a country which was carrying out a Leninist policy abroad and at home, nevertheless when its government under Kruschev proclaimed a unilaterial moratorium on nuclear tests — very embarrassing for the American imperialists who if they had ignored this and gone ahead with further tests of their own would have risked turning world opinion against themselves — I was able to think of the Soviet Union as a progressive country even though its leaders had deviated from Leninism. Then a year ago, at the time of the Berlin crisis when politicians from the German Federal Republic were intervening more and more in the affairs of West Berlin with the acquiescence of the occupying imperialist powers, and when as a counter-threat the Soviet government broke their own moratorium and resumed nuclear testing, 'for peace' Kruschev said, I saw them as crude imitators of the imperialists. Yet for almost a year after this I still could not totally believe that the country where the first successful working-class revolution in the world had occurred forty-five years ago had since then acquired leaders who had deviated so far from

Marxism-Leninism as to justify my demonstrating publicly against them. By taking part in the vigil I broke my very last ties of loyalty not only to the Soviet leadership but to the Party in Britain also. I finally and absolutely abandoned the old political life. My joy this afternoon assures me that the new poetic life has truly begun.

But I must not suppose that a true beginning of the new poetic life has been made possible solely by my final break two days ago with the old political life. It has been made possible also by my practice over the last few months of deliberately remembering my imaginings and imaginative impressions during the years before I first became politically active. I must not let euphoria persuade me now that there's no need to continue this practice in future. If I neglected this again as I did during the week before my almost neurotic despondency of a fortnight ago, I know I would be at risk of falling back into the same mood I was in then. I broke out of that mood by remembering how at my Prep. school my imagination developed in spite of all the constrictions and distortions which might have stunted its growth there; and the way I can best strengthen myself against the future obstacles which my new poetic life is bound to meet with is by continuing to think of how when I was young my imagination survived in much less favourable conditions than exist for it now. Let me think how it survived and developed during my time as a boy at my 'Public' school.

I have walked past the newsagent's and now I am walking past the Gas showrooms too. The bills can be paid to-morrow. Why is it that Elsie and I have always been so punctual in paying our bills, just as we've always seemed incapable of arriving late for meetings? I suppose we have anxious consciences. But if I were to turn back immediately and go into the Gas showrooms I might risk losing my hold on a remembrance which began to come to me a moment before I passed the newsagent's. It is of myself during my first or second term at Rugtonstead sitting at a table in the evening, seemingly alone, reading poetry. It may have been evoked by the sight of several red-covered commercial account-books among the other stationery behind the glass of the newsagent's shop-window. The poems I was reading were handwritten in a dark-crimson-covered notebook: they were my favourites which I had copied out from anthologies and I hoped to get to know all of them by heart eventually. But I cannot really have been alone as I read them. There was almost nowhere at this school where a boy could be private for long: in Dunton House, which I had become a member of because Rags knew its Housemaster Morphew, even the lavatories had doors whose lower halves were cut away so that at least the legs of the occupants could be seen from outside. The poems must have had so strong an effect on my emotions that besides freeing me temporarily from the unhappiness which the school normally caused in me they made me very nearly oblivious of other boys who must have been in the room with me and may have been sitting at the same table.

How was I able to sit peacefully reading there? Probably it was during the time when we were all supposed to be doing our prep. for the next day's lessons. At any other time I would have been unlikely to be free from interference of some kind for more than a minute or two. The hustle and the harassment during my first few terms were even worse than I had expected. I had known at my Preparatory school that 'fagging' went on at Public schools, which I understood to mean that the younger boys were forced to run errands for the older boys and to act as personal servants to them and were sometimes beaten by them, but I had got the impression — perhaps from reading unrealistic school stories in boys' magazines — that all this was more or less clandestine and illicit, and that the risk of punishment if it was discovered by the masters would prevent the older boys from carrying it too far. I was shocked to find that in reality fagging was organised by the Housemasters themselves. In each of the eight separate Houses into which the school was divided the Housemaster allocated his boarders to day rooms of varying sizes called 'studies' where there would be from two to five fags, and from one to three 'seconds' (who had been released from fagging after more than a year of it but who had no authority yet over boys who were still fags), and one studyholder, who could order the fags in his study to do what he chose and could beat them whenever and for whatever he thought fit. And although he was not empowered, unless the Housemaster had appointed him to be a House Prefect as well as a studyholder, to give orders or a 'bumming' with his ferruled cadet-corps swagger-stick to fags from other studies, he could and usually did compensate himself for this limitation by using the powers he had with a greater gusto than the cold-mannered and self-righteous-looking Prefects would have thought consistent with their dignity. I was lucky in having Selby as my studyholder; he was comparatively easy-going even though like other studyholders he believed that the fags should not be allowed to 'get above themselves', and sometimes in order to have a pretext for beating one or other of them whom he couldn't find fault with for any actual neglect of duty he would resort to tricks such as sprinkling fine ash from the fire on to the mantelpiece and on to the tops of picture frames when the fag who had already performed the duty of dusting them was out of the study for the moment. He didn't need to play tricks in order to find fault with me, as I was not a very competent fag; I was clumsy-handed at that age, and unresourceful — for instance when it was my turn to cook porridge over the study fire for all the members of the study in the evenings I more than once burnt it slightly, a fault I could have avoided if I had stirred it without stopping or if instead of using the old iron saucepan provided long ago by Morphew as part of the equipment of the study I had been capable like several other fags of acquiring from somewhere a double-saucepan in which the porridge could be steam-cooked with no danger of burning — nevertheless Selby did not beat me more than two or three times a term on an average. His manner was never harsh: when he said to me halfway through my first term 'It appears you are incomp' he said it with a not wholly unamiable though sardonic grin. Some of the older fags despised him a little because he was not good at games, and the news later on after he'd left school that he had been killed in France as soon as he'd been sent to the front did not seem to cause much concern in the House. The contempt in which I was held by the older fags for being incomp, and the taunts I constantly got from them, were much more bitter and upsetting to me than any beating Selby gave me. The ringleader among them against me was for a while Buscarlett, who had come from Marchfield a year before me. It was he who was always drawing the attention of the others to my incompetence and who took to calling me Auntie Flo, a nickname that the others readily adopted no doubt partly because my looks had something feminine about them, which I suppose I inherited from my father since he was called Nellie at school. I had quarrelled with Buscarlett during his last year at Marchfield and he had said to me that when I got to Dunton House he would be a year senior to me and would be able to make life hell for me there. I was very frightened by his threat, and the only way of preventing him from carrying it out that I could think of was by making a friend of him before he left Marchfield. I succeeded in this, and I persuaded myself I liked him, and after he left we exchanged letters which became increasingly warm, so much so that my mother felt bound at last to reveal she had been secretly reading the letters he'd written me and to comment that the friendship between him and me seemed — she used a German word whose meaning I could guess — a kind of Schwärmerei. She was right, at any rate as far as Buscarlett was concerned: I found when I got to Dunton House that under the influence of what went on there his attitude towards me had become consciously homosexual, and as soon as he realised I was not going to gratify him physically he turned against me and hated me still more venomously than he once had at our Prep. school. It's true he did no more than help to intensify the general disrespect which my ineptitude as a fag would have brought on me anyway. Even my friend Tilford who had left our Prep. school at the same time as I had and was a 'new bug' with me at Dunton House seemed to want to avoid associating with me. And the fact that I was quite good at football, which could have won me some approval in the House, was not discovered for a long time because I was always put down to play in 'Remnants' instead of in one of the House teams, the assumption being that someone as incomp as I was couldn't possibly be any use at games. It's a wonder that during my first two terms I didn't feel far too abased to be able to respond to the poems I read in the evenings. But they were a refuge for me, and after reading them I was strengthened inwardly against the hostile nastiness of my environment.

Many and perhaps most of the poems I'd copied into my crimson-covered notebook were about love. In the table of contents that I made on the first page I put signs against the titles to show which poems I thought good, which better, which better still and which best. The two poems I marked as best were Shelley's *Indian Serenade* and Herrick's *To Anthea, Who May Command Him Anything* (I did not detect the typical seventeenth century double entendre in the last two lines of this — 'And hast command of every part/To live and die for thee': if I had detected it I would at my age then have regarded it as an unpleasant anti-climax to the exalted feeling of all the preceding lines and I might have demoted the poem to 'better' or even to 'good'). Their poetic quality may partly have been the cause of my preference for these poems, but as Byron says of the young Don Juan's new interest in the beauties of Nature 'I can't help thinking puberty assisted'. The need for love was what caused poems about love to appeal so much to me, and they helped to give a poetically exalted quality to love when it came to me in actuality during my second term.

I fell in love with Young Jib. I did not call him by his real name, Shannon; I liked his nickname — which was ready-made for him because relatives of his who had been at the school before him had all been called Jib, though no one any longer knew why, and he was called Young because he had an elder brother still in Dunton House. He came to the school the same term as I did and he was in the same form as I was though not in the same study. He was rather shorter than me, had light blue eyes, was keen on poetry like me, and he had the same feelings towards me as I had towards him. Which of us was the first to feel love for the other I don't know, but whichever it was the other responded at once. My love for him was the only romantic love in my life that has ever been mutual. No doubt if we had been together in a day-school instead of in a Public boarding-school segregated from ordinary life, and if we had been able to meet girls, we wouldn't have fallen in love with each other. And our love was quite different from the love we would have had for girls: kissing him or holding hands with him would have seemed as abhorrently sentimental and unnatural to me as it would have to him, though I was very conscious of his physical beauty. Psychoanalytical theorists of the kind who have become fashionable under monopoly capitalism while bourgeois culture has been in decay would call our relationship sexual and would find more significance in the similarity than in the difference between it and the relationship I would have had with Buscarlett if I had done what he wanted, just as they would find more significance in the similarity than in the difference between the liking Lewis Carroll had for holding little girls on his knee and the feelings of a rapist of children, or just as some of them might use the term 'zoophilist' to refer both to the ordinary animal lover and the pathological case who has sexual intercourse with goats or dogs. My love for Young Jib certainly had an element of sexuality in it, but essentially it was poetic, and if we had become physically intimate even to the extent of merely holding hands its essence would have been destroyed. All the subtle and the intense and the delicate feelings which the reading of poetry about love had aroused in me found their living object in him. And the poem that seemed to express better than any other how I felt towards him — a poem I had first got to know as a song whose music made its words appeal still more to me — was *The Gentle Maiden,* and its opening line was 'There is one who is pure as an angel.'

The poetry of our love was before long subjected to attempts by other members of the House to smirch it. Buscarlett, guided by jealousy I suppose, was the first to discover that there was what in school slang used to be called a 'keenness' between Young Jib and me, and one day he came up to me and asked loudly in the hearing of a number of other fags, 'Have you and Young Jib had kittens yet?' Afterwards, strangely, he seldom taunted me in this way again; however the attack was taken up by others including one or two of the seconds though by none of the studyholders — most of whom probably did get to know about Young Jib and me but must have thought it beneath them to appear to notice the keenness between us. The worst of the taunters and sneerers were three older fags named Tetlow, Fisk and Barling, who were often in one another's company, and the most persistent of the three was Fisk, a crude sensualist lacking the courage to try to put his desires into practice with anyone except himself. Typical of the kind of thing he would say in jeering at me about Young Jib was 'I bet your handkerchief is so stiff you could stand it up on the mantelpiece as an ornament', and when he said this there was something of a plaintive wistfulness as well as malevolence in his voice. The other two were no less coarse than he was but Tetlow was harsher and Barling always had an exaggerated grin on his face as he delivered his taunts. They seldom attacked me physically, partly because they found I was quite strong and could fight back, though mainly because unofficial physical bullying was disapproved of in the House and they could have been officially beaten for it if the Prefects had caught them at it. I think that Young Jib himself, being a competent fag unlike me and having an elder brother who was a Prefect, was less often taunted about me than I was about him, and although we never said anything to each other about the taunts I had the impression that he did not resent them much and even that he was slightly flattered by them, as if he rather liked being thought to be a bit of a roué. But I was more unsophisticated than he was, and I felt wounded and dirtied by them. And at this time when they were at their vilest I got a letter from my godmother Margie that contained, besides several patriotic remarks about the war against Germany, the sentence 'I hope you have been able to make a good British friend at the school.' After reading this letter I bitterly repeated to myself again and again her phrase 'a good British friend', and a sense of irony awoke in me which was a beginning of the cynicism I was to feel later about the patriotic attitudes of my elders and which also had the more immediate effect of strengthening me inwardly against those members of Dunton House who wanted to smirch the purity of my feelings for Young Jib.

My enemies did not succeed in destroying the poetry of my love for him. On the contrary my poetic imagination was able to dramatise their malevolence and to show them to me as figures of evil, far larger than life, so that my love was enhanced by a feeling of being romantically alone with him on the side of goodness. In reality they were fairly ordinary middle-class boys for whom puberty was being made more difficult, and whose general development was being warped — just as mine was in a rather different way — by the Public school system. I saw them as innately base and vicious. Even their physical appearance seemed horrible: Fisk's rubbery sallow cheeks and his large mouth which was nearly always half-open, like a dog's except that he didn't visibly salivate; Tetlow's fat eyelids which closed to slits when he sneered at me, and his protuberant dark-brown cylindrically-shaped mole like an earth-worm beginning to emerge from the flesh just behind his ear; Barling's head round almost as a small football, and his face which though shiny red never looked clean, and the inhumanly un-changing and malicious grin with which he looked at me. But their talk was still nastier than their looks. It was not just mechanically abusive like the language of many other members of the House whose favourite expression when speaking to anyone junior to them was 'Damn your eyes': it was really venomous. However, I found the abusiveness of their talk less hateful than what I thought of as its immorality, by which I meant its pre-occupation with physical sex, though in this it was mostly a contemptible and sycophantic imitation of the talk of many of their seniors which I regarded as even more evil because more seriously lascivious. I sensed that the immorality in the House went deeper than mere talk, and it oppressed my mind and feelings at least as heavily as the attacks made on me by my particular enemies. The oldest of the seconds — his name was Lutworth and he never said or did anything unpleasant to me personally — seemed to me to be the most flagrantly immoral person in the House, not so much because of the stories I heard him tell, one of them for instance about prostitutes who wore nothing under their fur coats, and another about a well-known actress who according to him had once raffled herself among a group of young officers and had then copulated with the winner in front of the others, as because of his habit of doing solo dances in the hall, flicking his fingers and undulating his arms and writhing his rump like a woman's to music played on the piano at his request by a fag named Parsons (whom nevertheless I couldn't help envying for the skill at sight-reading which caused him to be in demand among his seniors including the Prefects whenever they wanted someone to play music for them). I did not realise until the end of my second term that the immorality in the House reached up to the very top of it, to the Housemaster Morphew himself. Though ordinarily he had seemed to me more aloof than the aloofest of the Prefects, he was the only person who during my first three weeks at the school had spoken with kindness to me and had said one evening when he caught up with me walking by myself behind other boys going in pairs and threes to chapel, 'I hope you aren't feeling too miserable'; but when the news broke in the House during the last week of my first Easter term that the Prefects had been carrying out an investigation among certain of the fags and afterwards had gone to report to the Headmaster that Morphew had been interfering sexually with several of these fags, 'tossing them off' as the saying in the House went, and when the official story was put around that Morphew would be leaving at the end of the term because he wanted to join the army, a story designed no doubt primarily to protect the reputation of the school rather than of Morphew himself, I felt no sympathy for him at all. Wholly unaware as I was then of the pressures which the war with its general undermining of bourgeois moral standards had exerted on him, a bachelor and possibly a natural homosexual who was no worse a schoolmaster for that and who might during normal times not even have dreamed of seducing any boy in his charge, I forgot his kindness to me as a new boy and I remembered only — with hindsighted understanding — how when I had had to go alone to his room to be weighed by him as all the fags in turn were (on the pretext that he wanted to make sure we

were none of us losing weight owing to war-time rations),
he had told me to get into my birthday suit and I had been
conscious of his strangely heavy breathing as he had kneeled
down in front of me to put the weights on the scales. His
downfall and disgrace made me think of the House as
having been a yet more evil place than I had already
realised it to be, but I was able to find poetic compensation
in the picture my imagination created of it as a hell through
which I together with Young Jib — though not with my
Prepschool friend Tilford who had been weak enough to try
to win the favour of the older fags by talking dirt like them
— was walking in heroic uprightness.

It was true that at nights when I was in bed in the
dormitory I myself was often guilty of private acts of
sensuality, but although these made me less easily able to
sustain my conception of myself as walking innocently
through hell they were not the cause of the general
weakening of poetic feeling in me that began during my
third term. Very possibly they would have caused such a
weakening if I had been really frightened by the warnings
contained in a book called *What a boy should know* which
my mother had given me and which said that the inmates of
asylums constantly practised self-abuse and that therefore
boys who did so would be likely to end up in asylums, but
fortunately I had enough commonsense to be able to
recognise that what I thought of as my lapses into
immorality were not doing me any physical or mental
damage. And sermons in the school chapel from preachers
who discreetly attacked the sin of 'giving way to one's lower
nature' could have slowed down my imaginative
development if they had influenced me, as they influenced a
few of the other boys, to make excessive and agonised efforts
to resist the overwhelming urges of puberty, but my
experience of Snell had immunised me against such attacks
from the pulpit. On the other hand my imagination might
have been coarsened and enervated if the puritanism which

was kept strong in me by my love for my home and by my loyalty to my childhood had not prevented my private acts of sensuality from becoming more frequent. It was not these acts that during my first summer term caused a lessening of my enthusiasm for poetry. It was the change that began one afternoon then in my relationship with Young Jib.

I was sitting on the grass bank near the cricket pavilion watching him bat in an Under 15 House match. He had made about thirty-five runs and was batting very steadily, without being too cautious and without giving any chances to the other side, and the hope came to me that he might go on to make his fifty, which would have been an exceptional achievement in an Under 15 match, but he was run out during the next over entirely through the fault of the other batsman. He showed no annoyance or disappointment as he walked away from the wicket, and the clapping from all the spectators on the grass bank began while he had at least twenty yards yet to go before reaching the steps of the pavilion. He went up the steps with self-possession, neither so slowly as to seem to want to bask in the applause nor so quickly as to seem over-modest, and at the top of the steps he stood still in the sunlight for a moment, undoing his batting gloves. While he stood there the gladness which his triumph gave me was suddenly annihilated by a feeling I had never had about him till then, a fear that I was going to lose him, that his success at cricket would make older boys regard him as someone they could allow to associate with them almost as an equal even though he was a fag, that he would be raised up far above me. When I congratulated him after the game the obligatory slang word 'graggers' grated on me as I spoke it, though I did my best to hide what I felt. I was sure I succeeded in hiding it, but I was aware of a slight remoteness and almost a graciousness in his look when he thanked me for my congratulations, and simultaneously I realised that this remoteness was nothing new, that it had been in his look for some weeks already during this summer term, and I guessed it meant he had begun to think of our friendship as something that might become a hindrance to his career in the House. I hoped I might be mistaken, but during the rest of the summer term he showed clearer signs of wanting to have less to do with me, and though his earlier feelings for me seemed to revive temporarily during the Christmas term — when I was becoming recognised in the House as a fairly good footballer — the unhappy process of falling out of love with him was never reversed in me. The poetry ebbed from my feelings towards him, while at the same time the love poems which had been my favourites and had helped to give my love for him its poetic quality lost some of their appeal for me. In the evenings of the Christmas term I did not so often take out my crimson-covered notebook from my locker in the study. I began to fall out of love with poetry as well as with Young Jib, but falling out of love with poetry was a process that was not irreversible. It was reversed during the Christmas holidays soon after I fell in love with Christine Dunbar.

I met her at a party in the Dunbars' house, and I was only gradually aware then of how dazzlingly different she was from when I had last known her eight years before at the kindergarten where we had been children together, though in some things she seemed very much the same — her dark hair was still plaited into two pigtails with a ribbon tied in a bow at the end of each of them, her complexion had not lost its childlike pink and white, her voice still had a slight gentle huskiness in it — and the sameness beneath the difference helped me to overcome the shyness which the difference would otherwise have caused in me. But when I got back home again after the party she became transformed for me into someone whom I seemed not to have known previously at all and who was so beautiful that the calmness I had felt while talking to her and dancing with her was hardly believable to me. I stayed awake in bed for much of that night and several following nights, going over in my mind everything I could remember about how she had looked and what she had said while we had been together, and during the days — except at times when I dared to walk or bicycle down her road in the hope (never fulfilled) of catching a glimpse of her at one of the windows of her house — I fed my love for her with daydreams about the coming party at our house when I would meet her once more, and also with love poems, mainly by Byron and Tennyson, which I often read to myself. Byron's poem beginning with the lines 'She walks in beauty like the night/Of cloudless climes and starry skies' seemed marvellously true of Christine whose eyes were so dark and yet so bright; and there were parts of Tennyson's *Maud* that seemed even truer, especially the part which began 'There is none like her, none,/Nor will be when our summers have deceased'. The words 'None like her, none' I repeated over and over again to myself, slowly, as I sat alone in the morning-room at home looking out of the window at the gravel path beyond the verandah, and also the words 'Just now the dry-tongued laurels' pattering talk/Seemed her light foot along the garden walk' which were especially evocative for me because we had laurels in our garden. When the day of our party at last came I had fears just before she arrived that my daydreams might have exaggerated her attractiveness and that her actual presence might be disappointing to me, but as soon as I saw her I realised that she was far more beautiful than I had been able to imagine. And though I danced with her only twice instead of three times as at the Dunbars' party, and though I did not see her again during the remaining days of the Christmas holidays, my love for her — and with it my revived love for poetry — was strong enough to survive after I got back to school for the Easter term, which during the first four or five weeks was the worst term I ever had.

I found when I got back that all the other boys who like

me had been in Dunton House for four terms were released from fagging, whereas I was still a fag. Ritchie, who had succeeded Morphew as Housemaster — he was nicknamed Scratch, because of the 'itch' in his name — took a more active part than Morphew had taken in running the House, and unlike Morphew he was a man with intellectual interests, but he evidently accepted the Prefects' estimate of me and thought that another term of fagging would do me good. The humiliation of being still a fag when my contemporaries had become seconds made fagging more hateful to me than it had ever been before, even though Burgess my new studyholder did not beat me; and I found no compensation in the fact that this term we were in a different and less dilapidated building — the authorities having come to recognise the unfitness of the old Dunton House for habitation — and that I would never again see the inside of my former study with its dirty walls and with the poker holes burnt into the brown-painted wood on either side of its fireplace, nor hurry along the worn floorboards of its dark corridors with their many corners and frequent steps and varying levels (like the corridors of the school described in Poe's story *William Wilson* that I had read at Marchfield), nor would I again kick a football across the yard which was in the middle of the old building and had high walls all round it with wire-covered windows in them and seemed like a prison yard, nor would I again smell the ominous fire-smell that had lingered on for so long in the dormitories after a fire discovered downstairs one night during my first Easter term by Morphew just as he was about to go to bed and just in time to save us all from being burnt to death, which we certainly would otherwise have been since no kind of fire-escape had been provided. The House at the beginning of my second Easter term, in spite of the different and better building and of our having a better Housemaster than Morphew, was anyway not much less savage than in Morphew's time. Although I was not beaten, others were; the hustle and the taunting went on as before; ball-fighting seemed on the increase; when we had hash for lunch, which was often, it was still spoken of among the boys as 'Squitter à la singe' though more usually now as 'Ma Scratch's babies' (Ritchie unlike Morphew was not a bachelor, had been chosen as Morphew's successor perhaps partly because he wasn't, and his wife had to act as housekeeper for the House); most of the boys behaved like swine to the matron, who was incapable of being strict with them, and they loathsomely bullied the red-headed boy from the village who was paid to clean their shoes for them; and whenever during the Saturday evening 'sing-songs' which Ritchie had instituted in the House we sang the song that has the chorus 'Adieu, adieu, adieu kind friends, adieu/I can no longer stay with you, stay with you' those boys sitting nearest to Shapiro, who was then the only Jewish boy in the House, would sing 'A jew, a jew, a jew kind friends, a jew/I can no longer stay with *you*, stay with *you*', and some of them — if Scratch was not looking their way — would add the gesture of pressing their forefingers horizontally up against their nostrils. The persisting nastiness in the House together with the humiliation I felt at being still a fag caused a depression in me which seldom lifted and which wasn't made any less genuine — though it was made slightly more tolerable — by the practice I adopted of going about always with a deliberate look of moroseness on my face: No one commented on it to me, and hardly anyone seemed to notice it, but I thought Ritchie did. However, during the third week of the term I developed a strange kind of skin disease which everyone before long noticed, mostly with revulsion. All over the backs of my hands and fingers small itchily inflamed patches appeared with yellowish blisters at their centres and became raw when the blisters burst; and the rawness was painful, especially at the finger joints. The matron put ointment on them but they persisted and became worse. Tilford, with whom I was friendly again after having partly got over my disgust at his readiness during our first term to play up to the older fags by talking dirt like them, suggested the good idea to me that I should go and see Dr Wolsey and ask him whether he thought I might be able to get rid of my blisters if I were allowed to go home to my parents for a while. Dr Wolsey was the younger of the two school doctors and he had the reputation of being more sympathetic than his partner Dr Crump — it was believed the Headmaster had once discovered that Wolsey was being consulted by boys who wanted to overcome habits of self-abuse and had demanded to know the names of the boys, but Wolsey had refused to reveal them — however, when Ritchie gave me permission one morning to walk down to the surgery in the village I hadn't really much hope of Wolsey's agreeing that I should go home, and I wasn't even sure that it mightn't be Crump instead of him who would see me. Luckily, after I had climbed the steps to the surgery — I think I remember it looked rather like a railway signal box, with a mass of medicine bottles indistinctly visible behind the horizontal window which extended along part of its upper half — I found Wolsey there. He examined my hands, didn't pretend to know what the disease was, said something about 'bad blood', and when I timidly asked whether he thought a week at home might help me to get better he brightened at once and said he thought it might. He wrote me a note to give to Ritchie, which I held in my hand as I went down the surgery steps and as I walked back up the village street, afraid I might crumple it or even lose it if I pushed it in among the other envelopes and papers in my pocket. It was my signed release from hell and my pass to the heaven of home and Christine. Two lines from Tennyson's *Maud* came into my head as I walked back — 'For a breeze of morning moves,/And the planet of love is on high' — and I had a feeling as though I was composing them myself, as though they were quite new and different from anything I had read. It was a foretoken of the feeling I was to have a week later, at home, when I began to write the first poem of my own that I had ever written.

The impulse to write. it came to me as I was sitting alone in the morning-room looking out of the window at the honeysuckle, leafless at that time of year, which partly screened the corrugated-iron garage beyond the far end of the lawn. I had just come in from bicycling along the road where Christine's house was. She had not been visible at any of the windows and I can't really have expected her to be, since I must have known that unless she was ill she would almost certainly be in school at this time of the morning; however, I wouldn't have dared to bicycle anywhere near her High School where the girls might notice me and guess I was interested in one of them and might even somehow discover which one it was. The crimson-covered notebook that I began to write my poem in was the same that I had used at Dunton House for copying out poems by other poets, real poets, and during the past few days I had also been trying to make drawings in it of Christine, but all of these had fallen so far short of achieving a likeness that I had finished each of them by changing it into a drawing of the face of a man with a moustache. I still know this first poem of mine by heart, and I think I would have been able to remember every word of it even if I hadn't read it again in my crimson notebook two evenings ago. The opening line of the poem was *When in dark dejection's dungeon I was thrown,* and after writing this down I decided that the poem as a whole was going to be a sonnet. I knew that sonnets had fourteen lines, but not that their metre was ordinarily iambic — I was even ignorant of what the word iambic meant — nor that they ordinarily had five accented syllables to each line. I was aware that there was a difference in form between a Shakespearean and a Miltonic sonnet, and the rhyming scheme which I found easiest to use in the first four lines of my sonnet was Miltonic, but although I was able to make the sixth and seventh lines (*I have prayed — my prayers were vain/Useless efforts of a worn-out brain*) rhyme as in a Miltonic sonnet with the second and third lines (*Nor God nor man could cheer my pain; When, by night, fever-tortured I have lain*), I couldn't make the fifth line (*Has seized my soul with dread unmeaningness*) and the eighth line (*I have thought, till thoughts were worth no more, no less*) rhyme with the fourth (*And dark terror of a vague and deep unknown*); however I was able, in compensation for this insufficiency of rhyming to write a ninth line (*Than black night of the abyss whose depths are bottomless*) and a twelfth (*Until in thee my heart found joy to everlastingness*) which rhymed with the fifth and eighth. My sonnet, like a Shakespearean one, had a couplet at the end of it (*And since that time my life has ever been/A dream of wanderings with the spirit of Christine.*) which did not rhyme with the tenth and eleventh lines (*Nor knew I any unto whom I might resort/when evil mood my spirit fought.*). I was not worried by my failure to keep to an orthodox rhyming scheme — nor by the general badness of the poem, which I was quite unconscious of. While I was writing it I had a sensation of wonder at the way the words came to me as if of their own accord or as if some power outside me were presenting me with them, and this is not surprising since in fact they were sometimes dictated to me by the need to make a rhyme and they were inspired throughout more by the words of romantic poems, particularly Byron's, I had read in Palgrave's *Golden Treasury* than by any actual experiences of mine at school or by my actual love for Christine. But when I succeeded in bringing in the word 'Christine' at the end of the final line I felt that the poem was my own, that I and not any power outside me was its creator. And together with the immediate keen thrill of love which came to me as I wrote down her name I had also a feeling, quite distinct from love yet rivalling it in intensity, of exultation at having become a poet. From that morning on until I had to go back to school again I was as eager each day to write poetry as I was to walk or bicycle past her house in the hope of seeing her at one of the windows.

Not all my poems were to do with love. The second one I wrote was called *Glory* and it contained the lines *He who after glory sought/Would live a life by fear distraught.* The third was called *Woodstock*: it was based on Scott's novel of that title and it praised King Charles I and was against Oliver Cromwell. The fourth was called *The Sinner (Victim of bitter remorse and repentance drear)*. I don't know whether I was consciously referring in it to my own lapses into 'immorality'. Several of the poems were about school; *The Lost Friend* may have been suggested by my drifting apart from Young Jib, and an untitled poem which began with the lines, *Traitors be they all, not one is true or staunch,/May they be destroyed, yea cut off root and branch/And he, his lying tongue, his taunts, his cutting jeers,/Let him have his taste of hell, let him drink his cup of tears,* referred both to such enemies of mine as Fisk, Tetlow and Barling and to certain fags who had been new boys with me and should have stood by me but who had sycophantically joined with those three against me. Besides poems, I began to write imaginative prose, usually in the evenings while I sat up in bed before going to sleep. By the end of my three weeks at home I had finished writing *The Book of Eitna*. It was modelled on *The Book of Artemas the Scribe*, a recently published topical skit in Biblical language about the war between the men of En and the men of Hu, 'Hu' being short for 'Huns' which was what the newspapers called the Germans. *The Book of Eitna* was about events at school and particularly at Dunton House, and the name 'Eitna' was my nickname 'Auntie' spelt in reverse with the 'u' left out. I got the idea of reverse spelling from Samuel Butler's *Erewhon* which I had just read. My scribe in the first chapter of *The Book of Eitna* had a vision of a great city in which there were eight palaces, and he saw a mighty angel come down from heaven clothed in a cloud who said unto him 'Thou must prophesy before many people and nations and kings.' In the second chapter Eitna looked even more steadfastly at the vision before him and he beheld many things that were corrupt and unseemly, and a voice out of the city cried unto him with an exceeding bitter cry— 'su evas, su evas', and Eitna was greatly troubled for there appeared unto him no remedy that he could offer. The cry came from the palace of Notnud, the ruler of which was called Wehprom. Subsequent chapters described how the Lord sent down fire and brimstone from heaven to consume the children of iniquity in the palace of Notnud and how, after Wehprom had attempted with the devices of man to lessen the flames, God had had mercy on the children of Notnud and caused the fire to cease, but Wehprom had continued in his evil practices afterwards until Ssob the great king learned of his wickedness and banished him for ever from the city. Another actual event which I gave an account of in *The Book of Eitna*, was the dismissal by the Headmaster of two young assistant masters who were said to have been carrying on pacifist propaganda among members of the Sixth Form. My sympathies at the time were far from being with these two masters whom I made Eitna describe as 'men of evil character in the land and cunning of speech' and also as 'two lewd fellows of the baser sort'. Why did I choose to write about school when I had temporarily escaped from it? I think because writing about it helped to exorcise my dread of it — (denouncing it like an Old Testament prophet gave me the feeling that I was raised above it) — and to strengthen me against the nearing day when I would have to return to it. After I had been at home for ten days the inflamed blisters were entirely gone from my hands. My father, who although he hated being a doctor was a more intelligent and competent one than the average in those days, was not much less scornful and resentful than my mother was of Dr Wolsey's diagnosis of my condition as being due to 'bad blood'. When the blisters disappeared my father decided that they had probably been nothing worse than a form of chilblains — and I am sure he was right, as I have had them at times since then during cold weather, though never so severely as during that Easter term — and he and my mother wanted me to go back to school, but I resisted and I persuaded them to let me stay on at home for another week. They tried to discover from me why I was so very unwilling to go back, but I could not bring myself to describe the vileness of Dunton House in sufficient detail to convince them of it, nor could I tell them that what more than anything else made me unready to go was that if I did I should lose the possibility of seeing Christine. I wrote a poem which began with the lines *Why do I hate that awful place?/They have sought the reason from me,/And I have lied — lied to their face/For I dared not speak of thee./Tied down to home by thy loveliness,/Thy sweet and infinite grace,/Tied down, yea and determined to stay/For the love of a beautiful face.* However, at the end of three weeks the fifteen or so poems I had written had given me sufficient strength to be ready to go back.

I found when I got back that Dunton House was slightly less vile than I had expected. For one thing, I had been let out of fagging: perhaps there had been correspondence between my parents and Ritchie and this was a result of it. For another thing, several members of the House who had hitherto looked down on me began to seek my company — not because I had become a 'second' but because of certain happenings in the House during my three-weeks' absence. *The Book of Eitna* contained a chapter describing how in the new palace of Notnud there were Pharisees, Sadducees and Essenes, the Pharisees being 'evil men who did every kind of wrong' (I was thinking particularly of Tetlow, Fisk and Barling), the Sadducees being men who 'put themselves out to annoy and did behave as babes' (I was thinking of my new studyholder, Burgess, among others), the Essenes — of whom there were very few — being men 'who were moved to do right' (I was thinking chiefly of myself, though also of Young Jib and one or two others such as Parsons the piano player), and in the next chapter Eitna recorded that the evil doings of the Pharisees were laid bare before Eichtir, the new ruler of Notnud, who meted out rightful punishment to these iniquitous men, and some of them were hard pressed to avoid being exiled from the land. I don't remember whether in actuality Tetlow, Fisk and Barlow or any of their associates were punished or threatened with expulsion by Ritchie, but certainly he had them up before him one by one in his study and afterwards they got together to try to discover who had betrayed them to him. They chose to believe without any evidence that Parsons, Young Jib and a few others including myself whose talk was less foul than the average had been the informers, and they organised a movement to put us into Coventry. It brought us, the Essenes, together and made me more cheerful than I had yet been at Rugtonstead, because I had not had as many close friends before, but it made Parsons so unhappy that he eventually went to Ritchie about it and Ritchie as a result announced to the whole House at prayers that the information he had received recently about the behaviour of certain members of the House had come to him solely from the Prefects. After this, Tetlow, Fisk and Barling could no longer keep us in Coventry, and Parsons and Young Jib and the other Essenes were no longer keen on having me in company with them and our group broke up and once again I became, as I had been before my three weeks at home, someone who was not thought much of in the House. The feeling which I had been made to have during my first year that because of my incompetence as a fag I was a kind of pariah began to revive in me, though in a less acute form now that I was out of fagging; but one evening something happened to rid me of this feeling for good. I was alone in one of the bathrooms — or bath compartments as they really were with their brown wooden partition walls and boltless doors — and I was having the weekly hot bath we all had to have. While lying in the water I thought of Young Jib and Parsons and the other Essenes. At the moment when I stepped out of the bath on to the wooden slats of the bath-mat the conviction came to me, as intensely as if it had been spoken to me in a vision, that I was not inferior to them but only different from them, and I knew I was glad to be different. I knew too that this conviction would not be a transient one, that it would last for the rest of my time at Rugtonstead, as in fact it did. I wish I could be as sure that the mood of joy which began this afternoon an hour ago while I was walking along the High Street will last for most of the remaining years of my retirement

The truth is that already the mood isn't quite so confident as it was an hour ago. Why? Not because of the continuing dullness of the weather: the grey-whiteness of the sky did nothing to prevent my joy from arising in the first place; and anyway the sea to-day does not seem dull to me with its unevenly advancing breakers shinily concave just before they topple and pouncing forward like feline paws as they level out on the beach — even though its roughness has caused its green to be tinged with the brown of the sand it has churned up and though the colour of its foam is a dirty cream. Perhaps the slight weakening in my joy during my walk along the shore this afternoon has been due to my remembering the unpleasantnesses of Rugtonstead; but these oughtn't to depress me at all now, especially as I have also remembered that moment in the bathroom when, no doubt mainly because I had become a poet during my three weeks at home, I was at last able to feel convinced that I did not deserve to be despised by the other members of the House. I think the real cause of my not having been able to sustain my joy fully has been a reviving at the back of my mind of the suspicion I had this morning that the poem I have been writing since my retirement may be too bleak and bare to be good. Very well, suppose the suspicion is justified (and it may not be), there's no need for me to despair of the poem. I could aim to make it richer as I go on with it and eventually I could return to what I've already written and try to enrich that too. I could aim to make it really alluring in itself, gem-like, though of course I should have to be on guard against treating it as a sort of art-object sufficient in itself and I should always have to keep in mind its secondary function of supporting the political struggle. Deficiencies in what I've been writing ought not to weaken my new joy; on the contrary this joy can help me to remedy them. And it should be strengthened not weakened by my remembering the vilenesses that my poetic imagination triumphed over while I was at Rugtonstead. I must think more about that time on my next walk.

6

One afternoon during my third summer term I was sitting
on the grass bank near the cricket pavilion watching a first
eleven match when Ritchie came and stood beside me for a
moment or two and said how beautiful the green of the
horse-chestnut leaves was at this time of year. I saw that he
was looking towards a group of trees beyond the high wire
fence on the far side of the cricket field. I had hardly been
conscious of them before, and certainly I hadn't noticed
they were horse-chestnuts, in spite of their conspicuous
creamy-white blossom candles. His face as he spoke gave an
impression of serious enthusiasm, an impression heightened
by the flush which as usual reddened the flesh close to his
nose on both his cheeks and which may have been due to a
mild eczema — perhaps this as much as the 'itch' in his
name was what caused him to be nicknamed Scratch among
the boys — and his voice had a passionateness in it as it
often had when he talked of things that interested him. I
had recently begun to admire him deeply for this
passionateness which I thought of as having a similarity to
my own feeling for poetry. I was impressed too by the
breadth of his interests and by the fact that although
chemistry was his speciality he was keener on literature and
music than most non-science masters were. I was sure his
passionateness was genuine, though I was aware also — and
even gratefully aware — that in speaking of his enthusiasms
to me he was trying to educate me. I would have liked to be
able to tell him that the chestnut leaves seemed beautiful to
me too, just as I had been able to tell him that I thought
George Meredith's *The Ordeal of Richard Feverel*, which he
had lent me to read, was a wonderful book. (Ever since he

had discovered from seeing a poem of mine in the school magazine that I wrote poetry he had been lending me his own copies of various books which he was enthusiastic about and which he thought I had reached the age to appreciate.) But though, in the scene where Richard Feverel is letting himself drift in his rowing-boat down the stream towards the weir and suddenly comes upon the lovely girl in her broad flexible-brimmed straw hat sitting alone on the bank, the dewy copse described by Meredith as being dark over her hat appeared exquisitely beautiful to my visual imagination, I could see no beauty at all in the chestnut leaves beyond the high wire fence on the far side of the cricket field.

After Ritchie had walked away from me along the grass bank to talk to other members of his House whom he might find sitting there — and I guessed he would suit his talk to each of them as he had to me, and it wouldn't be about trees but mostly about the cricket — I looked at the chestnut leaves again, for several minutes, trying to see in them what Ritchie saw in them, trying to forget that the trees they grew on were part of the scenery of the school and that only the wire fence and a small stream known to the boys as the Stinker separated them from the cricket field where I had spent so many afternoons of boredom or apprehensiveness. I had not often looked at leaves with such concentrated attention before, not even at home, but they remained unattractive to me and as dull as though I was seeing them through a mephitic haze that was rising up out of the Stinker in front of them. I could not dissociate them from the school, which poisoned my view of them, and I did not really want to dissociate them from it. To have found them beautiful would have been to have introduced a disruptive inconsistency into the emotional picture that during the past two years my imagination had been creating of the school as a place of monotony and pain, and would have detracted from the convincingness of those poems of mine which without using the crude word 'school' had referred to the wretchedness of my life there, for example a poem entitled *Going Away* that I had written at home just before the end of the Easter holidays. The final lines of this were . . . *how very bitter then it is/Leaving the quiet town/In the green hollow there, and proudly going/Where I shall find no peace, no love, but only/Raining and bitterness and gloom and snowing/And dreams most old, most lonely* . . . I recognised that the poem had its technical faults — 'snowing' was in it for the rhyme and 'raining' was in it to go with 'snowing', and I knew that my form-master was right when after it was printed in the school magazine he told me that 'how very bitter then it is' was a gallicism which some readers might regard as introducing a note of affectation into the poem, and I knew also that the way I had used the word 'most' in the last line was too obviously cribbed from the way Rupert Brooke had used it in his line, which I thought superb then, 'And your remembered smell most agony', but I made up my mind to avoid such faults in future, and I think now that the poem had at least the merit of being based on feelings of mine which truly reflected the reality of the school as I had encountered it. The school in its real essence was an ugly place, and to have allowed myself to see anything belonging to it as beautiful would have made me feel almost as I would have felt fifteen years later if I had allowed myself to be attracted by some aspect or other of Germany under Nazi rule.

I could have appreciated the chestnut trees if instead of their standing above the Stinker they had been somewhere near my home in Essex. There almost everything, even things that Ritchie might have regarded as rather ugly, seemed beautiful to me: for instance the small sawmill with black-painted corrugated-iron walls that could be seen across a field from our playroom window upstairs, or the pale brown hardened mounds of earth that were under the trees near the keeper's hut in the public park and were marked during dry weather with shiny paths made over their surfaces by the feet of children who had run up and down them. Home was beautiful because it was a place of freedom and also because everywhere in it and around it was associated for me with a childhood that in retrospect seemed to have been almost continuously happy. My poem *Going Away* and other poems I wrote during the same Easter holidays glorified and idealised my home, though the word 'home' was not used in them nor did they describe any of the actual details of my home or its environment: I may have believed that such details however moving to me they were in real life would be unpoetical in a poem. My Essex home together with my grandparents' home here at the seaside where we came every year for our summer holidays was transformed in my poems into a land I called Meremy, a name whose very sound was to have for me soon after I left school a suggestion of sentimentality which made me writhe, and makes me wince even now. Meremy was a summer-afternoon land, late summer and late afternoon, with a white half-moon already faintly in the sky, and children were always at play there, and trees to which I never gave specific names were always in the background, their foliage mistily green like the foliage in a Corot painting of birch trees, and 'dim' was an adjective I often used — without any awareness that it could ever be used in an unfavourable sense — to convey the mysteriousness of their beauty. But repellent though Meremy was soon to seem to me as a poetic idea, I recognise now that despite its distorting sentimentality it did truly reflect in part the happy actuality of my Essex home at that time and the actual beauty of the country near the seaside town where my grandparents lived.

That beauty is no less real at present as I turn to look back along the path by which I have come up the downs from the town in my walk this afternoon. And what I see elates me just as much as when I saw it in my boyhood, though now I may be more observant of the detail of it than I was then. I look at the whiteish-brown autumnal long grass which retains in its semi-defunctness, as a human beard in old age might retain, a trace of its younger colour, and at the wine-coloured bramble leaves, and at the fruiting ivy which is possibly the cause of an impression of olive green that the landscape gives in the middle distance, and at the sea far below on my left appearing even calmer than it actually is though with wind-scurries clouding its shine here and there and rapidly advancing in lines of changing shape, curving now forwards, now backwards — like unevenly aligned vapour-trailing aeroplanes — now becoming edgeless, now vanishing in the fall of small seemingly soundless breakers which shoot out their glassy laminae up the sand of the beach. I look at the dead carline thistle close to my feet with its bracts having the colour and the matt sheen of magnesium wire — or perhaps the sheen is not so matt and when I look again the bracts remind me of tarnished silver — and its pale yellow disk seeming downy like a baby's hair. I might have noticed fewer of all these things when I was a boy: my elation would have come from the scene as a whole, all at once, overwhelmingly, hazing my awareness of particulars, and with an intensity far greater — let me admit — than it has at present. Yes, what I feel now isn't really very like what I felt then: perhaps it is more like the elation that used to come to me from a cumulative awareness of details during my half-term holiday journeys down here before I retired from teaching, as on an evening at the end of October once when after getting off the boat I sat in the train at the station on the pier and saw above the platform the comfortable lights which made me think of Christmas, and a girl standing there whose turning of her head sideways when she spoke to the young man beside her caused the sterno-mastoid muscle to define itself as a firm slender column beneath the smooth flesh of her neck around which she wore a necklace of large dark red beads, and I felt a boundless generosity towards this young couple so that I could understand the pleasure of a man whose job it is to go to a small terrace house in an industrial town and announce to the occupants that they are the winners of a huge prize on the football pools, though I wanted to give lasting happiness not money, and to give it to everyone on the platform and elsewhere also as well as to this couple. But my present elation isn't really like that: it is less simple than that. There is something ambiguous about it. The truth is it isn't caused entirely by the details of what I see as I stand on the downs here. I'd better stop pretending that the scene seems as beautiful to me as it seemed in the past. In fact a wish to increase its appeal now was the reason why I have just been making myself remember how I felt about trees at school and at home when I was a boy. My elation is mainly due to something quite other and much more important than the beauty of this scene.

I am elated because the atomic war that seemed on the point of breaking out a week ago has, for the time being at least, been avoided. I have been reacting to the ending of the Cuban missile crisis with the same kind of excessive relief that most of the rest of our local C.N.D. members showed at our meeting in Dan and Myra's house yesterday evening, though I did argue then against the conclusions drawn by some of them, especially by Kevin. He said in his normal downright and assertive way, which probably because he is only seventeen never annoys me, that C.N.D. has been wrong and that the H-bomb had proved to be a deterrent after all, and when Elsie asked how he made that out he said that President Kennedy by being prepared to fight a nuclear war if necessary had forced Kruschev to climb down and to agree to dismantle the Soviet missile bases in Cuba. I said, 'But did he really climb down? Didn't he achieve exactly what he wanted to, which was to prevent American imperialism from invading Cuba?' Kevin wouldn't have this at all — he seemed to have completely swallowed the line of the capitalist news media that not the U.S.A. but Castro's Cuba and the Soviet Union were the potential aggressors. I said that Kruschev and the Soviet government had been abominably irresponsible when they had announced through their Tass newsagency that they had powerful nuclear weapons and powerful rockets with which they could assist any peace-loving state that came under attack (I nearly added that they had been abominably unMarxist-Leninist; however I checked myself partly because I didn't want to remind anyone that I had once been a Party member and partly because I still can't quite believe that the present leadership of the first country where a socialist revolution took place is not Marxist any more whereas I am), and Elsie said that Kruschev had made a similar threat to start a nuclear war in 1956 when Britain, France and Israel were attacking Egypt, though his bluff wasn't called then, but that the imperialist powers weren't bluffing about their intention to get in first with nuclear weapons if ever their vital interests were endangered, and I said that this was why we mustn't let the ending of the Cuban crisis lull us into thinking our campaign to ban the bomb in this country was any less urgent than before. I was rather taken aback for a moment when Denise Dobson asked whether we didn't think that the existence of the Soviet bomb might deter the American and British governments from being the first to use nuclear weapons. My answer was that it probably wouldn't deter the imperialists because they wouldn't care how many human beings they destroyed in the Soviet Union and because they might calculate that a country which still wants to be regarded as socialist would hesitate to retaliate by destroying millions of workers in America and Britain. I could see that this didn't convince Denise, and I wasn't quite convinced by it myself either. Myra came to my support by saying she had read in a Sunday newspaper editorial the extraordinary statement that the possession of the bomb by the great powers was the only guarantee that it would never be used, but in her opinion it would be less likely to be used if all stocks of it were destroyed and it ceased to exist altogether. Dan added that in his opinion the longer the bomb continued to exist and the further it was developed the more certain it was to be used eventually, by accident if not on purpose. Myra went on to say that though very naturally we all felt relieved and glad because war between America and Russia had been avoided, our gladness should not make us relax our efforts to get the bomb banned but should inspire us to redouble them. By the end of the meeting I was sure she had succeeded in convincing everyone, including Kevin and Denise, that our work for C.N.D. was more necessary than ever. The relief we all felt about the passing of the Cuban crisis had been converted by her into a stimulus for us. So why have I been thinking that the relief was excessive? And why should I think there is anything wrong with my elation as I walk on the downs this afternoon?

To be elated that millions of human beings have not been killed by nuclear bombs and that there is still the possibility for human beings to destroy the bombs rather than be destroyed by them is not wrong. What is wrong is that the view from the downs here has had no part, or very little part, in causing my elation. Political feeling — so powerful, so elementally human — has driven out poetic imagination. But does this matter, for once? It is not for once; it has been happening more and more often recently. If it goes on my poetry will soon seem totally insignificant to me in face of the vastness of world events. I shall lose my faith in imaginative creation, as I did during the nineteen thirties when war was approaching and the fight against fascism became all-important for me. I must not lose my faith again and I have found a means since then by which I can protect and strengthen it, a means which I have been inexcusably neglecting for the last few weeks — until just now when I made myself think of my Essex home and of the country around my grandparents' seaside home here as they appeared in my boyhood imaginings.

There were no girls in Meremy, not even half-hidden among the trees which were so often in the background of the pictures my visual imagination formed of it. There were children, whom I saw only as children and not as boys or girls. When I imagined Christine I saw her usually without any background other than a darkness against which her face showed vividly though only momentarily, or if there was a background with detail in it she appeared much less distinct against it and sometimes so indistinct as to be no more than a kind of warm luminousness (a 'luminence' I called it in one of my poems) and the detail was, or would have been but for the luminousness, often lugubrious — heavy clouds and sodden hillsides and leafless lanes. In my imaginings of her during the first week of the summer holidays following this term, the luminousness lessened and the lugubriousness increased. This was because I had seen her so seldom in actuality: I had met her twice again at parties during the previous Christmas holidays but not once during the Easter holidays in spite of my having bicycled often past her house then. The reason why there were no girls in Meremy was probably that they would have troubled the idyll, would have revealed the falsity of its cosiness, would have been symbols of my real deprivation.

I still wrote poems about her as well as about Meremy, but they became fewer, and increasingly they were melancholic, for example a poem which began with the lines, *I dreamt last night that as I slept/You thought of me, and softly stepped/The lonely passage to my room./Above the soft receding gloom/Your eyes seemed gazing piteously,* and which ended with *pain/Received my waking self again.* The satisfaction I got from such poems could not remove the painfulness of the deprivation that caused me to write them, and not long after the beginning of the summer holidays a day came when I made up my mind that at all costs I must find some way of meeting her before I went with the rest of our family for our three weeks at the seaside. But what way could there be? The most obvious one of simply going to her house in Western Road, ringing the front-door bell and asking to see her, seemed the least possible of all. If the strength of my feeling for her had been less I might have been capable of doing this: after all, I hadn't been afraid during the Easter holidays to call at the house of another girl, Barbara, whom I had first got to know at the kindergarten too and with whom I was friendly but not at all in love — though it's true I called there to return a book which she had taken the initiative of coming to our house to lend me. But to go uninvited to Christine's house would have seemed to me boundlessly presumptuous and like a blatant announcement to all her family that I was in love with her. Another way, almost though not quite as impossible, of meeting her again would be for me to loiter in or near Western Road for most of the day, and perhaps day after day, until I saw her coming out of her house and then if she was alone I could walk along and meet her as though by accident; but suppose she or her parents caught sight of me furtively lurking there, what sort of impression would I make? Nevertheless this is the way I would probably have chosen if an utterly unexpected invitation hadn't arrived by post at the end of July for Hugh and me to go to a party at her house in a week's time. The Dunbars had never before asked us to a party in the summer; perhaps the reason they decided to give one this year might have been that Christine, who was now sixteen, was finding not much less difficulty — even though her Girls' School was a day school — in meeting boys of a kind her middle-class parents wouldn't disapprove of than I found in meeting girls of any kind during the third of the year when I was free from my sex-segregated boarding-school. From the moment when I read the invitation, which was in a handwriting I guessed to be hers, my love-dream became almost as hopeful and as tenderly expectant again as it had ever been, and the long gap since my last meeting with her seemed to matter hardly at all.

If the invitation had been for seven weeks ahead the dream could have lasted and grown continually richer till then, but in fact it lasted only the seven days till the evening of the party. I saw a difference in her as soon as she opened the front door of her house to Hugh and me. I couldn't at first be sure what the difference was, except that it wasn't for the better. She was, outwardly at least, more rather than less welcoming than before; she was not so shy, not shy at all. She was self-possessed, and obviously had no difficulty in being so. But there had never been any real reason for me to suppose that her former shyness with me had arisen from feelings anything like those which had caused my shyness with her. If my presence now did not make her heart beat faster this was probably nothing new, since after all I had in the past never dared to say anything to her which might have revealed I was in love with her. What was essentially new in her became clear to me a minute or two after she had brought Hugh and me into the room where some of the other boys and girls whom she had invited, including Barbara, already were: watching her move among them I could see nothing remaining in her of the child I had known at the kindergarten and had been conscious of in her still, though dazzlingly transformed, when I had first met her again the Christmas before last. At sixteen now she looked a young woman almost. And this impression became final when her father who was in the room with us offered her a cigarette — he didn't offer one to any of the rest of us — which she took as though it was nothing unusual for her, and while she stood smoking it she rested one elbow on the edge of the mantelshelf and one foot on the fireplace kerb, the back of her high-heeled shoe sliding up and down her silk-stockinged heel without ever quite parting from it, her whole posture somehow angular. There was one small pink spot on her white chin, pinker than her cheeks, inconspicuous compared with the several squeezed red acne pustules which it reminded me I had on my face. I felt the beginnings of a disenchantment. But, just as on first meeting her again the Christmas before last I had not realised till some hours later how deeply I had fallen in love with her, so now I did not realise until this party was over how abysmally, how starkly, I had fallen out of love with her. While I lay awake in bed after I got home from the party my loss of love was made all the more unbearable to me by the thought that in all the months when I had been in love with her I had never once said or done anything to make her aware of it. However, this thought led me on to the thought that if I were to tell her now that I loved her, even though the truth was that I no longer did, the very act of telling her might have the effect on me of reviving my love for her. And the fact that I would no longer be inhibited by too intense feelings would make it less difficult for me to discover some way of telling her. As, after sleepless hours, I reached this conclusion, I felt that my love for her was already beginning to revive.

In my new love-dream during the next two days I no longer saw her as a momentarily effulgent and sublimely beautiful apparition against a background of darkness, nor as a diffused warm luminousness over a melancholy landscape, but as she had been at the party when she had stood smoking a cigarette and resting her elbow on the mantelpiece – still beautiful, though more of an ordinary human presence than previously, a physical being whom I ought not to feel intimidated from approaching. Nevertheless my renewed feelings of love lacked their former conviction until, three days after the party, I thought of a practicable way in which I could let her know I loved her. I would send her a present. During the last Christmas holidays I had written a sonnet starting with the words *I have no precious gifts to offer you,* and among its other words had been *I seek but, in your eyes,/ Remission for concealment of past dreams/And sweet acceptance of my humble art.* I certainly would not send her this poem, nor any other poems of mine, and not so much because they exhibited my feelings too nakedly as because I was afraid she might find them ridiculous as poems: I had few illusions about their poetic quality, though I believed that with hard work I could ultimately succeed in writing good poetry. It would end my 'concealment of past dreams' as she could hardly doubt the significance of a gift of this kind. In the same sonnet written during the Christmas holidays there had also been the words *Oh little have you guessed the hope that gleams/Beneath an outward mask! . . . /Or do I wrong your thoughts? Or silently/Have you returned my hope? Would God the door/Which holds your soul so jealously concealed/Might ope and all your purpose be revealed.* I thought that my sending her a book of poems would cause her to show in some way whether she reciprocated my love at all. I would not write my name in the book, of course, because if I did this I might seem too boldly confident that she would welcome a present from me and she might simply send me a polite letter of thanks revealing nothing, whereas if I didn't write my name she wouldn't be able to thank me formally but when we next met she would be conscious of me as the probable giver and then she would be able to see in my looks that I loved her, and — oh marvellousness almost beyond imagining — she might respond to my love. The book ought not to be too ordinary on the outside, I thought, so I went up to London to buy it from a big bookshop where I chose a copy of Palgrave's *Golden Treasury* which was softly bound in dark green suede. When I had brought it home and was looking through it before wrapping it up in new brown paper to post it to her, a sheaf of about ten pages fell out from the middle of it, but

I decided I couldn't bear the delay which would be caused if I had to go up to the shop again the next day and get the book changed for another and therefore I pushed the sheaf of pages back into the book and wrapped it up for the post, telling myself she wouldn't think I knew they were loose. Any doubts that had remained in me about the reality of the revival of my love for her were removed after I had posted the book to her; and during my three weeks at the seaside my love-dream, though it did not recover all its former visionary intensity, was less febrile and more constantly optimistic than it had been for a long time.

It became more optimistic still when I got home again and could feel that I was living within a quarter of a mile of her house, though I did not dare to walk or even bicycle along her road because to do so too soon after sending her the book might give an impression of overboldness were she to see me. I would certainly have at least bicycled if not walked past her house before I went away to school for twelve weeks of the autumn term, but three days after coming back from the seaside I got a letter from her. In it she said she had received a parcel containing a beautiful book, but 'unfortunately the person who sent it has omitted to enclose their name'. The letter was short and so neatly written that I guessed it must be a fair copy and suspected she might have been advised by her parents what to say. In my mind I heard the words 'unfortunately the person' and 'omitted to enclose' as though spoken in a tone of sharpest sarcasm, and I winced with disenchantment at the phrase 'their name', without recognising that it might indicate she had not written the letter at the dictation of her parents, or anyway not of her father who was a journalist and whose English grammar would be likely to be more correct. I found no hint of warmth in her words, except where she called the book 'beautiful', though this too might be sarcastic if when she wrote it she had discovered that some of the pages were loose: I quite failed to realise that perhaps

I had put her in a difficult position by sending the book anonymously, and that the fact of her having written to me at all might not be unencouraging. Her letter made me feel like a petty offender who had been found out; and a panic-need to exculpate myself at any cost caused me to write a letter back to her which I must have known would be almost certain to turn her — and her parents too if they read it — against me for ever; in fact, after this I never met her again in my life nor heard anything about her except when in the following Christmas holidays my mother told me that my father had had a letter from Christine's father about my letter, my mother's only comment being 'She is not worthy of you.' What I had said, ingeniously but implausibly, in my answer to Christine was that I too had recently received an anonymous present of a book — I didn't specify what book — and had thought it might be from her so I had sent Palgrave's *Golden Treasury* to her as a return present, but since sending it I had discovered that the present I had received had come from Mr Gardiner (I assumed she would know of this rather elderly solicitor who was a friend of our family and who took a special interest in me as well as being obviously though unavailingly infatuated with my mother, especially while my father was away during the war) and I ended my letter to Christine by apologising for the stupid mistake I had made. My full realisation, after I had posted this letter, that I had put an end to all hope of her loving me was bitter but it did not seem unbearable like my discovery after the party that I had fallen out of love with her. And in the sonnet I wrote next day I found a compensation such as I had not found in any of the poems I had written during the many months when I had been in love with her but unable to meet her.

The compensation came not only from the act of poetic composition but still more from the emotion on which the sonnet was based. The opening lines of the sonnet were — *It is the end: and all my gold is gone/And all my dream-*

domain of gold is crushed / Irrevocably to so much festering dust! I think I half-knew even at the time that this was one of the worst poems I had yet written; much worse than the first I ever wrote which also was inspired by feelings about her. Unlike that earlier sonnet it contained words I relished the sound of without properly considering their meaning: I seem for instance to have ignored — I can hardly have been ignorant of — the accepted meaning of the word 'heartless' in the third line of the sestet — *Haply you'll meet a heartless wanderer there* (the wanderer being myself in some after-life), though the word may have recommended itself to me partly because I wished I could feel utterly indifferent to her, just as the word 'premeditated' which I used no doubt mainly for its alliterative force in the sonnet's final line — *Of Pain's premeditated harsh regime* — may have been a foretoken of the deliberate cult of unhappiness I was soon to engage in. Even where words whose meaning I was vague about were by accident used more or less correctly, as in the concluding lines of the octet — *This is the hooded end to which love rushed, / This is the field of passion's gonfalon!* — there could be an unintended ambiguity ('field' might be heraldic or it might mean 'battle-field'). But any dissatisfaction I may have felt at the time with the poetic quality of this sonnet was soon superseded after I had finished it by the increasing satisfaction I got from the emotion which it expressed and which had caused me to write it. Seemingly the emotion was of sadness, and I did genuinely feel unhappy at having lost Christine, yet after I had expressed it poetically there was something consoling and pleasurable about it, and this was so also whenever in the following week before the end of the summer holidays the thought of her caused me to experience it again quite apart from the poem.

As a result of the satisfaction I was able to get from the defeat of my love, a new imaginative phase began for me in which I was able to get a similar satisfaction from other kinds of unhappiness too, even from the unhappiness of being at school when I returned there for the autumn term. If I had still been a fag the miseries of being one would have been too sharp and sordid to be converted into satisfactions by any sort of imaginative philosophising, no matter how perverse; but now that I was a 'second', and also had become a member of the Sixth Form this term, I was freed from most of the cruder harassments I had previously been subjected to and I was able to find pleasure in seeing the school as an abominable place. Not long after the beginning of term I wrote a poem with the title *Gloom*. Up till now I had not managed to write poetry at school, because of the general hustle and lack of privacy, but this term I was able to do it for three-quarters of an hour each week during a science class for non-science sixth formers which was taken by a newly-appointed master who didn't seem to mind our not listening to him provided we caused no disturbance. The first verse of the poem was *All in the silent autumn days/As I roamed bitterly,/It was still Gloom of leaf-starred ways/Came following me.* And the last verse was *And I loved Gloom, and dreamt with him,/And loved the tales he had:/Oh! and I've happiness with him,/For we are sad!* When the poem was published towards the end of the term in the school magazine, one of the masters — I forget which but I'm sure he wasn't Ritchie, who wouldn't have been so bluntly antagonistic to it — said to me that it was morbid. I felt gratified, because this was just what I had meant it to be. I had already consciously formulated the simple principle for myself that whatever the school upheld as wholesome ought to be detested by me, a too simple principle which inclined me to despise outdoor physical exercise and games, although I was considered good enough at football to be chosen several times to play in school first eleven practice games, and if I had shown enthusiasm I might have been chosen to play in first eleven matches also. Conversely, whatever the school was against I was for. I no longer disliked dirty talk — though I did not engage in it much myself, partly because in spite of its being officially disapproved of I regarded it as a product of the official attitude towards sex and therefore as a hardly less essential part of the public school system than fagging and beating, and partly because it clashed with my idealistic love of poetry. When Ronson-Smith, who was a second in the same study as I was and a hearty and amiable philistine, said that if he had had my gift for writing verse he would have used it to write some marvellous filthy limericks, I couldn't make him understand why I would feel I was prostituting myself if I did that. My attitude towards cheating in exams had also changed recently, but in this case although cheating might have been regarded as a product of the system no less than dirty talk was, I had had no qualms — other than fear that I might get caught — in taking with me into the School Certificate Scripture examination a crib which I had written out on the pages of a tiny booklet of my own making (however I didn't have to use the crib much, because the hard work I had done in preparing it had provided me with sufficient knowledge to answer most of the questions without cheating). The argument I inwardly used to justify my cheating was based on a statement — an incorrect one, though I didn't know this — by one of the masters that public exams were not competitive and that an examinee could get a pass if he reached a certain fixed standard no matter how many other examinees reached a higher standard than he did: so I would not be wronging anyone else by my cheating, and I would be preventing a failure which could make my future unfreer even than it was sure to be anyway. I used a still more specious argument to justify steaming off the piece of paper that sealed a missionary collecting box brought home by Vaughan in the summer holidays from Marchfield — I said that Rags had had no right to make him collect money for Christian purposes and that therefore we had every right to spend it for our own purposes, which we did (there was just enough in the box to buy a small model of a naval gun). I did not tell anyone at school about my cheating, except Tilford, or about the missionary box, nor did I try to convert anyone to my philosophy of Gloom. I remained almost as quiet and unassertive outwardly as when I had written in one of my earlier poems *They shall not know the thoughts of my heart,/Nor the depth of my sweetest hope,/Nor the anguish suffered, the lingering smart/Of the gold aims out of my scope,* — though inwardly my new philosophy had a far from quietening effect on me and the happiness it gave me was full of passion; *flaming ecstasy of gloom* I called this in a poem I wrote during the next Christmas holidays. Ritchie wrote at the bottom of my end-of-term report that I was much too self-effacing, which pleased me and upset my parents. Probably with the idea of helping me to become less self-effacing he promoted me to being a studyholder at the beginning of the following term, and this did make me more assertive, but in a way he may not have foreseen.

To the exultant bitter gladness I already got from my cult of Gloom I was able to add the satisfaction of using my new position to do what harm I could in a small way to the Public school system as it existed in Dunton House. Most boys who had been given hell as fags used to react when they were studyholders by giving hell to their own fags, whereas I chose to take my revenge not on the other victims of the system but on the system itself — though I didn't do this in a crudely obstructive way which might get me expelled from the school but in a way which would seem motivated entirely by highmindedness and would be less easy for Ritchie with his liberal ideas to take exception to. I started by telling the fags in my study that I had decided not to use them as fags and that I thought fagging was an abomination which ought to be abolished altogether in the House and the School. My decision probably had an element of genuine altruism in it, but if so this counted less with me than my wish for revenge, just as revenge counted less with me than my cult of Gloom, and my cult of Gloom less than my poetry. My behaviour towards the fags in my study wasn't absolutely consistent: I did beat one of them once, Levinson, for taking a very short cut in a House run rather more boldly and openly than any other of 'my' fags had hitherto risked doing, though my real reason for beating him wasn't this (nor had I any anti-semitic feelings towards him, at least nothing comparable to those which many members of the House with a bumptious young second named Ferrars as their ring-leader showed towards the two or three Jews amongst us) but I wanted to find out what it was like to beat someone, and I did not do it again. I can still see quite vividly in my mind the look that Levinson gave me when I told him I was going to beat him, a look not of fear or resentment but of surprise and of disappointment in me. During the following term I did something else which I soon regretted, and although it was not as bad as beating Levinson it was not helpful to the impression of highmindedness I had wanted to make on Ritchie: when Ferrars won the School diving competition I felt that his success would be certain to increase his bumptiousness beyond all bounds, and I organised a party of fags and seconds who had suffered especially from him and who in the evening soon after the House assembly at which he was publicly congratulated by Ritchie, seized him and brought him upstairs to one of the bathrooms where they dropped him fully dressed into a cold bath and held him there while the most junior of the fags were encouraged to give him a symbolic cleansing with heavy scrubbing-brushes normally used for cleaning floors. (He took this treatment in the best way that was possible for him — he was completely silent and unresisting, and when it was over I was filled with such admiration that I congratulated him and offered to shake hands; he properly refused, but for the rest of my time at the school he was very friendly towards me and became a follower of mine, and when I adopted a policy of behaving with deliberate slovenliness in the Officers' Training Corps as a protest against militarism he did the same and we were demoted together to be drilled among the new boys). Ritchie asked me the day after the ducking of Ferrars whether I had been responsible for it, and I said I had. He cannot have been pleased at such an act of unofficial punishment, even though he was almost certainly aware of how bullyingly bumptious Ferrars had been, but he made no comment. He evidently just wanted me to know that he knew. His refraining from reprimanding me made me feel that I was not already in his bad books for my other and apparently more highminded unorthodox acts such as abolishing fagging in my study, which no doubt he had been told about too. The idea that he might actually have been sympathetic to them did not occur to me until more than a year after I'd left school when he told Hugh, who had just won an Exhibition to Cambridge and who had been taking the same line as I had taken about fagging, that if he would stay on for another two terms he could have carte blanche as Head Prefect to run the House entirely according to the principles he believed in (but Hugh refused because he wanted to go to stay in France before going up to Cambridge). This offer may have been no more than an example of the old liberal tactic of trying to win over a rebel by giving him high responsibility within the system, but when I remember the passion with which Ritchie defended the Social Credit ideas of Major Douglas once at a Sixth Form Civics Class I wonder whether his views generally weren't more unorthodox than I then supposed, and whether — like a clergyman who loses his faith too late in life to be able to change his job — he hadn't in middle-age come to disbelieve radically in the public school system. He may have felt that I was not serious enough in my rebellion, and perhaps it was with the hope of making me more so that he invited me to dinner one evening to meet Angus, who before leaving school more than a year previously had as a Sixth Former become a socialist under the influence of one of the two masters sacked by the Head for pacifist propaganda during the war.

I was predisposed to like Angus, because of the notoriety as a rebel which his close association with the sacked masters had brought upon him, and I hoped to get encouragement from him in my own rebellion. I had long ceased to think that these two masters had been 'men of evil character in the land' as I had called them in *The Book of Eitna*, and I wanted to hear what Angus might have to say about them. But during all the time that I sat opposite to him at the table with Ritchie and Mrs Ritchie in their private dining-room he never mentioned anything that had happened at the school while he had been there. To start with he spoke very little, until Ritchie got him on to the subject of politics, and then he talked about the Bolshevik revolution in Russia, with calm approval. I regretted that throughout the whole evening he did not once attack the Public school system or even the British Empire whose rulers got their training at Public schools. I was surprised at the gentleness of his tone of voice: I knew he had had the reputation of being an outstandingly good speaker in the school debating society — though I had not heard him, because I never attended debates — and I expected his tone to have the austerity of his looks, of his extraordinary eyes deep-set in a broad face which appeared slightly concave with a prominent forehead above an unprotruding straight nose and with a prominent chin below a straight mouth. Perhaps his mildness was what enabled me, who normally had great difficulty in speaking at any length if I was conscious that more than one person was listening, to express quite fluently before the end of the meal such ideas as I had about socialism. I had just been reading Turgenev's *Virgin Soil* and had liked its pessimism about social progress. I outlined its story to Angus and said that I too believed that all attempts to ameliorate human wretched-ness were bound to fail. The theoretical position I took was not altogether different from that of certain comfortably-off adult intellectuals in the nineteen fifties — some of them subsidised, without knowing they were, by American imperialism's Central Intelligence Agency — to whom the idea of human progress seemed an illusion so utterly naive as to be almost unmentionable and who thought that the wretched of the earth would be no happier even if they obtained all the so-called benefits of material civilisation (however I couldn't be called comfortably off at Dunton House, in spite of my having become a studyholder and a Sixth Former, and perhaps my pessimism was more like James (B.V.) Thomson's who believed in fighting on without hope.) Angus entirely disagreed with my anti-progressivism, but he argued against it without heat. I sensed that Ritchie, who intervened hardly at all in the argument, was on Angus's side and was disappointed that I showed no sign of being influenced by Angus to adopt a less pessimistic view of life. When I went up to bed in the dormitory afterwards I felt pleased with the evening, not because I had disappointed Ritchie — although his wish to induce optimism in me seemed Public-schoolish and deserving of a rebuff even if the optimism he had wanted to induce was socialistic rather than of the conventional Public-school sort — but because my philosophy had become clearer and still more exciting to me than before as a result of my talking with Angus.

I did not find anyone who approved of my pessimistic rebelliousness and encouraged me in it until I got to know Richard, who had come up into the History Sixth at the beginning of the same term as I had, though he was almost a year younger than me. I called him Marple at that time, of course, and the public-school taboo against using any names other than surnames or nicknames was so formidable that my rebelliousness did not dare to challenge it until some while after we had both left school, nor did he call me anything but Sebrill before then. He didn't really agree with my philosophy but he approved of it perhaps chiefly because he felt it helped to make my poems excitingly strange. He was neither a pessimist nor was he an active rebel against the system — he used to say he was able to live within it fairly comfortably by means of cunning — but like me he had an ambition to be a poet, and poetry seemed to him as it did to me the supremely important thing. His admiration of my poems was far from being uncritical, however; and though he thought me potentially a very good and perhaps a great poet there were only two lines I had written so far which he praised without qualification: *But from the sea, silent, far-glimmering there,/Sadness commemorates a child's desire.* Nevertheless the way he had of laughing at my worst lines told me that he found even these attractive and somehow impressive. As for his own poetry, although he had been writing it for less than a year when I got to know him, I recognised at once that it was better than mine, more mature and technically much more competent. I felt hardly any envy, because almost from the first day when we got talking together in the school library — where with a small number of other Sixth Formers, unsupervised, we were supposed to be engaged in private study — such a friendship was established between us that any achievement of his came to seem as if it was mine also. We had no romantic feelings at all towards each other, but in the course of interchanging our poetic ideas and enthusiasms we created a shared imaginative world which grew larger and richer the more we were together and which gave me a deeper and less inconstant pleasure than any romantic love affair I was ever to have.

My cult of gloom, which had originated from the failure of my love for Christine, did not hinder me from falling wildly in love during my last year at the school with Stafford, who was then a first-year fag in Dunton House.

For a while I kept my intensifying feelings about him to myself and tried to sate them merely by watching him whenever I could, but a day came when I decided to let myself go even if everyone in the House including Ritchie got to know of it — in fact I wanted them all to know, and my love for him became a conscious part of my rebellion against the system. It was an absolutely 'pure' love, as lustless as my love for Young Jib had been, though whereas I had had no wish for any kind of physical contact with Young Jib I think I would have liked to hold Stafford's hand, but I never did. At fourteen he was very young-looking for his age and small-built, and he seemed to me a child, a beautiful Meremy child. I was too deeply infatuated with him to be able to concentrate on the work I was supposed to be doing in preparation for the scholarship exam I was due to take before long at Cambridge. I told myself that he was 'wrecking all my chances', and I was glad of it. But I was always conscious, as I had not been when I had loved Christine, that my love could not last, because before long I would be leaving school for good and anyway he would grow out of his childlikeness. However the sense of transitoriness made my love for him all the keener and also helped me to assimilate it into my cult of gloom. A bad poem I wrote in anticipation of the day when I should have to part with him for ever was called *The Assumption of the Child* and it began with the lines

He is dead; and children dead are sodden limbs at peace
After delight, in staid communion with the grave.
They are strange sallow bones shadowed in dank release
Of sullen hollows where no poppies wave.

The combination of pessimism with love in my feelings for him appeared also in a poem called *Phantom* I wrote two days after leaving school, though this was about Christine and about love in general as much as about him. Its ending was intentionally ironic:

158

There is strange peace now. All the woods are shrouded
With shadowy banners, and the swift unclouded
Sunlight stoops down to welcome you with gold.
You do return to gladness manifold:
You do return; and there is end of all
Aching and gloom and the insufferable
Thirsting for love. This is the day at last.
. . . There seemed faint whispering of feet that passed
Distant as wind. I have not dreamed in vain;
I always knew that you would come again.

At the same period when I was in love with Stafford I
began to read Walt Whitman, and I became enthusiastic
about him although there was nothing dismal or decadent
in him. His intention to 'nourish active rebellion' was what
appealed to me most. And he came much nearer to winning
me away from my cult of gloom than Angus had done.
Nevertheless, the passionate comment I wrote in pencil at
the end of his *Song of the Open Road* in my copy of *Leaves
of Grass* showed conscious irony as well as wistfulness:
'Come before you are ensnared. Come before the classroom,
the office, the sickening fever of money, the lure and
cataclysm of marriage have ensnared you. You have life
before you. You are unfettered: you are free to realise and
to escape for ever. You won't go the way that others have
gone before you, will you? Surely you will realise that life is
everything, that knowledge, and work, and money, are
disease?' The answer I gave to these two questions had a hint
of pessimistic recklessness in it which I think Whitman would
not have liked: 'Yes at this time of my life, when I have as
yet taken no decisive or irrevocable step, — I will determine
to find life, and damn the consequences!' In spite of my
enthusiasm for Whitman the thought that the road before
me when I left school might be an open and attractive one
occurred to me only once, and this was very briefly on the
evening when I heard I had won a scholarship to

Cambridge.

Ritchie came to my study with the telegram which gave me this news. After I had read it he said, 'Now you won't have to worry any more for a while about what you're going to do in life.' There was warm understanding in his smile: perhaps he had been shown a history essay I had written recently for Mr Holmes in which I had said something to the effect that all jobs in the modern world were shameful. He did not seem surprised — as I was — by my success, though he probably had some idea of how much more time I had spent thinking about Stafford than about my work. I supposed the scholarship must have been awarded to me on promise rather than on performance. I tried not to let Ritchie see how glad I was at the news he brought me. I did not try to disguise my gladness from Tilford when he came to congratulate me; however I pretended to him that what gratified me most was not the scholarship itself but its having come as if in answer to the anti-prayer I had said in his presence just before travelling to Cambridge to sit for the exam: 'Please God make me fail'. I had been propounding to him the joking theory that if a God existed He must be a God of Spite and Contrariness, and that since I had failed to get a scholarship to this school at the age of fourteen after praying for one (under the influence of Snell) I would be more likely to get one to Cambridge by praying not to get one. I did not mind showing gladness to Tilford at having 'spited Spite's spite', as I put it, but I avoided revealing to him the hope which had come to me that my life in future might be less unpleasant than at this school. It was a hope that lasted throughout the evening and also for a while after I had gone to bed in the dormitory.

This hope was unthinking at first, an emotion without visual images or clear ideas, but it began to resolve itself into ideas as I lay awake quite still in bed staring up at the iron tie-rod which extended from wall to wall across the shadowy dormitory just below the ceiling. Cambridge would be likely to be less nasty than school, I thought. I might even find it quite agreeable. Perhaps when I got there I might abandon my cult of gloom and become a hedonist like Marius in Walter Pater's *Marius the Epicurean* which I had recently been reading a few pages of for exam purposes. But mightn't this be bad for my poetry, since almost all poets who had been any good — the epicurean Lucretius was an exception, of course — had depended on unhappiness for their inspiration? 'Our sweetest songs are those which tell of saddest thought,' Shelley had said. The greatest poetry had been tragic. However, Cambridge might not be pleasanter than school; it might even be nastier, in a subtler, more insidious way. And in any case supposing it was likely to be moderately agreeable I needn't be alarmed that it might ruin me as a poet because at best it would be no more than a waiting-room where I would stay for three years before going out into the real life of working for a living. There was no risk of my finding a job I would be happy to do. In real life I was bound to be a misfit and a failure. Only by being so could I save myself as a poet.

At the moment when my thinking reached this conclusion an idea which seemed at first to be unrelated to it was suggested to me by the iron tie-rod which crossed the dormitory below the hipped ceiling and one end of which was almost directly above my bed. I saw the rod as a roost that birds could settle on if they were to fly in through the dormitory windows always open at the top at nights — shadowy, almost invisible birds; or perhaps just one bird, large, black-feathered, perching very upright, more than half as tall as the vertical iron rod that connected the transverse horizontal rod to the ceiling just above the 'teetotum', as the circular wash-basin stand in the middle of the room was called, a bird like Edgar Allan Poe's raven which sat on the pallid bust of Pallas just above the chamber door. But the bird I had begun to picture in my mind did not say 'Nevermore' like Poe's. It was not there to tell me I would never see Christine again as Poe's had told him he would never again see Leonore. It was absolutely silent. It was there to confirm to me that I was doomed to be a misfit and an outcast in life. I saw in my mind the tie-rod as well as the shadowy bird perching on it, and I felt that without much effort I could bring myself to see the bird on the actual tie-rod in the dormitory above the teetotum. I did not make the effort. There was no need to. The bird in my mind was as vividly and momentously present as if it had been suddenly perceivable in the external darkness. I repeated to myself again and again Poe's words 'And the raven, never flitting, still is sitting, still is sitting.' This bird that I was seeing would be with me for the rest of my life. It was my fate. Yet it caused no despair in me. I felt that it did me honour, conferred distinction on me. I was filled with the deepest pride.

What I felt that night in the dormitory seems pretty contemptible to me now. But I do not repudiate the imaginative aliveness that my feelings had then. On the contrary it's just such an aliveness I'm above all in need of now if I'm to make better progress with my poem than I've been making recently. Yes, let me admit to myself without any equivocation that my progress has been becoming slower and slower for the last three or four weeks. But has my thinking this afternoon about my poetic imaginativeness during my last year at Rugtonstead put me into a better frame of mind poetically as I hoped it would? The fact is I am as far from being able to feel poetically about the view from the downs here as I was before. Why? Perhaps because poetic sensitivity has been deadened in me by the cruder political emotion of relief at the passing of the Cuban crisis, but I don't think so. No, the true reason is that already before the crisis the poetic frame of mind which my rememberings of my past imaginativeness had enabled me to develop and sustain was not helping me as effectively to get on with my poem as it had helped me up till two or three months earlier, and how can I expect to sustain poetic feelings now if they don't make the writing of poetry easier for me? Some change in the poem itself may be necessary before a poetic frame of mind can help me with it again. Haven't I recently been suspecting more and more that although the 'gemlikeness' I have been trying to introduce into the third and fourth sections of the poem has gone some way towards getting rid of the bleakness I was so worried by in my first versions of them, nevertheless they are essentially trivial? What they require, what the poem as a whole requires, is not more surface polish, not to become a coruscating 'art-object' — though certainly the first versions of the third and fourth sections were too lustreless poetically — but to be given more depth politically. I must change the content, make it less commonplace and more significant. When I have worked out how to change it I shall be able to begin to rewrite the third and fourth sections — the first two I still think are satisfactory — and then a poetic frame of mind will no longer be useless and I shall have no difficulty. in reviving it to help me get on with the rewriting. The poem will still need it. Without it politics could, as in the nineteen thirties, bring my writing to a stop.

There will have to be a change not only in the political content of the poem but also in my political work as a member of C.N.D. To continue to campaign solely against nuclear weapons as we did before the Cuban crisis will no longer be enough. The imperialists may be deterred from ever using the bomb by the prospect of the too huge destruction of property it would cause, and even by fears that it might bring about their own destruction, but there are many other anti-human harms they can and will do and are doing. It's the whole monopoly capitalist system we need to campaign against. This is what Elsie and I will have to begin to convince our local C.N.Ders of. Otherwise as the threat from the bomb seems to become less imminent they may drift away into inactivity.

7

It wasn't to think about politics that I began this inland walk along the embankment of the disused railway across these low-lying meadows in early spring. I came to sensitise myself poetically by seeing once again the yellow and the silvery male and female catkins on the goat willows, the ladysmocks which really are 'silver-white' here as Shakespeare calls them and not mauve as I have most often seen them elsewhere, the alighting lapwing with the white-tipped separated primary feathers of its rounded wings resembling broken ribs from the skeleton of some small animal, the group of ten tall and as yet leafless poplars in a row close to the embankment each of them leaning at a different angle and each robed from foot to almost crown with spiralling ivy, the small river winding towards the low black iron railway bridge and becoming smoothly transparent like curved grey-brown glass as it goes over the weir soon after passing under the bridge, the birches whose budded twigs were wine-coloured already in autumn against the hill bordering this flat valley to the north and the light green of whose foliage has a tinge here and there of still remaining purplish-brown rather as the hoodlike upper leaves of a red dead-nettle have a tinge of dark crimson, the heron rising from a reedy ditch and flying with its long-necked head retracted on to its shoulders and with deep-flopping grey wing-beats and only gradually gaining height till at last it perches on a high tree on the south side of the valley quite far off where it surprisingly appears a large bird still. But ten minutes ago, as I was looking at a clump of red dead-nettles growing among grass beside these brown ballast stones which are all that remains of the former railway track, I had the thought, for the first time since my retirement, that perhaps I ought to give up the new poetic life which I have aimed at living and ought to begin to live primarily for the political struggle again as I did in the nineteen thirties when I was a member of the Party. Since I walked on after looking at the nettles I haven't yet succeeded in convincing myself that this thought was utterly wrong.

Where did it come from? Not from the sight of the red dead-nettles, though strangely they seemed more rather than less attractive to me after the moment of its coming. No, the thought had been growing underground in me for quite a while, for a year perhaps, for two years even. It began to germinate at the time when the Chinese Communist leaders first openly criticised the Soviet government. Elsie and I could hardly believe our eyes when we read in the newspapers those statements issued one after another by the Chinese who were using exactly the same arguments against the Russians which we had used fifteen years before against the revisionist and non-revolutionary line of the British communist leaders and which resulted at last in our being forced out of the Party. Since our defeat then I had almost come to think of ourselves as political cranks, as puny eccentrics who had claimed to be better Marxists than the whole of the world communist movement and who even if our arguments were right would be swept away by history like the minutest of dust specks, ludicrously insignificant. But suddenly we found that a communist-led country with seven hundred million inhabitants was on the same side as we were. It was this discovery which started the growth in me of the idea, fully conscious at last this afternoon, that Elsie and I might one day be able to rejoin — not the Party, because it does not look like ever being able to cleanse itself of its revisionism — but the Marxist-Leninist movement which I believed I was joining when I became a Party member thirty years ago, or that if such a

165

movement has hardly begun to exist again yet in this country we ought to help to revive it.

Oh, the attractiveness of the idea is understandable. How glorious the opportunity would be of cancelling out the sorrow which became fixed in me, as it did in so many other left-wing intellectuals of my generation, when almost every Communist Party except the Chinese betrayed its Leninist principles and degenerated either into an oppressive bureaucratic elite as in the Soviet Union or into a mainly electoral organisation as in this country. How stimulating the effect would be, even on my poetic imagination, if I could feel now as I did during my early days in the Party when I became freed from my individual woe and was one with all those in the world who were battling for the cause of humanity. I was able to begin writing poetry again then, better poetry than I had written before, and sterility returned only after the Party had begun to turn revisionist. But was the Party's degeneration really the reason why I once more stopped writing? Or did I stop because too much of my energy was taken up by the political struggle which was what I believed I ought primarily to live for? If I were to decide to live for it now the same result could follow. I dare not take that risk. I must live for poetry as I did in my pre-Party days; though secondarily I must without fail continue the political struggle, since my not taking part in it was the main cause of my not being able at last to go on writing then. I must live for poetry with the same conviction as I had already begun to towards the end of my time at Rugtonstead and during the three years when I was an undergraduate at Cambridge. I must never abandon the new poetic life, and whenever it loses strength I must reinvigorate it by coming to look at such sights as these that I can see from the disused railway in springtime here and by going back in thought to pre-Party times when I lived primarily for poetry.

The poetry I was writing during my first year at

Cambridge was of a kind that I'd had the initial idea for in the previous summer holidays on the afternoon when my grandmother came into the dining-room looking for her spectacles while I was standing at the book-case reading John Clare. My realisation then of how unempathetic (though at that period I couldn't have used such a word in my thoughts because I'd never heard of it) my affection for her had been throughout my childhood and schoolboyhood led me on to recognise how shallow in feeling the poems were that I had written during my recent five months at Rouen. I decided I would try to give greater depth to my next poems by bringing back into them with a new intellectual and passionate explicitness the philosophy of gloom which had been emotionally alive in the poems of my later Rugtonstead period but which had lost its vitality in those I wrote at Rouen (where I had been happy), though my Rouen poems used the same kind of imagery as my Rugtonstead ones — tombs, lichen, leprosy, toads, lych-owls, putrefaction, and the rest, with various additions suggested by my reading of Villon and Baudelaire. Whether Cambridge would be sufficiently dislikeable, however, to sustain in me the state of feeling I would need in order to make my new gloom poems convincing, I couldn't be sure until I actually went up there, but after my first few weeks there I was able to say in a letter to Richard who was still at Rugtonstead, 'If school was unmitigated hell, Cambridge is insidious hell. Cambridge is a blasé monster which attacks you when you are off your guard and before you know where you are all poetry and individuality have been drained out of you, and you become a motor-bike or history maniac.' This really meant I was already confident that Cambridge wouldn't prevent me from writing the kind of poetry I had been thinking of; and before the end of the term I made a new friend, Desmond, who after I'd got to know him spent almost as much time in my college which he wasn't a member of as he did in his own, and whose company helped me to intensify within myself the emotions I wanted for my new poems.

Desmond's large eyes and shining golden hair gave him the look of a romantic poet, and soon after I first met him (in the rooms of an Old Rugtonsteadian named Wentworth who knew him because they were both Geography students) I described him in a letter to Richard as 'the man with a soul'; but he did not actually care much for poetry except when it was pornographic — he put himself to some trouble once to get hold of a poem he said was by Byron which was called 'The Dream' and of which I can remember only three and a half lines about a girl of just fifteen lifting waist high her crinoline for some fond boy to ply with joy his readily erected toy — but the cynical view he took of the university authorities and of the virtuous and the conformist among the undergraduates gave support to the anti-Cambridge attitude in me that I considered essential to my cult of gloom, and so did his own unvirtuous and unconforming conduct. He owned a four-cylinder Brough Superior motorbike which he rode dangerously fast, and he was a daring College-roof mountaineer — he once persuaded me to accompany him on what he called 'a beginner's climb' but I did not go far before turning back, though some months later he succeeded in teaching me how I could get into my College at night after lock-up time by climbing hand-over-hand up the stay-wire of a telegraph pole with my knees against the high back wall of the College and then by sliding blind down a similar wire through the top foliage of a tree on to a lawn on the other side of the wall. Sitting with him and his other friends in the evenings in rooms that had medieval mullioned windows, often playing poker, listening to obscene stories, always drinking, I had moments when I thought of him and them as resembling the companions of Villon in medieval Paris. Not that Desmond or any of his friends was a thief or was likely to end on the gallows, though they weren't in very good odour with the authorities and Desmond I knew was disapproved of also by the socially élite group among the undergraduates in my college who were members of the Chess Club — which for some reason unconnected with chess was the most exclusive club in the college and its few members were almost all of them either rich or socially well-connected or outstandingly good at physical games or athletics. I heard that one of them who had met him suspected him of cheating at cards — though there was no justification for the suspicion, and his success at cards was due solely to his above-average skill as a player — but Desmond's having been educated at a Grammar school instead of a Public school would by itself have probably been enough to earn him their disfavour. He relished the name I invented for them — 'the poshocracy' (a name which, judging by the eventual behaviour of some of them towards me, I think they may have got to hear of, possibly through his mentioning it to nearly everyone he knew). The attraction that Desmond had for me was increased by the poshocracy's dislike of him, and the attraction that his friends had for me was increased by the thought that they would have incurred the same dislike if the poshocracy had known them as well as I did.

There was one drunken evening I spent with them and him in his college when the decadent mood I was cultivating for the sake of my poetry seemed to become much more strongly established in me than it had been before. During an interlude in our poker-playing I recited to them a crude Publicschoolboyish dirty limerick composed by me which ended with the line 'So he climbed up and rogered the ceiling', and Desmond said critically to me, 'Perhaps you could illustrate just how he did that.' Pearson in whose rooms we were and who was Desmond's closest friend after myself asked 'Will anyone bet me five quid that I couldn't?' Desmond said yes, and immediately Pearson went over to an open bookcase in a corner of the room and removed the books in armfuls from the shelves, then he pushed the bookcase along the wall towards a small cupboard on to the top of which he managed with face-reddening effort to lift it, while Desmond but no one else jeered. He had a strongly-built, though short, body and when he clambered up from a chair on to the cupboard and from there on to the bookcase the structure beneath him swayed, but he was still several feet away from the ceiling so he got down again to fetch the chair, which he lifted by stages till he laid it on its back on the top of the bookcase, and then he very cautiously tried to lie with his buttocks on the front legs of the chair and found that he was not yet near enough to the ceiling and he got down once again to fetch up a thick cushion which he placed over the chair-legs before slowly settling his buttocks on them a second time, while Desmond, pretending to lose interest, picked up another cushion and was moulding it with his hands into the shape of a huge vulva, but he stopped doing this when the chair began to totter — without falling, however, and Pearson undid his buttons and arched himself up and was able very briefly to make contact with the ceiling. He climbed down smiling modestly to cheers from everyone except Desmond who looked surly and soon showed he had no intention of ever paying out five pounds, but Pearson good-naturedly did not press him for them, and my indignation at Desmond's bilking lasted no more than an instant because I was already beginning to go off into the kind of dream I had often had — though never so potently before — when drinking with Desmond and his friends, who had become my friends too, a dream in which time was as if slowed down and each second was not only marvellous in itself but brought memories of the marvellousness of the second that had preceded it and I sang to myself over and over again the line 'Oh the great days in the distance enchanted'. The room was filled with beauty, my friends' talk seemed to have a meaning which was not in their words alone, there was a breath of sublimity in their jokes about Pearson's achievement. I had the conviction that behaviour and language like theirs even when — or perhaps most of all when — repulsive by ordinary respectable standards were not really so but were a revelation of humanity in all its immortal (a favourite word of mine at that period) richness and variety, its wonderful confusion of lewdness and kindliness, of blindness and insight. I said to myself as we helped Pearson to move the bookcase back into its place that if I could describe in a poem what I felt this evening I should produce a masterpiece for all time, and I asked myself how long I should have to go on understanding so much without being able to express it fittingly.

The state of feeling which was necessary for my new poetry was sustained also by something else Desmond provided me with besides the company of his friends and himself. As he had been educated at day schools instead of at single-sex boarding-schools like me, he was free from my kind of romantic timidity about girls, and he led me out hunting for them one evening along the lamplit autumn streets during our first term soon after we had got to know each other. We met a pair of them quite soon and the one I found allotted to me — perhaps he judged that the other looked as if she would be sexually more enterprising — was the one I would have chosen. She had a small and rather childishly pretty face, and though her name, Milly, did not seem at all poetic when she told it to me in the cinema where all four of us went on together to find seats right at the back with no one behind us, I felt as I kissed this first girl I had ever kissed that I was at long last kissing Christine, but all next day it was Milly's face I saw in my mind and I seemed to be as yearningly and idealistically in love with her as I had been with Christine — yet I was well aware that idealistic love couldn't help me to write the cynically decadent poems I wanted to. However, the romantic exaltation she made me feel was brief and it quite subsided after I had met her four or five times more, and none of the other girls to whom I introduced myself on the streets of Cambridge — Doreen, Doris, Edna, Molly and the rest — ever revived it in me even briefly, except Betty whom I met during my last year one night when I was very drunk and whom I talked to for only ten minutes and to my despair did not turn up next evening to meet me again as she promised she would. To have revived that exaltation in me they themselves would have had to show some response on the same romantic level, which none of them except Betty did; nevertheless, though I could not romantically love them they were poetically enlivening to me in a way not altogether different from the way Desmond and his friends were. They were the girls of a medieval town, and there was a spice of risk in meeting them because of the Proctors who patrolled the streets at night in long black gowns and each of whom was attended at heels by two 'bull-dogs' — athletic-looking college servants wearing tail coats and top-hats. Desmond said that these bullers were such good runners that they had once been able to catch a well-known Running Blue whom the Prog had sent them after; he also said that if a Prog saw you with a dubious-looking woman he would stop you and ask to be introduced to her. What would happen then Desmond evidently thought too obvious to be worth telling me, but I assumed that if she spoke with a lower-class accent you would be progged, punished in some way, perhaps by being 'gated' inside your college for the remaining evenings of the term, or if the woman was discovered to be a prostitute something worse would happen — you might be rusticated or possibly sent down from the university for good. Once when I was walking with a girl — I think she was called Monica — whom I would have expected to seem dubious-looking to a Prog, we inescapably met one with his two bullers as we rounded a shadowy corner, but he passed us by apparently without a glance. No doubt he would have stopped us if I hadn't been wearing a cap and gown as the rules required or if she had really looked like a prostitute; however the girls I picked up weren't prostitutes, not even amateurs. They were working-class or lower middle-class teenagers — who were probably virgins and remained so as far as I, frustratedly, was concerned, though in my mind I pictured them poetically as drabs (a John Masefield word) whom a poet ought naturally to associate with rather than with upper-class ladies such as the poshocracy sometimes allowed themselves to be seen with. Even if these girls hadn't known the difference between 'good' and 'bad', a difference which at least two of them when I was handling them asked me whether I didn't know, and even if somewhere more practicable for coition had been available than the back seats of cinemas or more comfortable than farmers' fields or more securely private than a punt on the river moored against the bank under the semi-concealment of weeping willows up a creek which Desmond always referred to as 'fornication creek', I doubt whether I would have dared to seduce any of them completely. But often my frustration was compensated for by a feeling of half-cynical yet at the same time ecstatic detachment in which I saw myself as a young and probably 'immortal' poet lying with a drab in his arms under the stars.

The poetic appeal for me of my encounters with these girls was heightened, just as the appeal of the company of Desmond and his friends was, by my awareness that the poshocracy knew and disapproved of my going with them. Why did I feel so hostile to the poshocracy? I wasn't envious of them and I hadn't been excluded from their circle; at least, not from their lower circle, the Young Visiters Club, as they whimsically named it after the title of Daisy Ashford's best-selling juvenile novel. During my first or second term at the college I was initiated into this club in a silly ceremony based on words taken from the novel. I had been persuaded to let myself be put up for membership by Cyril Ainger, who had come to the college from

Rugtonstead a year before me and whose brilliance as a history scholar, together with his general elegance and the fact that he had an uncle who was a bishop, had ensured him immediate acceptance by the poshocracy; he let me understand that I too had qualities which would make me eligible — good looks, a good Public school, good football, and a history scholarship (if not good family connections, though he tactfully did not allude to this lack). The poshocrats were far from being total philistines, they read other books besides Daisy Ashford's novel, even books of poetry, they could talk too about painting and music, but I soon recognised that none of them — with perhaps two exceptions — was serious about any of the arts, that they were triflers and poseurs, and this antagonised me immeasurably more than if they had held poetry in wholehearted contempt. However, I did not find their company altogether stultifying to my poetic imagination. The hostility I privately felt towards them, which caused me to observe with vivifying scorn and in minute detail their facial expressions, their vocal intonations, their slightest gestures, the theatrical artificiality of the laughter of one of them and the way another would nonchalantly kick a stone as he stood talking in the quad, was not without a poetically satirical quality, though they could never be as strongly stimulating to my imagination as Desmond and his friends were.

I still got imaginative excitement from the company of Desmond and his friends even after Richard Marple came up to Cambridge from Rugtonstead, which he did a year later than me, but it was incomparably less subtle and various than the excitement I got from being with Richard. Unlike them he was a poet, who could understand and share my poetic feelings as I could his. And unlike the poshocrats he took art seriously (we often referred to our poetry-writing as our 'art') and we encouraged and criticised each other's practice of it. The fact that the recently written poems he brought with him to Cambridge seemed, as his poems often had before, much more competent technically than mine were did not make me despair — at least, not for long — but gave me the hope that I would be able to learn from them how to improve mine. He himself, as usual, was excited by mine, though I soon detected that he thought rather more highly of some of my earlier ones than he did of some of my latest and most decadent such as one that began with the line *While I waste in the confine of my grave* and ended with *The cobra looms, the spectral bird swoops dim*. The poem I thought he seemed to prefer above all my others was one I had written only just after leaving Rugtonstead and before I went to Rouen — *The Hymn to Truth*, in which significantly the main message was *It is not good that we desire to see/The naked world through veils of poetry:* Truth was invited, only half ironically, to arise from God *with confluent streams* and to purge me of all my futile poetic dreams. The final lines were *At heart I tire of beautiful desires/Of countrysides at peace, sky's twilight fires,/Girls' hands, the steep downs dwindling into blue,/Far seas that pause* (an image that Richard particularly praised), *fields' anadems of dew./Fountain of Truth, perpetual radiancy,/Bring on brave streams and wholly cover me;* however it wasn't solely dreams of a romantically idealistic Meremy kind that I was asking Truth to destroy but also dreams of a decadent kind, as I made clear a few lines earlier on in the poem when I said *prosper the wife, consume the whore* (the whore being, from a decadent point of view, more admirable than the wife). And during my second year at Cambridge I came to think that none of my decadent poems was any good. I was enabled to reach this correct estimation of them partly by Richard's criticisms, far from damning though these were, and by the fact that my cult of gloom on which they were based was ceasing to seem valid to me. I was finding that the company of Desmond and his friends no longer helped me to sustain it — there was one crucial occasion when two of them actually aroused disgust in me, by urinating into their champagne glasses after drinking from them; and my meetings with drabs couldn't keep the cult alive in me either. Increasingly I felt the longing to meet a girl with whom I could fall totally and undecadently in love. Towards the end of my second year I decided that my poetry could never become any good until I was able to base it on a less artificial, less negative, more normal and more 'sincere' attitude to life.

My disenchantment with almost all the poems I had written hitherto did not make me despondent. The exhilaration of the hours I spent each day with Richard in talk about poetry and life kept me confident that before long I would discover how to write far better than before. In the meantime, because I wanted to avoid getting out of creative practice, I did not abandon decadent writing altogether, but it became a game which I played with Richard. We began to write stories for each other with titles such as *The Leviathan of the Urinals, The Horror in the Tower* and *The Loathly Succubus*. He would write a story and put it on the table in my sitting-room late at night when I was asleep in my bedroom and I would read it with delight at breakfast, and a morning or two later he would find a story by me on his table. *The Leviathan of the Urinals*, which was the first I wrote, was about a very drunk young man going down after midnight into a public lavatory where he sees lying on the copper grating over the drain in one corner of the urinal a small shaggy seaweed-coloured object which as he urinates grows rapidly in size until it becomes a gigantic and fungus-covered fishlike monster — my detailed description of its growth owed something to the tale of the fisherman and the genie in the Arabian Nights and perhaps something to Keats's *Lamia* — and before he escapes up into the outer air again it touches him with one of its fins; and next day he discovers he has syphilis. *The*

Horror in the Tower, written by Richard, was about a coprophagist — Kester, eleventh Lord Wranvers, one of whose similarly depraved ancestors had added to the family mansion a tower at the top of which was a water-closet with a secret compartment immediately underneath it, and he insisted that his guests, whom he fed with very rich and pulpy food to which cascara sagrada was sometimes surreptitiously added, should 'use the tower' in the day time but never at night because it was haunted then by the ninth earl; however the hero, Starn (I don't remember why Richard chose to give himself this name in his stories, or why I called myself Hynd in mine), guessing the truth, goes up to the tower closet at night and fires several rounds from his revolver at the bespattered face of Kester when it appears in the old-fashioned valve-aperture at the bottom of the pan. Our intention was to make these stories as bluntly and ludicrously disgusting as we could: obscene farce was our answer to the kind of namby-pamby delicately indelicate pseudo-pornography — James Branch Cabell's *Jurgen* was an example of this — which was fashionable with some members of the poshocracy; nevertheless we only once showed any of our stories to a poshocrat, Cyril Ainger, and his high-mindedly disapproving reaction made us angrily sorry that we had. Our stories were an attack on the poshocracy in another way too: several of the most nauseous characters we invented were based on actual poshocrats whose affectations we more especially resented. (Richard, it is true, did not dislike the poshocracy quite as deeply or see in them as great a threat to genuine art as I did — he was something of a social success with them — but out of loyalty to me and also because a simulated detestation of them gave extra force to his stories he at least equalled me in the revoltingness of his characterisations of them.) However, what our stories were above all directed against was the study of History that we were supposed to be engaged in here at Cambridge: they attacked this both by being a substitute activity taking the place of the History reading we ought to have been doing, and by having as the most odious of all the depraved characters in them an imaginary typical historian, whom we called Laily — a word which we got from the old ballad about the 'laily worm' and which according to a footnote in the Oxford Book of Ballads meant 'loathly'.

I can remember many of the lines of a satirical poem called *Tale of a Scholar* which I wrote about Laily. It was headed by a fake quotation, 'The Vidange is coming, hurrah, hurrah!' — vidange being the name given to the municipal lorry with the big cylindrical tank on it which used to be driven round to houses in Rouen for the purpose of sucking out sewage from domestic cesspits through its long metal hose. The Tale was full of deliberately ludicrous overstatements, though its beginning was comparatively unextravagant:

> *Morning, a garish half-light filtering down*
> *Through interminable fog, wakens the town*
> *With draymen's brawls and muted echo of hoofs*
> *And aqueous flares that star the salesman's booths*
> *And snowball globes lit in the doors of shops*
> *Where draper bows or butcher flings his slops*
> *Or, stooping stiff and decorous and drab,*
> *The aproned poulterer sluices his blood-streaked slab.*

After this the exaggerations really started:

> *Always in Cambridge town it seems to me*
> *Morning's like midnight in a cemetery;*
> *Beneath these sooty spires that prop the sky*
> *Death's sordid bones and pashy ordures lie;*
> *Fog clasps the tombstone towers and, darkly gowned,*
> *Men walk like shapes escaped from underground.*
> *Wonder it is that all men here are not*
> *Foredoomed alike to idle and to rot*
> *Careless of life and death;*

The tradition that work is ungentlemanly still influenced quite a number of undergraduates at this period and probably it had more to do with the idleness of Richard and myself than we were aware.

> *yet* one *I knew*
> *Who nobly lived his three or four years through*
> *In this same town, a famed historian*
> *Well-schooled in details of the grief of Man,*
> *Skilled to eschew the passions that possess*
> *And cheat men living, and are profitless;*
> *Laily his name and premature his birth.*

The thing beyond all else that made us hate History as it was presented at Cambridge was what seemed to us its fact-grubbing passionlessness, its dull indifference to human suffering, its lack of love, generosity, beauty or poetry — even though there were certain Latin phrases to be met with in Medieval and in Constitutional History which we found poetically exciting, and the words 'Habeas Corpus' caused me to write a poem beginning with the line *You have the body of my only love*. In an ironic *Prefatory Epistle to my Godson on the Study of History* Richard told this imaginary godson that the acquisition of The Historical Method was the most important ideal of human endeavour and invited him to consider as a parable of that Method in operation the story of the Valley of Bones which was set forth, 'though, I must warn you, with some degree of unscientific levity', in the Old Testament. 'The bones are clear, ascertained facts, lying, each a separate entity, in the valley — but the life-giving breath of the historian transforms them into coherent skeletons, where each bone bears a relation to its neighbour, without losing any of its original value as a fragment of ossified matter.' Most unfortunately for the truth of the original tale, Richard's epistle went on to say, the transformation did not end there; the skeletons were clothed with flesh and inflated with wind, and their 'exact precision' was thus seriously impaired. History at Cambridge was all the more lifeless for us because of the contrast between it and the History we had been taught at Rugtonstead in the Sixth Form by Mr Holmes who was a genius as a teacher and knew how to give the subject an appeal to the individual tastes of each of his pupils — for instance he got me interested in the Renaissance by presenting it to me as a time both of artistic greatness and also of revolt against conventions: History as he taught it had a relevance to my experience of actual life in a way it was not to have again until I became interested in Marxism some years after I'd gone down from Cambridge (and Marxism helped me to respect the work of several of those Cambridge historians whose lectures I had cut as an undergraduate — especially the work of the great medievalist G. G. Coulton whom I discovered to be far from indifferent to human suffering.) Richard and I did not however hate our History tutor at the college, Andrew Gorse; on the contrary we found him the most human among all the 'dons', with his shyness and his interest in literature and his outbursts of invective. We weren't conscious how right-wing his political views were, and if we had been they would have made no difference to our liking for him, because we regarded all kinds of politics with an equal contempt. One of the main vilenesses we found in History books was their concern with past politics. Laily was our imaginative representation not of any actual existing don or undergraduate, but of the spirit of Historical studies at Cambridge as they appeared to us then.

> . . . *His witty converse and his kind retorts,*
> *His rapid pacing through the college courts,*
> *His glance assured, as who should say — 'I'm Laily;*
> *I have the air of Benjamin Disraeli,*
> *Or Byron, rather. Yet I'm more than these;*
> *For there's no extant proof that Byron's knees*

> *Were soft and pinkish, or that Dizzy's foot*
> *Was graced with so impenetrable a boot*
> *As this I wear — and bought dirt cheap it was.'*

Evidence begins to come out at this point in the poem that though I believed myself to be a total rebel against the English Public-school mentality I was not yet free from some of its nastier prejudices. When I went to Rugtonstead as a new boy, boots had recently gone out of fashion and any boy who still wore them instead of shoes was likely to arouse a detestation surpassed only by the detestation felt by the majority of the boys for certain physical peculiarities which unlike the boots could not be changed, and which I was not above holding against Laily in my poem — though I also implied that he was to blame for trying to improve himself physically by using Tatcho (I added a footnote explaining that this was a much-advertised depilatory) to remove the hair from his knees.

> *Dizzy and Byron lose to me because*
> *Tatcho and Woolworth's were unknown to them;*
> *And where's the proof that Byron chewed his phlegm,*
> *Cackled, or gargled spittle, or conceived*
> *This pose of grimness I've so well achieved?'*

Perhaps Laily could have changed his habit of cackling and could have stopped being a poseur but the characteristics that the poem next attacked him for having were not his fault, and the attack seems fascist-like to me now:

> *Laily was proud, yet must have felt the want*
> *Of some infallible deodorant,*
> *And often dreamed of an electric ray*
> *Potent enough to take his curls away —*
> *His oily curls, from which no barber's art*
> *Could comb the lingering essence of a fart.*

I inconsistently added:

> *Handsome he was, yet lust and history books*
> *Had done some mischief to his boyhood looks . . .*

Soon I still more inconsistently went on to accuse him of not being motivated in his studies by a love of History.

> *. . . And largely in the background seemed to loom*
> *The haven of the examination room;*
> *For, to be just to him, let me confess*
> *He loathed pure History worse than cleanliness,*
> *But loved competitive exams and prizes*
> *And all rewards the History Board devises —*
> *High marks and hinted praise, promises muttered*
> *To those who know which side their bread is*
> *   buttered.*
> *Honours he relished, yet found joy no less*
> *In others' failure than in his success,*
> *And gave God thanks that in exams at least*
> *One does not lose by stinking like a beast,*
> *And that the kind examiners subtract*
> *No marks for sweating like a sexual act . . .*

I never finished the poem, partly because it did not seem serious enough to be worth the effort of finishing, but in the last few lines of it that I did write I was beginning to return to what would have been my main accusation in the poem as a whole against Historical studies at Cambridge — that they had no heart, were devoid of any feeling for the sufferings of the human race — and this accusation if I had developed it further could perhaps have made the poem more serious.

> *Yet I should wrong both accuracy and art*
> *Should I suggest that Laily had no heart;*
> *His mind indeed was overstocked with dust*
> *And grimed with dreams of profit and of lust,*

> *And true, his body would have won disgrace*
> *Had it not aptly matched his feet and face;*
> *But always, let me say, his heart was good*
> *And duly drudged to pump the daily blood*
> *With systole regular and diastole*
> *Seldom perturbed or flurried by a soul . . .*

'Systole' and 'diastole' were impressive-sounding words I had found in a poem by Whitman and used here without checking up on their pronunciation in the dictionary; my assuming that they rhymed with 'soul' was the kind of blunder which made my poetry technically inferior still to Richard's. Nevertheless *Tale of a Scholar* now seems to me technically better than any of my decadent gloom-and-doom poems. It seemed so also at the time, and in spite of my unseriousness when writing it I felt that perhaps it had brought me a step nearer to solving the problem of how to write a less artificial and more normally human kind of poetry. I would have liked other people besides Richard to read it, but it was too obscenely subversive to be published by any of the undergraduate magazines, and I didn't let Desmond or his friends see it because I was afraid they would have regarded it in the same way as they did the occasional dirty limericks I wrote for them. I decided I would show it to Sugden, the only other undergraduate Richard and I knew who wanted more than anything else in life to be a poet. We had not had a high opinion of the verse he copiously produced until one day he let us read a short poem of his entitled *Immortality* which I immediately recognised to be immeasurably superior to anything I, or even Richard, had yet written, and I knew that he was a real poet. In taking my *Tale of a Scholar* to him I half-hoped that he might say something about it which would give me an idea of how I could go on from this negative kind of poetry to the new positive kind I needed to write.

When I went to his college one afternoon at tea-time with

the Tale in my pocket and found him in his rooms, he was glad to see me — gladder it seemed than ever before, no doubt because at our last meeting I had told him of my admiration for *Immortality* — though his smile as usual was oddly slow to spread from the corners of his mouth over his soft and evenly pink cheeks. The look of his eyes too was soft as he sat listening in his wicker armchair while I read the Tale aloud to him. Before I got to the end of it I sensed that he did not like it, but when I'd finished he was at pains to avoid saying anything about it which might wound my feelings. He gave as a reason for not being enthusiastic about it that he had never been able to appreciate satire. I realised that he was perfectly genuine in saying this when he went on to tell me that parody or any other kind of slighting made him miserable. He wrote his poems straight down, he said, and he could never bring himself to alter them in any way afterwards. He seemed unhappy about something — perhaps it was the criticisms that Richard or I had made to him of many of his poems before *Immortality* which had impressed me so much. I quoted to him from the passage in *Adonais* where Shelley regrets the over-sensitivity to criticism which had reputedly hastened Keats's death: 'Where was then/Wisdom the mirrored shield, or scorn the spear?' He reacted to this quotation by going on to talk more revealingly about himself than I had ever known him to do since I had first met him. At his Preparatory school, he said, he had seen visionary faces on the wall in the dormitory and had spoken to the other boys about them. He had believed the faces were real. The headmaster heard him speaking about them and gave him a severe telling-off which made him weep, and afterwards he managed to throw off these visions for ever. Later he became a pantheist, and still was. All men's minds are a part of God, he thought. He said he was afraid of going mad, though there was no madness in his family. He had a dread that he might see faces at the window of his college bedroom, in spite of its being three storeys above the ground. Every night he looked under his bed before getting into it, and also he looked inside his trunk which he kept in his bedroom. He could never sleep unless the right-hand corner of his towel on the towel-horse was lower than the left. I began to suspect there might be some truth after all in Freud, whom I had hitherto regarded as a charlatan mainly because Cyril Ainger and several other of the poshocrats were modishly keen on him. What Sugden said about his towel made me think of the human testicles. But there was a difficulty here, since the left testicle in fact hangs lower than the right. A solution occurred to me suddenly: Sugden was seeing the towel as though it was a naked man frontally exposed to him and therefore the drooping right corner of the towel could correspond to the man's left testicle. That he had the image of a man at the back of his mind as he looked towards the towel-rack seemed to me to be proved when I asked him whether he was sure it was the right corner of the towel that had to hang lower and he explained that the lower corner must be on the right *facing him*. I asked him whether he had read Freud at all, and he said he hadn't. This fully convinced me that the account he had given me of his Preparatory school visions and of his bed-time ritual at Cambridge wasn't just an invention intended to impress me, though it did impress me. I forgot I had come to see him in the hope of getting some suggestion from him that might help me to write a new kind of poetry in place of the decadent kind which I had decided could never be good. The need grew in me as he talked to go and find Richard as soon as possible afterwards and to report to him the disturbingly amazing things that Sugden had been revealing to me.

On the evening of the same day, when dinner in the college hall was over and I was walking alone with Richard round the New Court towards his rooms, I said I had had an interesting conversation that afternoon with Sugden, and

Richard told me he had had one with him too — for five minutes in the street outside the Union. 'This *sincerity* of his,' Richard said with a laugh, 'is really too humorous.' I disagreed, and said I was moved by it. I didn't ask what Sugden had talked to him about, because I knew from Richard's tone that it couldn't have been anything as extraordinary as I was going to report. I began at once to tell him of Sugden's bed-time ritual and of the towel which had to hang always with its right corner lower than its left. As we were passing the entrance to the passage-way which led out from the New Court to the bicycle shed I said: 'You know, Freud was right after all.' I said it with a deliberately sinister intonation, and after saying it I was startled to recognise a Freudian ambiguity in my use of the word 'right'. Richard immediately slowed in his walk and we came to a stop. His face in the semi-darkness had a terrified look, which I assumed he was putting on as deliberately as I had put on my intonation — we often indulged in dramatic mimicry of various extreme emotions to amuse each other. Then he began to run, fast, towards the part of the court where the staircase to his rooms was. I followed him but didn't catch up with him till he got into his sitting-room at the top of the stairs, and there I became sure that whether or not his fright had been partly factitious to start with it was wholly genuine now. He told me that at the same moment when I had spoken the word 'Freud' he had seen the stars above the court and that they were unutterably white and seemed to flicker violently in the wind. I explained to him that what had converted me to Freud had been my realisation that Sugden saw the corners of his towel as though they were the testicles of a naked man facing him. I could feel that Richard's fright increased after I'd said this, and soon it infected me also. We heard the wind against the turret just above his rooms. He said that the constellation Orion hangs down to the left too. We agreed that to think of this in relation to Sugden's towel was ridiculous, yet the thought was somehow horrible. We had in some dim way touched on the elementals. The panic we felt, Richard said, was like the true classic panic which used to be felt by the followers of the god Pan. Except that we were possessed not by Pan but by Freud. Freud. We kept on repeating the name. Sigmund Freud. Or alternatively, Tod (this word which was derived from the German for Death had become a favourite with us ever since Richard had used it in a story of his to name a character who when the historian Laily tried to rape him turned out to be a dressed-up skeleton). Mr Tod. Or God. Freud was God. No snuffling Viennese mountebank (why did I think of him as 'snuffling'?), but God. You know, Freud was right after all. Horror and death. The death of all poetry. Laily's hand had put out across the stars and they were gone. I couldn't get up the courage to walk back to my own rooms in the Old Court until well after one o'clock. And in the morning, although I was able to think of my panic as having been a fairly trivial experience, I could not reverse my unwilling conversion to Freud, and I sensed that this was going to increase my difficulties in achieving the new positive kind of poetry I was so slowly feeling my way towards.

I didn't achieve it till some months later at home during the Easter vac, after a term of deepening despondency and of rather frequent drunken evenings, sometimes on my own, which usually ended with my writing down in almost illegibly spiky handwriting in my journal admonishments to myself such as 'Let me wither if I betray the trust given to me in youth.' (Richard and I had recently both started keeping journals at the same time, inspired by Barbellion's *Diary of a Disappointed Man*). The poem I wrote ignored Freud. It was called *Religio Poetae*, though the religion in it had — so I thought — nothing to do with conventional Christianity, which I continued to abhor. It avoided the word 'God', in place of which it used the word 'Love' — but only once and as the first word at the beginning of a line, where the capital 'L' wouldn't seem too obtrusively metaphysical since any word in that position would have had a capital letter. However, nowhere in the poem was there an overt suggestion of the longing for sexual love that was almost as strong in me as my longing to be a poet. It's true that spermatozoa were mentioned, among other poetically interesting if not so surprising things — such as the falcon and the dragon-fly, the brag of glittering streets, the fife's Jubilate (a word I'd learnt from the Catholic poet Francis Thompson), spires and cranes, skylit vanes, thunder and lilies, frogs, the sewer rat's domains, the Marquesas towering green from breakers' white — things which the poem said Love had created. I had read hardly any philosophy, and I didn't know how philosophically commonplace the idealism of my main theme was.

> *In the rain's shadowy pace, in the wind's cry*
> *I feel your strength that shaped to live and die*
> *All forms that ever were in earth or sky . . .*
> *Within the stone long-dead your strength yet reigns,*
> *Within the swallow's skull some dream remains,*
> *Some shadow of your bounty that sustains.*

In the last nine lines of the poem, after blaming myself for my former cynicism and contempt for 'faith', I ended by claiming that even at my worst I hadn't really betrayed Love.

> *I have not failed your trust, I have not strayed,*
> *Since of your very fancy you have made*
> *My life, and the mind's meanest gesture weighed.*

I wasn't as dissatisfied with this final rhymed triplet as I ought to have been. What I had wanted to say in it was that Love who had created me had predetermined all my thoughts and actions however wayward these had been. I considered altering the last line to *My life, and all my faithless acts foreweighed,* but this *sounded* worse, in spite of its getting slightly nearer to the sense I wanted. So I let the line stand as it was, with its inexplicit 'the' and its ambiguous 'meanest' and its wholly inept 'weighed'. Technical incompetence was evident also, not so glaringly as here, in several other parts of the poem, where I wasn't aware of it at all. I believed that *Religio Poetae* was the best think I'd written yet. Richard seemed to rate it highly too, though he was impressed less by its philosophy than by its imagery which had much the same kind of 'strangeness' that he had found exciting in the decadent gloom-and-doom poems it was repudiating. But by the third or fourth week of the term following the vac during which I had written it I came to think that it was no good. This happened chiefly as a result of my attending the lectures on literary criticism given by B. K. Wilshaw, which had begun to change my whole conception of what modern poetry ought to be like.

He seemed an amazing genius. Richard, who was still doing History after I had escaped from it to do English at the beginning of my third and last year at Cambridge, also came to hear him and was equally impressed. There were other English lecturers whom I found very good, and Richard sampled several of these too and agreed with me that their lectures were as full of life as most History ones we'd attended had been full of death and no doubt if the college authorities hadn't refused the request he made to them at the start of his first term to be allowed to transfer from History to English he wouldn't have been sent down from the university at the end of his second year for writing impertinently comic answers to the questions in the Tripos examination. But Wilshaw's lectures came home to us with especial force because they dealt with poetry not just as something achieved in the past but as something still to be achieved in the present. He soon convinced us that the kind of contemporary poetry most in fashion since the end of the war — the post-Victorian romantic and predominantly iambic kind that had most influenced my style, particularly

189

in *Religio Poetae* — was out of keeping with modern life. He wanted a poetry which would use the rhythms of normal speech and would be compatible with a scientific outlook on the world. There was only one important thing in his theory that I couldn't easily accept, and it disturbed me increasingly as his lectures continued. He thought that poetry ought not to be regarded as referring to anything in the external world. He told us that people with a scientific training — and there would be more and more of them as time went on — couldn't be expected to see much point in lines like Coleridge's 'The hornéd moon with one bright star/Within the nether tip', unless they could be brought to recognise that poetry was 'emotive', 'emotive' being the key-word he habitually used to convey his view that poetry was concerned essentially with states of feeling, in contradistinction to science which was 'intellectual' and was concerned with objective reality. At last, after the end of one of his lectures, I dared to go up and speak to him of my doubts about this part of his theory. I spoke with an artificial intensity, to overcome my nervousness, and his face seemed to have a faint smile at first as he listened; but when, after I'd told him I would fully agree that what I would call the prose sense of a poem — which I explained as being the sense it would retain if it were translated into prose — was only one thing among others that gave the poem its appeal to the reader, I went on to say I thought the 'prose sense' was the most important thing because it informed the reader what the poem was about, he interrupted: 'You should have attended my earlier lectures.' I wanted to answer that I had attended all of them and also to let him know how enthusiastic I was about them, but his tone had an impatience in it which inhibited me, and I turned away and went out of the lecture-room without saying anything more. I didn't stop attending his lectures after this but I never tried to speak to him again. His view that a poetic statement could not have any external

m, had very likely planned the whole thing
ey had got drunk. I saw my broom leaning
uppermost against the mantelpiece where
have transported it from my other cupboard,
of it suggested a method of revenge to me
diately put into practice. I smeared butter
s, which were soft, and then went quietly
oshocrats and buttered the backs of their
None of them seemed to notice — they must
drunk or else the general crush in the room
de them insensible to the soft contact of the
s even able to butter the front of The
harles Gedge's jacket without his realising
ing. Having buttered the jackets of all those
aged in messing up my room, I then took a
r in my hand and exultingly went to the
witch by the door and I turned off 'the light
and flung the lump as violently as I could into
When I switched on the light again I saw a
yellow medallion stuck on to the black satin
e Padlow's jacket. He was already aware of it,
felt the impact of it. He was a big rugby-
, and he looked frowningly around the room,
ho had thrown the butter till one of the other
nted me out to him. He came towards me and
head down determined to hit him before he
fended me off with one hand while with the
ved the medallion from his lapel and rubbed
o my hair; then I managed to close with him
ll him, but someone parted us. Several other
l been watching the episode and I turned on
ed to tell them vehemently some of the things
ag time thought about them all; and, while I
em, Messiter, who had taken a packet of
out of my cupboard, was experimentally
xes one after another with a hammer which

'referent' was, as I came to realise before long, central to his whole poetic theory. No wonder my doubts had irritated him a little. I realised too that this view was absolutely unacceptable to me and that I would never succeed in writing a satisfactory poem unless it was about something. So although his lectures did me good by destroying my attachment to contemporary post-Victorian romantic verse and by convincing me that I ought to create a verse-form closer to the rhythms of ordinary speech, they didn't give me the information I most needed if I was to succeed in the struggle which subsequently began for me to write poetry in keeping with modern life. They didn't help me to discover what this poetry could be about.

I soon knew that the struggle was going to be still more difficult than my previous one which had ended in the writing of *Religio Poetae*. I knew that the gap I would have to cross in order to achieve a truly modern poetry would be far huger than the gap I had crossed between my cynically decadent poems and *Religio Poetae*. The few preliminary attempts I made at poems in speech-rhythm, none of them getting farther than three or four lines, were all of them rightly damned by Richard when I showed them to him. I became increasingly depressed, and though I still spent very much of my time with Richard and we laughed as often as ever, I went out drinking by myself on more evenings than before. In the pubs and streets of Cambridge my own angry wretchedness about my poetic impotence and also about the frustration of my endless yearning for a girl I could fall utterly in love with, helped to give me a keener sympathy than I had hitherto had for the comparatively far greater wretchedness of so many other and older people. One evening in a pub which was also an hotel I saw a very old waiter, and a farmer with a bowler hat tilted over his eyes who looked ill, and in the hotel lounge an irritated ageing commercial traveller searching through his papers, and I heard music and the shouts of drunkards, and I asked myself how men like these could bear up. Phthisical and old, what made them strong to endure the injustice and monotonous misery of their lives? Alcohol and tobacco: that was the answer. Or, perhaps, religion. But I had nothing, — I overlooked the fact that I was drinking and smoking at the time — not even the courage to kill myself. Soon after leaving this pub I saw in the lamplight a man with locomotor ataxy coming out from a passage-way. (I recognised the disease from what I had read about the three stages of syphilis in my father's medical books.) He was struggling along with the aid of a kind of staff which had a thick rubber ferrule at the bottom of it — 'if a ferrule can be rubber', I said to myself. He advanced spasmodically by means of a shakily lunging movement while his free arm swung curvingly upwards and forwards not unlike the arm of a bowler at cricket. Saliva dribbled from his colourless lips and a dog barked at him. When I got back to my college rooms I wrote drunkenly in my journal, 'Oh if only I were strong enough to end this blatant injustice, this motiveless system which produces cretinism and phthisis and cases of locomotor ataxy such as the man I saw to-night.' Next morning the idea came to me that I might be able to solve my poetic problem by trying to write about people like that man and the old waiter and the farmer who looked ill and the ageing commercial traveller, and to write about them in a way which would have none of the negativism or quaintness of my decadent poems and would be positive without any of the religiosity of my *Religio Poetae*. I could try to write poems of human sympathy, and the work of Wilfred Owen would be my model, though I knew all too well that I could never come near him in genius.

After this during the remainder of the Michaelmas term I did not succeed in writing a poem but I cultivated sympathy towards other people in myself and was even able to feel it for a while towards the poshocracy who after all would not

be immune to eventual
been aware when I had
poem, *Nor do you gue*
who laugh in rooms o
poshocracy reached its
evening of the college C
the term. After the din
had sat next to one of
that the only sexual re
rosy-cheeked butcher-b
Richard, both of us ve
surprised and flattered
seemed, many of the po
a thing that very few
while. I welcomed them
them all, and soon I wa
ink on the starched sh
Warder, whom I had n
musician. Warder look
wrote out all four ver
belle/Qui remplit mon
heart. Not long after
poshocrats in the ba
objects in my room —
pictures from the wall
drawer in my table and
usually gave this sor
contemptuously, when
things out from the c
crockery. Gedge went
butter with my bread
butter towards the ceili
soon joined him, using
in my drunkenness, wa
Suddenly I become angr
had obviously come up t

of spoiling t
even before
with its hea
someone mu
and the sigh
which I im
over its bri
among the
dinner jacke
have been t
must have r
broom. I
Honourable
what I was
who were e
lump of b
electric ligh
for an insta
the darknes
large circul
lapel of Ge
had no dou
football pla
not knowing
poshocrats
I went for
hit me but
other he re
it violently
and tried to
poshocrats
them and s
I had for a
was telling
match-boxe
hitting the

he'd also found in my cupboard, causing white smoke to spurt out from each box, so I spoke directly to him: 'perhaps now you would like to *bugger* the pictures, Messiter.' I emphasised the word 'bugger' because he'd always seemed to me to have an epicene look about him, though I knew of no evidence whatsoever to suggest that he was actually homosexual except in the non-practising way in which so many Public school young men at the university continued to be. He got my meaning, and I was gratified to see a flush come up over his rather pale face — whether of anger or of embarrassment I never knew, as my attention became distracted by a movement which other poshocrats in my room had begun to make towards the door. I realised that they were leaving. I hurried over to the door myself, and as they went out, ignoring me, I apologised to them magnamimously for having buttered their clothes, rather in the tone of 'Forgive them, for they know not what they do.' Everyone who had been in the room, except myself, was leaving it, Richard among the rest. I had hardly been aware of him during all that had been going on — he had been sitting somewhere in the background, talking with Maurice Warder, I seemed to remember — and now he was suddenly grinning at me as he went out, extremely drunk and supported on one side by Maurice. Why hadn't he come to my aid? He can't have been so drunk as to have been totally unaware of what the poshocrats had been up to. Why hadn't he made at least some gesture against them, however ineffectual, given some sign that he was on my side, not on theirs? He had just sat there, neutral. Or worse than neutral, an accomplice by default. My anger at his disloyalty steadily rose as I stood alone in my room after they'd all gone. Then there was a knock on my door and Plummer, who had been among the first of the poshocrats to walk out of the room, came in again and asked if he could help me to clean up the mess. If he had been one of those who had been prominent in causing it I might have hesitated to let him absolve himself so simply, but I couldn't remember his having caused any of it at all, so I said yes. He worked with me for what must have been not much less than half an hour at getting the room in order again. I wondered why he was helping me and I supposed it might be because he was a History Scholar of the same year as myself and knew me better than most of the other poshocrats did and was a bit ashamed of the way they'd behaved. When we'd finished I said to him, 'You at least are a gentleman. I like you.' At that period I still thought it a compliment to call someone a 'gentleman'. He said expressionlessly, 'Thanks' and left me. I felt I could forgive him for being a poshocrat, but I could not begin to feel forgiving towards Richard. I could more easily forgive even those poshocrats who had messed up my room — after all, they knew I was no friend of theirs, and at least they had been civilised enough to refrain from overpowering me physically and throwing my trousers out of the window — than I could forgive Richard who knew I was his friend. My indignation against him continued to increase after Plummer had gone, and it seemed to me that the whole of the imaginative world we'd been constructing and living in together was fraudulent. I sat down at my table and wrote him a letter in which I broke with him for ever.

But in the morning I didn't deliver the letter, because I recognised that his failure to support me against the poshocrats could have been due mainly to his drunkenness then, and also because the rage he had caused in me was wholly supplanted by another feeling which came over me while I was packing my trunk in my sitting-room after breakfast in preparation for my return home that day for the Christmas vac — a feeling about which I was later to write in my journal: 'I was miserable beyond telling. I did not care whether or not my name died with me.' My misery began from my realising as I packed my notebooks into the trunk that my seventh term at the university had ended without my having achieved a single poem in my lifetime yet which would have the slightest chance of surviving after my death. I had failed. I had failed in the one work I was fitted for, in the aim I had set myself ever since I had written my first poem at the age of fifteen. And I was too miserable to care that I had failed. But this wasn't true; I did care. I cared for nobody and for nothing except poetry, and I would never give up the struggle to be a poet. Yet I had a dread that one day I might change. Another man with my name and body would betray the trust given to him in his youth. He would laugh pleasantly at his son's poetic ambition, and say that he too had once intended to be a Shakespeare. If futurity held such a man, let him remember what I was thinking now. Across the waste of time (the pun at this point in my thinking was unconscious) I damned him. I wished him death and ten years of physical agony before death. But on the other hand if the 'I' that was to be should keep the faith, I wished him immortality as a poet and I knew my wish would be fulfilled, and if when he remembered these thoughts of his he was poor, old, ill and unknown, let him find a sufficient reward in them and be comforted by them.

Which of those alternative future I's is this man, no longer even middle-aged, though in good health still, walking along the disused railway here across the low-lying meadows in early spring, interested in flowers as I never was at Cambridge except as a vague springtime background that was more exciting, I have to admit, than they are to me now when I see them in detail and know them by name? I am neither the philistine betrayer of my youth that I dreaded I might become nor am I the poet assured of poetic immortality that I hoped to be. I don't fool myself that I am one of those English poets alive to-day whose work will still be read in a hundred years' time. As for betraying my youth, when I was in the Party I did after a while allow politics to get the better of art in my poems and this eventually stopped me writing poetry altogether, but that time is past and I am a poet again now. And if I mean to go on being one I must defeat the wish which I had at the beginning of this walk, and which I am not yet wholly rid of, to make the political struggle my primary concern once again. It's true my attitude towards politics can no longer remain what it was when my retirement began, now that the Chinese (whatever they may do in future) have given new life to Marxism-Leninism throughout the world by their attack on the revisionism of the Soviet leadership. I recognise that the political struggle is far more important than poetry. Nevertheless, if I am to give of my best to the struggle, poetry must still come first for me.

8

It isn't any lack in me of poetic sensitivity to my surroundings this afternoon that I am uneasy about as I walk through these woods high above the sea. Admittedly my imagination may be less exaltedly awake than when fifteen years ago here during one of my holidays before I retired from teaching I turned from this path I'm on now to go down towards three white poplar trees at the edge of the cliff with the sea beyond them and with the pale undersides of their wind-lifted leaves showing, and suddenly I entered into a different existence (as I described it to myself later), on earth not in heaven but incomparably better than I had been experiencing before, an existence in a world where monopoly capitalism with all its anti-human crimes had been ended for ever, and though I knew this was an illusion I felt utterly justified in trying to keep it alive in me for as many minutes as I could, because I believed it prefigured the reality of the future and could strengthen me in supporting the fight to bring that reality nearer. My state of mind at present may not be visionary, yet I am imaginatively interested still in the detail of these woods, in the ivy which is on the ground almost everywhere except along the paths where brown leaves fallen from the trees are thick and which seems to leap up the slenderer trees as abruptly as flames would if the floor of the woods were on fire, in the flowers of the ivy mostly finished now and with none of Shelley's yellow bees visiting them and none of the metallic-blue flies I have sometimes seen on them, in the fruits of the ivy that have the shape of the ends of sewing-machine bobbins, in the stout and goblin limbs of the ivy with their hairy-looking adhesive roots that grasp and climb the trunks of the bigger trees, in the oaks that are multi-elbowed like the Indian god Shiva, in the patches of lichen whose green is so pale that they appear as though sunlit on the bark of the branches even where sunlight doesn't penetrate to them, in the moss whose green is so dark on the branches even where the sun does shine on it that it suggests to me a velvet livery worn by the footmen of a shadowy mansion. I don't much like that image 'footmen of a shadowy mansion' — I suspect it of being derivative, perhaps from Walter de la Mare — but my uneasiness this afternoon is not due to any doubt in me about my ability to think imaginatively, nor to misgivings about the poetic quality of my imaginings. No, I am uneasy because I am unsure whether there can be any justification for my engaging in imaginative activity at all, either during my afternoon walks or when it takes the form of poetry-writing at home.

What validity can there be in my imaginings or in my poetry at a time when American imperialism every day is bringing slaughter and torture and destruction to Vietnam? No matter how good the poem I've been writing for so long may be — and at worst it's certainly far less bad than I'd feared it might become, and in reaching the final section of it yesterday morning with only a seventh of the poem still to write I've made steadier progress with it than I expected when my retirement began — what support can its poetic quality give to the Vietnamese? Ever since our C.N.D. group eight months ago helped to organize our first public 'teach-in' here on Vietnam, I have been asking myself increasingly often the old question I used to ask when I was in the Party, 'Why write poetry at all?' And my answer has always been 'I write primarily in the hope of giving to the reader what poetry specifically can give.' But wouldn't I do better to concentrate all my energy on helping to get across to as many people as possible the truth about the abominations, the napalm, the gas, the fragmentation bombs, the torturing of prisoners, the 'zapping' of villages, the chemical destruction of crops and forests — which the richest and most technically advanced nation in the world is inflicting, with the 'unswerving' approval of Britain's highly religious Labour Foreign Minister, on Vietnamese peasants and workers, men, women and children indiscriminately? Yes, if the sole purpose of my poem were to give the reader what poetry specifically can give I would do better to abandon it at once and devote myself wholly to political activity, but I have been able to assure myself that my poem does secondarily support the struggle against imperialism and if only it doesn't take me too long to finish it could prove to be more effective politically — even though this isn't its primary aim — than any primarily political activity of mine could be. Yet as soon as I have convinced myself that I can aid the political struggle best by putting poetry first, the disturbing question poses itself to me whether the intensity of the political feeling in my poem may not have caused damage to its poetic quality, and perhaps so much damage that the poem could do a disservice to the cause which it is secondarily intended to serve and which I might have served far better by writing a prose pamphlet. May not the impression I still sometimes get from the poem that it is altogether too bleak and bare be due to the prevalence of politics in it?

No, if the poem really is too bleak — and often I think it isn't — this is not because it's about politics. Some of the greatest and poetically richest poetry ever written — by Shakespeare for instance — has been essentially political. If my poem is bleak this is because I have not yet wholly recovered from the effect of the years when political activity was my first concern and when the politics in the poems I tried to write overruled the poetry. My full recovery can best be brought about by my continuing the practice of going back in thought, whenever I have doubts about the validity of poetry or of the new poetic life, to my imaginative activity during the years before I put politics first. The absolute belief I had then in the validity of poetry — even at times when I found myself unable to write it, as I was for quite a long while after I came down from Cambridge — can revitalise my belief in poetry now that I am able to write it once more.

The intention I formed towards the end of my last term at Cambridge to try to write poems of human sympathy did not survive the subsequent holiday period during July and August when I was with the rest of my family at our home in Essex and at the seaside. One reason for this may have been that I saw no such sights as I had seen while I had been pub-crawling alone along the streets of Cambridge, and I realised that even if I were to see such sights in my home town the comfortableness of my life at home would prevent me from writing about them with anything remotely like the depth and sincerity of feeling with which war poets had been able to write about sufferings that they themselves had shared. In the autumn after Vaughan and Laura had gone back to their boarding-schools and Hugh had gone back to Cambridge I became aware of a subject that I thought I would be able to write poetry about more genuinely than about consumptive waiters and ageing commercial travellers. This subject was my home. Since my childhood I had never been here in November — I had always been away at school or at Cambridge — and the house and the streets seemed extraordinarily beautiful, magical, as though I was seeing them again just as I had seen them when I had been a child. I conceived the idea for a poem which would be something like Rimbaud's *Bateau Ivre*, a fantasised and ecstatic remembrance of childhood, though it would be rather closer to external actuality than Rimbaud's poem had been. It would mention such things as the piebald rocking-horse and the yellow varnished toy-cupboard in the nursery; the many small green-framed engravings of the faces of musicians that were on the wall above the baby-grand piano in the drawing-room; the bowl of lavender that was always on the windowsill there; the golden privet and the laurel and the euonymus growing along the garden fence; the road outside leading downhill in one direction past the cypresses of the cemetery to the market place and downhill also in the other direction towards the public park; the park itself with its two very large ponds, one shaped like a spoon and full of reeds and the other with a bend half way along it and with an island of tall trees in the middle of it where ducks and swans and moorhens and a Chinese goose apparently lived when they weren't on the water. But the more I thought about this idea for a poem — and I thought about it for several weeks without getting a single satisfactory line of verse down on paper — the less ecstatic and the more nostalgic it became. This was because the longer I stayed at home the greater the difference seemed to be between the immediate actuality of home and my memory of what it had been like in my childhood, and especially between what my mother and father had been like then and what they had recently become.

I didn't for a moment feel that my presence at home was anything but welcome to them, however, nor did either of them show any sign of thinking that I ought to begin to look for a job by which I could earn my own living: on the contrary my father more than once told me he was glad to have me there, and my mother — who took a pride in trying to make the house a place where her children would always want to return — showed in various ways that she too liked me to be there, and I knew both of them were as keen as I was that I should succeed as a poet. What was different was that in my childhood they had not seemed to quarrel with each other, though in the past few years they had certainly begun to — if not so frequently or bitterly as now — and perhaps even from the start of their marriage there had been fundamental disagreements between them but they had not allowed these to drive them into open hostility then. There had been two early incidents which my father fairly recently had told me of for the first time: the earlier of the two had happened just before they were married when they had gone up together to a big London store to choose furniture for their house, and the salesman had shown them an attractive but expensive imitation Sheraton dining-room suite and she without asking my father's opinion had said to the salesman 'Yes, we'll have that', causing my father to feel alarm for the future even though she had an income of her own; the second incident had been when they had attended a point-to-point race meeting and he had heard one county-type young man remark to another about them 'The grey filly seems the better horse there'. My father felt humiliated by this, knowing as he already did that he was not going to be master in his own house as he had been brought up to believe a husband should be. My mother who before marrying him had travelled on her own in Europe and America and in Palestine and Egypt, and who had been an actress for a short while and also a hospital nurse for a short while, could not willingly accept the restrictions on her freedom that having children and running a household meant for her, and to compensate herself as best she could for what she had lost she aimed to make something exceptional of her home and also of her children and of her husband, all of whom she became constantly more critical of as they failed to come up to what she hoped for, her husband especially. No doubt he did give her something to complain of by conventionally believing that the male should dominate the female, though in practice he gave way to her on most points of difference between them and didn't prevent her from having us christened in church or sending us to boarding-schools where we were more unhappy than we would probably have been at the less classy day schools he would have preferred for us. No doubt she wasn't unreasonable in not liking the crude new friends he had made at the golf club after the war who called him Doc and with whom he drank and played cards as well as golf. The quarrels between him and her were imposed upon them by the world outside the home, and my having to listen to these at meal-times with no one else present except sometimes Ethel our maid — previously when I had heard my mother and father quarrel it had been during the holidays and one or both of my brothers and/or my sister had usually been in the room too — brought me to realise how ridiculous my idea for an ecstatic poem about home was, above all in its assumption that home was a place that could be insulated from an outer world of which Marchfield and Rugtonstead and Cambridge were, like the golf-club, a part.

Although home as I would have viewed it in the ecstatic poem I never wrote would have been much as my mother would have wished me to view it, she seemed to me to be more to blame than my father for starting the quarrels which made me unable to write such a poem. I could not sympathise with her in her aggressiveness, because I did not recognise then what it was essentially due to — the position of inferiority which bourgeois society imposed upon her as a woman. I can remember two of these quarrels in some detail since I recorded them in my journal at the time, partly as an outlet for the indignation I felt that my parents who were both of them by nature gentle and kindly should talk in such a way to each other, and partly as an aid to preserving a detachment favourable to the writing of the nostalgic poem I hoped would be possible instead of the ecstatic one. Most often the quarrels happened at lunch-time when my father had called in at the golf-club for a drink on his way home after finishing his morning round of visits to his patients, and one typical minor quarrel began with my mother saying to him as he sat down to the table: 'I saw a very smart car outside Dr Browne's this morning.'

'Probably a chauffeur who had strained his wrist starting the car,' my father said, forcing a laugh.

'No, it was a young couple.'

'They may have been friends of the Brownes'.'

'No, they were patients.'

'How little you know about these things,' my father said, beginning to show anger.

'I'm certain they were patients. The woman was carrying a baby.'

'Well, anyway, what's your motive in telling me this? What do you want to make me feel?'

My mother smiled faintly and did not answer him. It was very obvious she wanted to make him feel that Dr Browne had a better class of patient than he, with his golf-club manners, was able to attract. They went on arguing for a long while mostly repeating what they'd already said though my father did add the new suggestion that the woman with the baby was a niece of Mrs Browne's, till my mother ended her part in the argument by saying 'Well, anyway, one thing is certain — that your theory is totally wrong'. My father laughed loudly, trying to give the impression that she seemed merely ridiculous to him. Though quarrels like this were temporarily disturbing to me they did not inhibit the nostalgic mood I needed to cultivate for the poem I wanted to write about my childhood at home, but one or two other quarrels my mother and father had in my presence made inner detachment harder for me, one especially which resulted from my mother's having bought a new couch to replace the shabby old leather-upholstered ottoman used by my father in his surgery for examining patients. This quarrel too happened at lunch-time, my father having gone into his surgery for a moment before coming to the dining-table.

'I particularly asked you before I went out,' he began in a tone of pathos, 'not to move anything in my room.'

'But nothing is moved,' my mother said. 'You will find the cupboard behind the screen.'

'What a lie.' (He was referring to her first sentence.)

'I haven't touched it.' (What she meant by 'it' wasn't clear to me.)

'Oh my god, I really can't go on living in this house with you.'

'I had to look after it. What would the other person think about her predecessor if she found everything at sixes and sevens?'

'What other person?'

'The one who will have to see to your room when I'm gone, who will have to clear up all the mess.'

'You're the most self-centred person I've ever known. Always thinking about what others will think about you.'

'Very well, I am the most self-centred person you have ever known.'

'What I object to most is your damned impudence.' At this point Ethel came into the dining-room but my father went on without taking any notice of her: 'I particularly asked you not to move anything. What right have you? What am I to do? If I were a proper husband I should knock you down and stamp on you.'

'I can't think what's come over you to-day. I suppose that's how they talk up at the golf club.'

'What am I to do? I've got absolutely no control over my own house. What can I do with the woman?' He seemed to be appealing not to me or to Ethel but to some invisible audience of just men.

'You said you wanted a new couch months ago.'

'But that was only an idea, something in the future. I didn't expect you to dash up to London and buy one. Especially without consulting me at all.'

'We talked it all over months ago, and you said you wanted one.'

'O my God.'

'I suppose you'll say you didn't.'

'Yes. I shall say I didn't. You do everything in secret, behind my back.'

'All right, I do everything in secret, behind your back.'

'It's your damned impudence in interfering. One of us will have to go.'

On the same day later when I was sitting alone with him in the morning-room while my mother was in her room — the drawing-room — he said of her 'There is no one on earth I hate more.' (He was nevertheless to live with her for the remaining twenty-five years of her life, and the new couch she had bought with her own money stayed in his surgery till he retired from practice.) He took down a book by Rudyard Kipling from one of the bookcases in the morning-room and read to himself from it for a while without saying anything more to me about her. Kipling was the writer to whom he usually turned when his practice or his marriage seemed unbearable to him, though recently he had also been able to find consolation in T. S. Eliot who hadn't yet become a High Anglican and whose *The Love Song of J. Alfred Prufrock* he assumed to be the work of a cynical misogamist of the same age as himself. While he sat reading I thought 'I will never marry.' I thought too that as the antagonism between him and my mother had probably existed already in the early stages of their marriage even if it hadn't often come out into the open, the nostalgic poetry I hoped to write about my childhood might give almost as untrue a picture of my home then as the ecstatic poetry I had decided against writing would have given of my home in its latest actuality. However, after my parents' quarrel about the surgery couch I did not immediately stop trying to write a nostalgic poem, and a few weeks before Christmas I succeeded in finishing one.

I conceived it on a rainy morning while walking for exercise down South Street towards the railway station, and I began writing it as soon as I got back to the house. Only the first two lines still sound at all genuine to me:

> *How desolate the bridge against the sky,*
> *The rain-dark stone, the cloud, the unmoving*
> *train; . . .*

though the real bridge was built of brown brick not stone.
But the next two lines, besides being displeasingly
ambiguous — the words 'dead . . . to' in the third line
might mean 'totally oblivious of' or they might mean 'dead
in comparison with' — seem to me now to give a foretaste of
the artificiality which becomes still more obvious as the
poem goes on and which reveals the factitiousness of the
poem's nostalgia:

> *How dead this town to that remoter town*
> *Whose roofs yet vaunt their sunlight in the brain.*

I did not actually remember having noticed sunlight on
the roofs as a child; and the fourth line, flaunting its fancy
word 'vaunt', carries no emotional conviction. The third
quatrain, almost bracing in its tone and archaically using
the word 'fare' for the sake of a consonantal rhyme with the
word 'before', seems even less genuinely felt.

> *Stone and the street shall crumble in my mind,*
> *I shall outlive this time as that before;*
> *Still with life's strange assurance I shall fare*
> *Towards the town where time shall end my war.*

After finishing this poem I knew that it would not do at
all, and that I was on an altogether wrong track, not only in
trying to write nostalgically about my childhood but also in
giving the poem a form which although it combined
consonantal rhymes (of a kind first used by Wilfred Owen)
with ordinary rhymes (several of them much too easily
predictable) was old-fashioned, neo-Victorian, not least
because of its iambic metre. I recognised again how right B.
K. Wilshaw had been at Cambridge to demand that
contemporary poetry should use the rhythms of

contemporary speech. Mightn't he also be right in his theory that poetry ought not to aim at referring to the objective world? My inability to find anything I could convincingly write about led me on to think that he might be, and to experiment with what I called 'non-referential' poetry. Most of the non-referential poems I tried to write never got beyond six lines, and most were full of echoes of other modern poetry. The least bad of them was longer and deliberately echoed T. S. Eliot. It was nothing more than a crude parody, but there were some not wholly dead lines in it:

> Mr Ferruginex sat in the park at Vladivostok
> Circumambulated by nursemaids and abrupt
> bankers
> And feculent paralytics terrified by swans . . .
> They will say, 'his nose perhaps is painted by the
> cold.'
> They will hint, 'his voice should be a ratchet-wheel
> Muffled by scabrous craters of the moon.'

My more serious attempts were duller, such as:

> Never the absolute, the one-toned
> Drum paring desiccation in a hall;
> Rather the doll-stocked teetotum,
> Chairs on the esplanade, the water's sign
> Under runged wood, bearded with weed . . .

This wasn't even properly non-referential, though B. K. Wilshaw wouldn't have disapproved of its hostility to the Absolute. The nearest I came to being properly non-referential was in the one or two brief prose poems I next went on to write, which while they were based on real experiences succeeded in destroying almost all clues that might have revealed to the reader what the experiences were. I myself cannot guess now what experience — if any — gave rise to a passage I can still remember from one of these prose poems: '*Hooligan actuality blasting tin reverberations scatters the never shadows and no doom is hinted but all generic corpses green-wander in old honey river and drowsing inclination casts back on bridge and park — something we were before whisky astigmatised all distances and for the terror in the picture sooted the glass.*' Stuff like this I knew to be mere froth which was bringing me no nearer at all to being able to write the kind of poetry I wanted to. By the end of November I was beginning to feel that nothing I had written so far since the summer could justify my continuing to live at home, and that after Christmas — unless by then I had achieved at least one reasonably good poem — I ought to get a job somewhere. I would have to get one sooner or later anyway, and it might as well be sooner. Not that I could think of any job which I had the least desire to do, and in spite of my parents' frequent quarrels I found home pleasant because of the complete leisure it gave me. The job might be some way from London, perhaps abroad, and I would no longer meet Richard almost every weekend as I had been able to since I had been living at home. We had met usually at his home in Kensington, had sometimes gone together by train on expeditions to places our notion of which excited us — like Canvey Island, or Southend with its mile-long pier, and always our talk was inspiriting to me whether it was about poetry or about the things and people we saw or whether we engaged in inventive amusements such as imagining a pack of cards with extraordinary names, an idea we got from Eliot's Notes on *The Waste Land* in which he said that one of the cards in the Tarot pack was called the Hanged Man. (How many can I remember of the cards we invented? The Colonial Physician, The Aztec King, Resurrection Morning, Prophet's Country or the Dice and Nails, The Colony of Apes, The Property Crocodile, The Geometrical Instruments, The Stifling Cathedral, The Fox with Paper Bowels, The Corpus of Poetry, The Accident to Travellers,

The Photograph of Nero, The Bald Tutor, The Boy sacrificed by a Sheep, The Box of Confectionery, The Authority of Galen, The Phthisical Excursionists, The Pure Intelligence, The Defective Scales, The Spirochete, The Hunting Rector, The Novelist's Synthesis, The Newspaper printed in Blood, The Subsided Monument, The Agent for Careers, The Parable of the Nine Monoculars, The One Valid Assertion, The Masked Goat.) I could stay on at home if I liked — both of my parents seemed very willing that I should be there for as long as I wanted to be — and the longer I stayed the more uninviting the idea of getting a job was becoming for me, but I felt I ought not to continue living at their expense. Besides, a job away from home might bring me advantages in spite of depriving me of most of my leisure: it might enable me to meet a girl I could fall totally in love with, someone not only beautiful but genuinely interested in poetry or better still a poet herself — there seemed little chance of my meeting such a girl while I remained at home — and the very dislikeableness of the job might, together with my being in love, stimulate me to make a stronger and more successful effort, in what spare time I could get, to solve my poetic problem.

All the same, I was glad to find that the tutoring job I got in Cornwall after Christmas (through the Scholastic Agency which Richard had nicknamed Rabbitarse and String) was not dislikeable, and I soon had to admit to myself that it ought not to make poetry less easy for me to write than if the job had been a really grim one, like teaching in a Reformatory school for instance. There were no more than two pupils for me to teach, a brother and sister, both of them amiable, civilised and willing to be taught, and my teaching was only in the morning — Mr and Mrs Norman were enlightened as well as comfortably-off parents who sensibly believed that the longer a schoolchild's working-day was the less the child would learn during any part of it, particularly during the later part of it, and this was one of the reasons why they decided (perhaps less sensibly) to have a tutor for their children instead of sending them to the local school — and after finishing work each morning I would return for lunch to the lodgings which Mrs Norman had found for me at the far end of the village and in which I had a sitting-room to myself, and for the rest of the day I was free to do what I liked, read, go for a walk, write. I had to admit too that I need not be hindered from writing poetry by the fact that the Normans showed friendliness towards me instead of treating me like an expensive servant as some other comfortably-off employers would have treated me, nor by the interest they took in the arts (one of their reasons for engaging me as a tutor had been that Rabbitarse and String had mentioned I wrote poetry), nor by their introducing me to their friends in the district most of whom were painters or musicians or writers or potters or handweavers, nor by their taking me along with them to the Arts Club where I met girls who, unlike any of those I had been able to meet at Cambridge, were not indifferent to poetry and who all of them practised — this was a condition of membership of the club — one or other of the arts or handicrafts. Within three weeks of my coming to Cornwall I was in love. But though the emotion was of a kind which seemed close to poetry and could have stimulated me to write poems expressing it, I knew that the poems would have been other than non-referential and would have been a regression to romanticism, so I made no attempt to write them.

It wasn't till I met Tessy for the second time that I began to hope she was someone with whom I was going to be able to fall totally in love. My first meeting with her had been at the Arts Club when I had been introduced to her by another girl, who had walked with Mr and Mrs Norman and myself from their house to the Club in the evening along the cliff path, a girl I had been immediately attracted by because of her lively friendliness and her good looks — her resemblance to one of the girls in Botticelli's *Primavera* made me give her this name in my journal and in my letters to Richard — as well as because the Normans had told me beforehand that she was a talented violinist. I had taken little more than polite notice of Tessy when I had been introduced to her, as I had been too much pre-occupied with Primavera. But on that same evening I had given up hope of Primavera when she had introduced me to Maurice Beale — a tall, easy-mannered and charming young man whom she undisguisedly admired and who she said was doing musical research; and another thing which disposed me to take more notice of Tessy when I next met her — at folk-dancing in the village Institute — was that since the evening of our first being introduced to each other I had guessed from a remark about her made by Mr Norman to Mrs Norman that she was an artist. When I came into the Institute with the Normans she was already there, and she and I briefly recognised each other across the room and I felt a sudden hopeful excitement. Before long someone, I think it was the folk-dancing instructress, got us to dance together, and afterwards as we sat on a bench against the wall I said that the tune the violinist had been playing for the dance was nice and she quite eagerly agreed and went on to say it reminded her of something from *The Beggar's Opera* but she couldn't remember what. 'Can you?' she asked. I said that I couldn't but that I was sure there was a tune in *The Beggar's Opera* very similar to it. Then, because I was exhilarated by our having established that the same tune appealed to us both and that both of us knew *The Beggar's Opera*, I asked with a premature personal emphasis for which I felt like biting my tongue out a moment later, 'Do *you* play?' 'A little,' she said coldly, and though the coldness might have been due merely to modesty about her playing I decided that when on some future occasion — it wouldn't be this evening — I dared to ask her about her painting I would at all costs avoid saying anything which might suggest I was more interested in her as a girl than as an artist; and certainly the truth was that my interest in her was above all aroused by my hope that she would prove to be someone who cared as much about her art as I did about mine. However the crassness of my emphasis did not seem really to have offended her, and we went on talking without constraint, mainly about folk-dancing, until she got up to join in a dance, probably a morris, which I was afraid to accompany her in because it was difficult and I was too much of a novice. She wore a brightly striped skirt and a blue velvet coatee, her posture was very straight though with no suggestion of rigidity, her bobbed hair was strikingly dark, her face was gently serious. As I watched her dancing I became convinced of her beauty, which had been less immediately obvious than Primavera's but was far subtler and more appealing than hers now that I was aware of it. I felt the blood throb in my throat, and the urge to let myself fall boundlessly in love with her came almost irresistibly to me but I restrained it for fear of the abyss of disappointment I should drop into if I did not restrain it and then later on found her mind to be conventional and commonplace.

When I got back to my lodgings that evening I wrote in my journal, 'Oh for a formula by which one could discover at first meeting whether the met was a living soul or a gramophone'. I did not get a chance to talk with her alone until more than a fortnight after this, and even when the chance came — at the Arts Club, to which the Normans took me again — I wasn't able to become finally sure she was what I most longed that she should be. I asked her to dance — the dancing here was ball-room not folk dancing — and she said with all kindness in her look, 'No, I'd rather not, if you don't mind, but don't let that stop you,' and I said also, 'No, I'd rather not,' assuming, rightly as it turned out, that she had refused because she was not keen on ball-room dancing. I began to tell her I too disliked it compared with folk-dancing, though this wasn't true and I would rather have danced the foxtrot with her than any morris as it would have enabled me to hold her more closely. 'Perhaps we are jealous,' she said as we sat down while others began to dance. 'Yes,' I agreed; 'I certainly have seen ball-room dancing done in a way that . . . ' I was afraid to finish the sentence lest she would think me a philistine. It was she who pulled aside what in my journal afterwards I described as the 'sham curtains' between us: she mentioned *The Beggar's Opera* again, and we were soon talking of things that really interested us. I was so glad to find she was intelligent that I almost laughed. We were both excited and could hardly keep our smiles from breaking out into a kindness — as I called it in my journal — which would have been obvious to everyone in the room. What did we talk about? One thing I know I said was that I disliked John Drinkwater's play *Abraham Lincoln*. I thought I would never be able to forget the tone of her 'But why? Why?' — plaintive and controlling laughter. I said that the scene with the profiteer was cheap, or did I in fact say 'chea-', hesitating to sound the final consonant for fear I might seem to be expressing my opinion too assertively? I also took the risk of saying that I didn't like Drinkwater's poetry, and I was glad that this time she agreed: 'Nor do I. Except one thing . . . I can't remember . . .' 'The one about the apples at the top of the house,' I suggested. 'Yes, yes,' she marvelled, and I controlled my delight, though by now there hardly seemed to be a valid reason why I should control it. We went on to talk about music, and to find that our musical tastes agreed, though she gave the impression of not being so keen on gramophone records as I was ('the gramophone noise', she said), but she didn't mention painting and I didn't dare to. We were together for half an hour almost. When she got up to follow her mother who had beckoned to her she turned to look back towards me for a moment as if in gratitude. But it wasn't till more than three weeks later, after I had been to her house for supper at her mother's invitation, I allowed myself to believe with hardly any reservation at all that she was what I hoped she was.

There were four moments during the evening at her house which when I considered them afterwards became decisive in enabling me to believe. The first of them was within a minute of my coming into the house and while I was trying not to look naively impressed by the surprisingly large entrance hall: her mother said to me, 'We have rolled back the carpet so that you and Tessy can do some folk-dancing practice later on if you want to,' and Tessy almost in an undertone, for my ears rather than her mother's I thought, corrected her, 'The mat, you mean,' and I recognised in the correction a true if slight indignation against a pretentiousness she had detected in what her mother had said. The second moment was when she and her mother and father and I were at the table in the dining-room having supper — 'supper' was what her mother had unpretentiously called this excellent meal when inviting me to it, the more fashionable word 'dinner' being out of favour among the artistic middle class in this part of Cornwall — and Tessy asked me, in a tone of earnestness it seemed, 'What do you *do* all day?' I felt that she might not have asked me this if we had been alone, and that if she had it would have been a lover's question. 'Read,' I answered. If we had been alone I would have gone on to tell her I was reading Proust and was filled with wonder and astonishment at his genius, but this seemed too emotional and intimate a thing to say in front of her parents. The third moment was when we were getting up from the table at the end of the meal and her mother said to her, almost in an aside and ending a sentence the first part of which I hadn't clearly heard, 'since you are now so dissatisfied with all your work', and I inferred from this that she must be suffering from the same grief about her art as I was about mine. The fourth moment was after we had gone into another and larger room for coffee and she took me over to the far end of the room to see her collection of gramophone records, and as I sat on my heels to look at the records on a lower shelf I felt an electric recognition — so I was to describe it next day in my journal — pass between us. We said nothing for at least a minute, until she asked if I would like to hear the Bach concerto for two violins. Her voice was tender and quiet. We listened to classical music on the gramophone for much of the rest of the evening, and we did not practice folk-dancing at all. When the time came for me to leave she offered to, see me to the gate with a lantern, the garden path being long and winding, and I thanked her but said I thought I could find my way in the dark all right without bringing her out of the house in her indoor shoes. She did not insist; and I can almost feel regret still that I didn't let her guide me with the lantern and missed the opportunity of kissing her on the way to the gate or at least of putting my arm through hers, though most probably if she had come to the gate with me I would have done neither because I was sure that her offer was a bona fide one and I would have been afraid that by kissing her or even touching her I would have caused her to think I assumed the offer had been made with an ulterior motive and she would have felt belittled. In any case, I was so filled with bliss already that there seemed no need to attempt to increase it then.

It was a bliss that remained in me, seldom far from the forefront of my consciousness, for days afterwards. It was hardly weakened at all by my not getting an opportunity of talking with her alone during any of the folk-dancing practices at which we met during the next three weeks, the dances being too vigorous and communal for private conversation to be possible even when we were partnering each other, and sitting-out between dances was communal too in the alcove-less conditions of the Institute in which we danced, and I wasn't able to walk back with her when the dancing was over because I felt bound to go with the

Normans with whom I had come and in any case her mother was there each time. At last, nearly four weeks after the evening of the supper at her house, I came upon her standing by herself at a bus-stop one afternoon. I was sure she had seen me, but I was conscious of blushing so hotly that I had to turn away to let the blood fade from my face, and when I turned towards her again I saw from the vague soreness in her look that she had momentarily thought I was going to cut her. I stood close to her and could not control the trembling of my knees. I stammered stupid words, asking if she was waiting for the bus. I felt that the blush had quite gone from my face and that I must be looking as white as a corpse. Luckily at this moment a friend of hers, Miss Lightwood, came up to us, and equally luckily did not stay with us long, saying before she went 'I must be getting along to my class.' This, after she had gone, gave me something a little more sensible to say to Tessy: 'Is it an art class?' I guessed. 'They call it that,' Tessy said, and added with what in my journal later I described as 'strange passion': 'They talk of everything *but* art there. They discuss flowers . . . But I am getting on to dangerous subjects.' I did not try to persuade her to say more about this, filled as I was with a new calm exaltation. We went on to talk of modern art, of Epstein, of Bourdelle (she was disappointed when I admitted that I knew little about him), then of Paris, of Massanet and of L'Opéra (I had the strange wish, which I resisted, to tell her how I had once walked for half an hour round L'Opéra looking for a lavatory). By the time her bus came, 'gratefully late' as I was to say of it in my journal, I was confirmed in the belief I most wanted to have about her — that she was a serious artist, and I was more completely in love with her than I had been even on the evening of my going to supper at her house. But when I next saw her, at folk dancing a week after our bus-stop meeting, and once again was not able to talk with her alone, though I was able to partner her in several of the dances, I felt for the first time since I had known her a frustration which may have caused at one moment a brief coldness in my manner towards her. Three days later she was not at the concert in Penzance which she had told me she would be coming to, and soon after this I heard that she had gone to stay with relatives in London, and I wondered whether my coldness could have made her decide to go earlier than she had previously intended. I did not know I would not see her again for seven weeks; and the desperation which would have grown in me sooner if I had known was intensified, when it did grow, by my unhappiness at not having succeeded in starting to write poetry again yet, but was mitigated by the prospect of a visit from Richard who was to come down from London at the end of my tutoring term to stay at my lodgings and to see the Cornwall I had been fantastically describing in my weekly letters to him. This desperation was mitigated also by my invention, which I made a few days before he came and which served as an almost compensatory substitute for actual poetic creation, of a new theory about what modern poetry ought to be like.

According to my theory a tragic view of life, formerly essential to the writing of the greatest poetry, had ceased to be possible during the period since the ending of the 1914 to 1918 war, and no one now however much of a genius could hope to write tragic poetry on a level with Wilfred Owen's; on the other hand, if the poet were to write nothing but non-referential verse he would be ignoring the continued existence of griefs and horrors in real life. My theory demanded that from now on the poetry I would write should deal with these, or at least with some of them that I knew something about, for instance diseases, road accidents, marital hate, but should not treat them as specially important, should even give rather less emphasis to them than to other more trivial actualities, should denude them of any suggestion of grandeur, should present them as quite unremarkable aspects of modern life. I did not ask myself what Wilfred Owen would have thought of this theory. When I expounded it to Richard soon after he arrived in Cornwall at the end of my term he was excited by it, and later that year it had an influence on the poems he wrote; also it had the more immediate effect of stimulating him to write something a few days after his arrival, though this wasn't poetry and its content showed no sign of being affected by my theory. He called it 'Vision of Scilly', and he began writing it while we were on the ship at Penzance quay waiting to start out on the visit we had suddenly decided to make to the Scilly Isles. 'Our steamer was not the *August Timmernaben*, an angular black ship, startlingly tall and lifting in chains against the granite wharf. *The Zennor Captain* lay unwatched by idlers in the shelter of a corrugated iron shed. The gangway was still in place.' A feeling of apprehension (the sea looked like being rough, the ship was small and the Isles were twenty-five miles out in the Atlantic) was combined at the beginning of this prose piece with an excited expectation of marvels awaiting us. 'Richard had imagined the Isles in the hush of tropical summer, the green snake languid under the palm, the panther behind ropes of blossom . . .' When we got to the Isles we found them almost more astonishing than we had expected, though in a different way, the reality in its unforeseen detail seeming far richer than the most exotic inventions our imaginations had been capable of. We decided to stay for a week instead of for a weekend as we had originally intended. On our motor-boat trips from island to island and on our walks in the islands we talked most of all about poetry and our plans for future poems, and also about experiences we had had and people we had met since last seeing each other, but I told him very little about Tessy, because what I could have said about her wouldn't have been amusing or amazing. When we got back to Cornwall again after our week in the Scillies I saw her as we sat in the train which had stopped at St Erth on our way to London. I was reading Freud's *Introductory Lectures on Psycho-Analysis*, given to me as a present by Richard. I looked up and she was standing on the platform only a few yards away from the window through which I obliquely saw her, wearing the broad-brimmed brown felt hat that suited her so well, saying good-bye to a bright-faced strongly-built young girl carrying a 'cello in a black case whom I thought might be a cousin of hers she had once spoken to me of and who was getting into a compartment two or three doors ahead of ours. Tessy did not seem to see me as the train moved off and the window of our compartment passed within hardly more than a yard of her sideways-turned face, but the sight I had had of her — I didn't mention it to Richard — abolished in an instant all the desperation her seven weeks' absence had caused me and established a confident gladness in me which made the London houses appear clean and happy as I looked at them from the taxi window on my way from Paddington to Liverpool Street, and which never quite left me at home in Essex throughout the remaining two and half weeks of my Easter holidays — even though I did not succeed in my efforts to start writing a poem of the anti-tragic kind my new theory demanded.

As the unlikelihood of my succeeding before the holidays ended became more and more clear to me, so the growth of despondency in me was checked and countered by an increasingly happy awareness of the nearing time when I would be able to meet Tessy in Cornwall again. A few days after my summer term began I went with the Normans to folk-dancing, and finding she was not yet there in the room where the dancing was to be held I waited trembling inwardly like a taut string, perhaps outwardly too, much as I wanted to avoid causing the Normans to notice how tense I was. Ten minutes, twenty minutes, a half an hour later she still had not appeared, and pure misery and hopelessness came upon me, but just when I had decided that all was over for the week she walked rather quickly into the room, not seeing me, not trying to see me. I went across the room towards her, and she gave me an oddly surprised stare as if my coming over so quickly to speak to her was a social impropriety: 'this really is incredible,' her stare seemed to say. I danced with her, once, but wasn't able to talk to her much, nor did she appear to want me to; then we were divided and she went to join a sculptor named Gerald Doyle and his wife, and he partnered her in the next dance, after which she found other partners than myself for the remaining dances of that evening. And it was no better the following week when there was folk-dancing at the Doyles' house: again she danced with me only once and she left early without giving me a chance to say goodbye to her. I thought she might have decided, since her return from London, to have as little to do with me as she politely could: perhaps while staying with her relatives there she had been introduced to a man she liked better than me and who wanted to marry her. But by good luck three evenings after the dancing at the Doyles' I met her when I came away from an amateur performance in Penzance of the *Importance of Being Earnest* to which I had gone mainly in the hope that she would be there: she was with her mother at the bus stop, and although her manner towards me was reserved at first it changed not long after we had got on to the bus — which was very crowded, so that while her mother managed to find a seat we had to stand all the way, and since among the people immediately around us there was no one who knew us I could talk to Tessy as though we were alone. I was physically closer to her than if I had been partnering her at folk-dancing, so close that I could only with difficulty prevent myself from being pressed frontally against her by the others near me in the bus whenever it swayed. I talked of my visit to the Scilly Isles and I could see her kindle to my account of it and I was filled with such a joy that though there was one moment when I did think of asking her whether it mightn't be possible for me to see her more often,

I did not in fact ask her: being with her in the present was sufficient for me. But my next meeting with her, at folk-dancing again, was my unhappiest yet. It was in the open air, on the asphalt of a school playground; we danced together and her hand seemed icy to hold; we talked and our voices were dull; I was wearing a too thick woollen pullover under my jacket, which made my face sweat, and I thought I could see she didn't like that; when the dancing finished she left without saying goodbye to me and walked off, very eagerly, it appeared, in an opposite direction to the one I would be taking to get back to my lodgings. A recognition grew in me during the next few days that since the evening half-way through my previous tutoring term when I had gone to supper at her house there had been retrogression rather than progress in my relationship with her, our recent closeness on the bus back from Penzance having been no more than a brief exception that proved the rule. I had nights and mornings when I lay awake in bed with images coming into my mind of myself putting the hard cold revolver muzzle to my temple, pulling; of myself lying dead, after the sick bang and the incredible roaring expansion of everything. Every morning and every night I had the same wish: Oh take me away or take it away from me. I wanted no more of this endless fuss. I imagined the exploded brain lying hidden by the trailing brambles of the cave's mouth and the feet crossed in coloured socks on the sand. Someone threw down a rock, but what was broken could not be broken any more. I wánted Tessy. 'Oh quick, quick. Tell me what makes your life tolerable, what you believe in, what you feel. Why do we waste the little time we have with each other? Why not speak?' Thoughts like these would probably not have come to me if I had been seriously considering suicide at this time: they were a kind of poetic creation, a substitute — a very poor substitute — for the anti-tragic poetry I had not yet succeeded in starting to write. They could not compensate me in the least for a poetic impotence which was all the more grieving to me now that my hope of becoming Tessy's lover was no longer strong enough to help me, as hitherto, in my struggle to overcome it. However, I did find a partial compensation for the frustration both of my efforts to write poetry and of my love for Tessy. I was able to become absorbed during my afternoons and evenings in adding to my anti-tragic theory a further poetic theory which while not having any apparent logical connection with it did not contradict it.

Essentially my further theory was aimed against B. K. Wilshaw's view that poetry could not be said ever to refer to anything, a view which continued to anger me, no doubt partly because his lectures had caused me for the first time since I had started writing poetry at the age of fifteen to enter upon the phase of almost complete poetic sterility which still persisted (though I had to admit to myself he had helped me recognise the truth that my poetry-writing had been on a totally wrong track), but more because I considered his view slighting to poetry. Wilshaw had made a distinction between what he called 'intellectual' statements which he defined as always having a 'referent' and 'emotive' statements which had no 'referent', poetry being 'emotive' while science was 'intellectual'. My new theory countered this by applying the term 'explanations' to what he called intellectual statements, an 'explanation' according to my definition being any communication in words, symbols, physical gestures, music or paint which could be presented in more than one way without significantly altering the message it was meant to give. The message of a poem on the contrary not only couldn't be conveyed, my theory claimed, in any other words than those the poem actually contained, but also it was a type of message which no 'explanation' however intellectually precise was capable of conveying. It directly evoked feelings, and feelings were at least as important in the world as ideas. I was not altogether satisfied with the term 'explanations', however, since it might suggest that my theory was in agreement with the views of people who made remarks like 'Beauty is all the more beautiful for being inexplicable' or 'There are many things that science will never be able to explain'. I did not believe anything existed which of its nature was unsuited to being scientifically explained, and I was in favour of explanations provided they were true (religion also used explanations, which were false, as were some of those that scientifically-minded intellectuals like Wilshaw used) and provided they didn't become substitutes for the things explained, as when in imaginative writing the writer aiming at an emotional effect described it instead of producing it in the reader. 'Symbolisations' might be a more exact term, I thought, but it would lack the slightly derogatory suggestion that 'explanations' had, and I wanted to hit back in my mind at 'explainer' Wilshaw who had slighted poetry by saying that it didn't refer to anything. Working out my theory became an occupation for me during my afternoon walks and during solitary evenings at my lodgings, and it lifted me sufficiently from the depths of my frustration to enable me to make the decision that as soon as I got the chance I would ask Tessy to come out with me — perhaps to the cinema or perhaps even for a walk — a decision which allowed me to become hopeful again about the future of my love for her.

My hopefulness was helped by my next meeting with her. I arrived before she did at the house — I've forgotten whose, Miss Lightwood's mother's house perhaps — where the dancing was to be, and when she came into the room she saw me at once and the quick smile she gave me had a warmth that put an end to my recently increasing doubts whether she was really interested in me at all. After I had partnered her in the first dance she told me she would be going camping on her own at Zennor for the next eight days and there would be folk-dancing on the third evening in the field where she would be setting up her tent. 'Will you be there?' she asked. This invitation, together with her telling me she would be on her own at Zennor for the next eight days, seemed so full of the most wonderful promise that I felt there was no need for me to carry out my intention of asking her if she would come for a walk with me one afternoon. But the evening of the folk-dancing at Zennor was in actuality a failure. I arrived early, almost half an hour before the dances were due to begin, only to find her father and Mr and Mrs Doyle with her outside her tent, which was beside a stream. She and I danced together twice, we hardly spoke at all and when I went back to her tent after the dancing had finished for the evening the Doyles were still there, sitting on canvas-seated stools which she had provided. There was a third stool, which she insisted on my having, and she remained standing till I suggested half-jokingly that she could sit on my raincoat — I had left it lying on the rather damp ground when she and I had gone across the field to join in the dancing. She knelt on it in front of the Doyles, saying to me after a while, 'Your mackintosh is getting wet.' The frustration I felt at not being alone with her influenced me to answer quite crudely, 'Never mind. You'll dry it.' The Doyles pricked up their ears (as I was to say in my journal). I noticed surprise in her look, and I knew I had destroyed any slight chance there might still have been that evening of my being able to make myself ask her if I could see her again while she was at Zennor. When I got back to my lodgings I realised I would almost certainly not see her till the next folk-dancing practice, which was ten days ahead. What 'in blood's hell' (as I frantically worded it in my journal) was I to do till then? I must wait and let my feelings slowly subside. My love for her, I thought, was like the rising and falling telegraph wires that could be seen alongside the railway track from the windows of a train, but the motion was reversed — instead of a slow steady rise of the wires until they were whipped down again at the pole, there was a sudden ecstatic lift followed by a gradual fall.

The day after the dancing at Zennor I went there again and sat on a hill from which I could look down to watch her tent beside the stream. I sat among the bracken and the foxgloves for at least three hours and saw her come out of her tent twice, and I did not for a moment dream of daring to go down to pay an uninvited visit to her. I was startled several times by a bird-call which I thought might be a stonechat's and which sounded something like a hoof striking on rock: what would I be able to say for myself if her father, riding his horse — as I had seen him doing recently — were to come up behind me and find me there? My watching that afternoon only increased my love-misery during the remaining nine days before the next folk-dancing practice, at which I had taken for granted I should meet her again, but she didn't come, and as I walked back to my lodgings I took an oath in my mind that I would never beget a son to go through what I was going through. She was at the Penzance festival four days later, however, where I was able to sit for a while with her and Primavera and Maurice Beale on a plank in a corner of the field. She told me there would be a fair nearby the following week. When the dancing was over I got her to walk back alone with me to the bus and I asked her whether she would be going to the fair. 'Yes,' she said, 'with Mrs Doyle'; and as if she felt her going needed to be justified she added, 'I was there last year, sketching.' I suddenly risked asking 'Did you do that picture I saw in the hall at the Doyles' house, of a roundabout?' 'It was only a sketch,' she said so deprecatingly that I was deterred from telling her how good I had thought it. — 'So you *are* going,' I said. — 'Why don't you come?' she asked, but did not invite me to join her and Mrs Doyle — 'I should like to. I think I shall,' I said. And a week later I did go to the fair. I was on my feet for five hours there, saw her distantly three times, was afraid to pursue her and impose myself on her and Mrs Doyle, then saw her a fourth time and made up my mind to get to her at all costs but was held up by the crowd and lost sight of her finally, almost wept, walked the seven or eight miles back to my lodgings. It seemed I had never yet been so deeply in love with her and I believed I would continue to feel like this even if she were to snub me when at our next meeting I at last asked her, as I absolutely must not fail to do, whether she would come for a walk with me one afternoon.

But when I did actually meet her the following week at the Village Institute in the evening it was she who invited me to come with her to join in a folk-dancing demonstration which was to take place the next afternoon, and I was stupid enough to tell her I didn't think I would because the afternoon being an ordinary workday one I would be likely to be the only man there. Her look showed that she was hurt, and I decided afterwards that I would go to the demonstration at all costs, even though only as a spectator on my own and not as a participant with her. I did go and, as I wandered sicklily off the field when the dancing was over, she — to my boundless gratitude — followed and caught up with me and we walked for more than twenty minutes together back towards my lodgings. I remembered how I had resolved to ask her when I next met her to come for a walk with me one afternoon and I realised that now there was no need for me to ask her since we were in actuality walking together: I needed nothing beyond the immediate joy of being with her. Lying in her arms hidden by bracken on a hillside was something that might or might not become possible in the future: I had no wish to force the plant of love. 'Let it happen when it will', I thought, 'so long as it has the opportunity to happen.' But after this walk with her I began to wish that during it I had taken the opportunity of asking her to come for another walk on another afternoon. More than a week passed without my being able to talk to her or even to see her again, and when I did eventually see her, at one of the several folk-dancing festivals which were taking place at this time of year, I was unable to dance with her and she walked off the field on her own at the end without our having talked together at all. She was walking fast and I ran after her and just before overtaking her I called out her surname 'Miss Baker, Miss Baker', (I still didn't dare to say 'Tessy' — usually I avoided naming her, though she showed little hesitation in saying 'Mr Sebrill' to me). She turned to me with a glad look, and once again we were walking together and once again I was so happy that there seemed no need to make any demand of her for the future, but when we arrived outside my lodgings — this time she came all the way there with me — I did manage to make myself say, 'I wish you could come to tea with me.' I said this in a tone which while it could at a stretch have been taken to mean I was inviting her into my lodgings conveyed also my regretful awareness of the unlikelihood that she (in this village of watchful Wesleyans) would feel able to accept. She gave me a long look of understanding, and said, 'I think you had better come to tea with me.' I walked back with her to her house, where her parents seemed entirely glad to see me and where I met her cousin for the first time. I fell in love with her parents and her cousin and the room in which we had tea and the view of the sea through the wide windows. I felt utterly at home, as though Tessy had just announced to her family that we were lovers and they had been very pleased. When I said good-bye and walked away up the path to the garden gate she called out after me, 'See you again next term', and though this reminded me that I wouldn't be seeing her again for at least seven and a half weeks it didn't give me the least pang of unhappiness, both because the emotion of that afternoon seemed more than strong enough to last me through till the end of the holidays and because her mention of next term was like an assurance that our love would develop further then. Actually I was to meet her again the next day, at the Penzance public library with her mother. We did not say much to each other, though she did ask me what she should read and I recommended the modernised Everyman edition of Chaucer's *Canterbury Tales*. (She hadn't read any Chaucer and perhaps I half-consciously hoped he might help to bring our relationship down to earth more), but I had no feeling of anti-climax.

I mightn't have been so undespondent at the prospect of not seeing her again till the autumn term if I hadn't been looking forward to the fortnight's holiday in the south of France which Richard and I had arranged to have together and during which I should be able to talk to him about the continuing unsuccess of my efforts to write poetry — a problem that mattered even more to me than love. The only imaginative writing I had achieved throughout the summer term, other than the fantasised descriptions I included in my letters to him of my life in Cornwall (though not of my feelings for Tessy, because these were too obsessional and repetitive and too deadly earnest for me to be able to be imaginatively playful about them), was a fragment of an unserious prose piece which I called *Charade* and which began with stage directions containing sentences of Joycean parody such as 'Siberian horns with shrill farheard tundra legato sketch the opening phrases of the Ensign Battersea leitmotif. They seethe decrescendo while a solo flute temporises with portraits from the Hainwort folk theme, hinting at *Turkelony* and *Pepper is Black*. Final light on the ebbing snake weeds at the inn wallfoot sets off the viola's evening blandness in the *Green Pools* obligato. Ensign Battersea wearing forged Crimean medals gropes out from the private bar and fumbles belching for the entrance of the iron latrines.' I had failed to make a start on the first of the anti-tragic poems I wanted to write, though I had spent many hours thinking of what it was to be about. I intended it to describe my home town as viewed day after day from the window of the bedroom where Hugh and I had slept as children. Among the things seen would be the body of a small raggedly-clothed boy laid out on the pavement with something white — was it cloth or was it paper weighted down on either side with stones? — covering his head. He had been swinging on the coupling rod between a steam traction engine and its trailer, had fallen off and the heavy wheel of the trailer had crushed his head. My anti-tragic theory required that this dead body should be given no greater, and preferably less, emphasis than other things pictured in the poem such as the black saw-mill on the far side of the field, Mr Holt the furniture remover standing in a green-baize apron at his gate with a large woman on either side of him, the short gravel drive behind him curving back to the gabled chalet-like house, the cattle being driven towards the market place on Wednesdays, the telegraph pole against a high brick wall behind which were trees only half as tall as the pole; but I could not succeed in developing my conception of the poem to a point where it was sufficiently satisfying to enable me to begin to put it down on paper. Always the dead boy, no matter how casual and brief my intended presentation of him might be, disrupted the unity of my conception, introduced a sensationalist if not a tragic note into it. I discussed this difficulty at length with Richard during our second day in the south of France while we were on the paddle-steamer going, interminably it seemed, round the lake at Annecy — I discussed it at too great length, with the result that eventually he became irritated and accused me of excessive fastidiousness and he prophesied that I would never achieve anything except perhaps one slim book of verse in the end. I was deeply wounded by his prophecy, fearing it might be all too true, but the quarrel it started between us did not last more than two or three hours and was not the cause of our decision two days later to separate and go our own ways for the rest of the holiday: we decided this because he had met someone in the corridor of the train who was going to Chamonix and whom he had since felt more and more that he needed to pursue, and I didn't want to be in his way while he did so. Before we separated, however, he suggested a solution to the difficulty I had been having with the poem I wanted to write about my home town: he said I could avoid seeming to emphasise the boy's death if I were to make the poem considerably longer than I'd hitherto intended and were to include in it many more details about the town, several of which could be just as grim but most of which would not be. I soon came to feel that his suggestion was right. When I got home from France I worked out a plan for a new and longer version of the poem, and although by the time of my return to Cornwall for the beginning of the autumn term I hadn't managed to make a firm start on the actual writing of this version my confidence in it remained strong, partly no doubt because I was filled with a general optimism by the prospect of meeting Tessy again soon.

In Cornwall after I got back there my imagination wherever I walked made me seem so near to her that I was not much worried at not seeing her in actuality during the first week of the term. But I did not meet her during the second week either, and I began to wonder anxiously whether she might be away in London. I could not bring myself to ask the Normans where she was, for fear they would guess I was in love with her. I might have asked Primavera or Maurice Beale when I went to the cinema one evening with them at their invitation, but their purpose in inviting me was to introduce me to Tibbie, just home from America (they were probably aware of a forlornness in me and wanted to do me a good turn), a girl with wild red hair whom I was to describe unjustly in my journal as 'vivacious to the point of sub-hysteria' and in whose presence I felt inhibited from mentioning Tessy. Soon after the four of us had come out of the cinema I noticed another girl in the semi-darkness on the other side of the road who was going in the opposite direction to us and who looked rather like

Tessy: as we walked I let myself become increasingly certain that she had been Tessy, and I was surprised that instead of feeling unhappy at having missed the chance of crossing the road and speaking to her I was able to find an almost satisfying substitute pleasure in thinking how near I had been to meeting her. But next morning I woke and wished myself dead. No compensatory daydream devices, such as planning to call at her house on the pretext that I'd mislaid my umbrella and wondered whether I'd left it there at the end of last term could give me any comfort. I knew that the utmost I would ever be able to bring myself to do would be to continue roaming the lanes around her house as I had been doing every afternoon for the past week. I believed I understood my nature and what I had to expect from it in the future. I would never get anything I wanted. I could see nothing but disgust and apathy ahead of me, and the best I could hope for was that perhaps in time my death-wish might become strong enough to cause me to forget to look out for traffic when I crossed the road. The only con-solation I could find was in Proust, whom I was still reading. With infinite calm he repeated the things I felt. He forestalled and corroborated me, he described my love and foretold the course it would take. He sometimes repeated almost my very words: one afternoon for instance while I was slinking down the lane that passed her house I thought 'Well, anyone can use this lane,' and in the evening I read 'Mais après tout la rue est à tout le monde,' which Proust's central character said to himself in circumstances not very different from mine. At last there was an afternoon when I did see her, from the window of the bus in which I was going to Newlyn, and I thought she saw me. She looked up at the bus as it passed, and her cousin who was with her did not. Immediately my whole picture of the world was changed. Misery was transformed into happiness as suddenly as an apparent depression in a landscape viewed from a hill can be transformed into a sunlit acclivity by the shifting of a cloud-shadow. She was living and she was here, not in London. I should meet her within a few days, at folk dancing or at the Arts Club, and when I met her I would tell her I loved her.

In fact I met her the next afternoon. She and her cousin got on to the bus in which I was going to Penzance. I was able to keep entirely calm as they came over to sit on the seat in front of mine. She turned to speak to me with her head bent down, and for the first time I realised that a scent I had sometimes noticed before was hers. She asked how I had liked Annecy and she said that she had been staying in Somerset. She had been rather disappointed by it. 'Pretty', she explained in an aside to her cousin. In the shadow of the broad brim of the brown felt hat that suited her so well the lobes of her ears and the under-curve of her nostrils seemed to my imagination to have a dimly luminous bloom on them as of ice. I was filled with an exalted excitement, which I sensed that she was aware of and was not embarrassed by. Outside the window of the bus the sunlight was like white fire on the sea in the bay. I felt that nothing I wanted would be impossible for me: that I would become her lover, that I would write my poem and it would be a masterpiece. Unexpectedly she and her cousin left the bus before it reached Penzance, at Marazion. As they began to walk away from me towards the door of the bus I was able to say to her, with the suggestion of a query in my tone, 'See you at the Arts Club on Saturday', and her look answered 'Yes'. On Saturday evening, she, on her own, got into the bus in which I was already sitting with no one occupying the seat beside me and she deliberately, I was sure, did not see me and went past me to sit at the front of the bus as far as she could from me. I was not indignant, or not for more than a moment, because the thought came to me that she might very well be just as shy as I was and that I had done little — and said even less — in the past to encourage her to be more forward with me. When the bus stopped at Newlyn I waited for her and we walked on together towards the Club, but the plan I had had of telling her as soon as possible this evening that I loved her did not seem immediately practicable after the shyness she had just shown. I asked with a painful yearning to know more about her, 'What are you doing nowadays?' — 'Nothing special,' she said, then remembered, 'Oh, I'm learning to play an oboe. But I can find no one to teach me.' There was a casualness in her tone that made me silent. After a while she asked, 'Have you been to the Penzance Library lately?' — 'Yes. Have you?' — 'No' — 'Are you going?' — 'Not that I know of,' she said with what seemed cold surprise, as though she felt insulted by my question. A bitterness rose in me. Her shocked rejection of my tentative attempt to arrange a future afternoon meeting alone with her made me think that all my love for her had been an utterly naive waste of time. 'The meanness of a coquettish Wesleyan,' I said to myself (though she was not a Wesleyan and I had no grounds for regarding Wesleyans as mean or coquettish). In order to give Tessy time to feel her pettiness if she could, I said nothing to her; and at last she went on, 'I liked the Chaucer very much . . . do you remember?' — 'Oh yes,' I answered indifferently though her tone had become warmer, and perhaps she had not been shocked but only surprised by my question which could very well have seemed odd to her if she hadn't immediately guessed what was behind it. Yet if she had failed to guess this her failure was a sign at best of an unpromising slowness in her, and anyway the renewed hopes I might have had of her were decisively prevented by what she said next, 'I have also been reading Charles Lamb's letters. They are so *companionable*'. That word, emphasised by her as though she was pleased with having thought of it, made me feel almost physically sick. Once before, on the day when the General Strike had come to an end and she had told me she was glad it had, I had briefly suspected she might be a dullard (a favourite word of

Richard's and mine) with a conventional mind — not that I was consciously for the strikers then but I was against the Government just as I had been against the poshocrats at Cambridge — and now her dullness seemed proved. However, later that evening at the Arts Club where I wasn't for a moment alone with her I gradually realised how unjustified I had been in feeling disgusted that she, who knew much less about literature than I did and probably almost nothing about academic literary criticism, should have used such a loathsome word as 'companionable' in praise of Lamb. She would have had nearly as much right to have been disenchanted with me on the occasion when I had shown ignorance of Bourdelle. My disgust was due to sheer literary snobbery. Fortunately I had said nothing to her to reveal the disenchantment I had felt, so now that I was recovering from this it need not be an obstacle to my telling her I loved her. I could still tell her; and though I wasn't able to during the remainder of that evening because I couldn't get her on her own the prospect of telling her next time we met became something I thought I could live for.

Next morning I had the suspicion that I might be deceiving myself about her and that she might be a dullard after all. But I realised that even if I were almost sure she was one I would not have the courage to give her up. My love for her had become too strongly rooted in me, and I had 'dovetailed everything else into it' (as I said in my journal). I should have to go on trying to deceive myself that she was one of 'earth's best'. But in the next few days I began to have doubts whether, even if she were one of earth's best, the kind of free-love relationship I wanted could ever be possible with her — or with any other girl. I, or both of us, would have to find some slavish job to keep ourselves, and before long our relationship would become indistinguishable from a marriage with all the miseries my parents' quarrels had made me think it must bring. I became aware now that from the start of my love for Tessy I had not really expected anything would come of it in the end, and this was the reason for my diffidence and hesitancy with her which in turn might account for hers with me. Yet however delusive my imaginings of a life of love and freedom with her might be, I believed I would not be able to bear to go on living without the hope of such a relationship, any more than I could live without hope of eventually writing at least one good poem, though that too was beginning to look as though it might be delusive. I had better kill myself, as my uncle Edmund, the only professional writer yet produced by our family, had recently killed himself. At the age of sixty he had shot himself in the heart with a B.S.A. airgun (which did not require a licence) and I too could buy one from a shop. I was proud of him, of his courage and of his having been able to remain unadapted to society for so long. During several days after the evening when Tessy had called Lamb 'companionable' I was inspirited by the idea that I could end myself by the same method as he had used, though I would do it much earlier in life.

But I soon knew that my hope of committing suicide was only another self-deception, that I had neither the nerve nor probably the genuine wish actually to shoot myself. I descended into a melancholia which must have been evident to my landlady and to the Normans, and if it had deepened it might eventually have become a pathological condition in which suicide would not have been impossible for me. Proust helped me to prevent it from deepening and so did a philosophical book I got out of the Library at this time by the mathematician A. N. Whitehead. Although his view of reality was even more warmthless and colourless than mine had yet become, the intellectual effort I had to make to understand what he was saying was stimulating to me. B. K. Wilshaw, while assuming that human beings could know nothing of the world as it really was outside their sense-impressions of it, did consider their sense-impressions to be of very great importance; whereas Whitehead, while devaluing external reality by reducing it to abstract processes and to what he called 'prehensions', seemed to want to rid it of perceivers at the same time. He defined a prehension as an uncognitive apprehension, a definition that was followed by several pages of explanation which I summed up as saying that a prehension was like a perspective without a viewer, and later he said that the actual world is a manifold of prehensions and that nature is a complex of prehensive unifications. I began to think in these terms, and increasingly to see the world as something dead and boring, and the result might soon have been a deadening also of the intellectual stimulation I got from reading Whitehead, but before this could happen my philosophical thinking indirectly gave rise to an idea in me for yet another new kind of poetry. If the actual world was dead and boring why not base my poems on dreams? Not on actual dreams, such as I assumed Freud's patients' dreams had been, but on consciously constructed dreams, which could be made much richer than those. This idea was all the more attractive to me because I felt it would be easier to put into practice than my plan to write a long anti-tragic poem about my home town.

During the remainder of the 1926 autumn term I invented several dreams: I remember in one of them there was a background of dunes and marram grass and a brown cave out of which came a mammoth-like yet globular-shaped animal whose skin was human and whose proboscis had a telescope lens at the end of it that the dreamer could look through to see men moving about inside the animal's stomach, some in bowler hats, others in bathing dresses and one in complete polo kit. I sent prose versions of these dreams to Richard in my letters to him, but I didn't manage to make a poem out of any of them. I wrote no poetry before the end of the term or during the Christmas holidays. In the Easter term however I was able to write some light-verse which was quite undreamlike. I wrote it for Tibbie, whom I had begun to meet sometimes in the afternoons and to go for walks with alone. I was not in love with her so I was not inhibited by any shyness from asking her to come out with me, but I liked her well enough to feel some jealousy when she told me halfway through the term that she would soon be travelling up to the Midlands to stay for a week with a girl who was an old school friend of hers and that they would be going to several dances and enjoying themselves generally. The jealousy inspired the light-verse, which I entitled *The Holiday Girl's Companion* and which suggested various cheap tricks a girl could use for getting off with men during a train journey and afterwards. The tone of it was repulsively facetious, and even the two least bad quatrains I can remember nauseate me now:

> *Bring books to impress all types. When you're aided*
> *To shift your bandbox on the rack*
> *See that Plato is artlessly paraded*
> *Beneath Wisden's cricketing Almanac . . .*

> *. . . Above all, let your eyes seem elusive, my dear,*
> *And gently retreat from his avid inspection:*
> *But let them retreat towards the window where*
> *They can counter-inspect in a modest reflection.*

She understandably didn't like my light verse, and after she returned from her holiday I didn't write any more of it. Nor was I able to write the dream poems I wanted to, but she came out with me increasingly often and this lessened the grief my unproductiveness caused me. She was the pleasantest-natured girl I had met anywhere. I tried to believe I was falling in love with her and I behaved towards her as if I was, but she knew I wasn't. During the next ten months I never got farther with her than fondling — 'petting' as she called it, a word she had learned during her American trip: I did not really want to go farther though I thought I did. I was not prepared to involve her in a serious affair with me. I did at last tell her I was still in love with Tessy, though the truth was that I was becoming gradually less so. I continued to see Tessy at folk dancing and at the Arts Club but I made no more attempts to get her to meet me alone, and she no doubt knew that Tibbie was going for walks with me. She was away several times for a week or more in London and her absence caused me no pangs. During one of these times I saw an etching by her on the wall of the dining-room in Miss Lightwood's house when Tibbie and I went to tea there: it was of a barge beside a quay with warehouse roofs sharp in the background against the sky, and I thought that it had vision and that a dullard could not have done it. My longing for her was revived for a while, but also I became more certain than ever before that nothing could come of it, that I would never get to know her, let alone live with her. After this I began to feel I ought to decide to leave Cornwall where I had discovered that love could not, as at Cambridge I had still believed it eventually might, solve the problems of my life, and where I had made no progress with my poetry. As it happened I didn't have to decide, because Mrs Norman decided for me: half-way through the 1927 autumn term she told me the children would be going to a local school after Christmas. I wonder now why the doubts which my melancholy and my tongue-tied diffidence in company must have aroused in her about my fitness to tutor the children hadn't made her give me notice before. I felt relief when I knew for certain I would be leaving Cornwall soon: and I was able to convince myself that my poetic frustration had been due to the unreal kind of life I had been living there — unreal because it was so different from the kind most people everywhere were forced to live — and that this life had been the cause of my attempting to write dream poems, and that such poems could never be anything but trivial. I was also able to convince myself, two days before the end of my last tutoring

241

term there, that my earlier plan to write a long anti-tragic poem about my home town was still possible and exciting.

But at Christmas time when I was back home in Essex again after leaving Cornwall for good something happened which turned me against the whole idea of anti-tragic poetry. Laura and Hugh and Vaughan were at home too — Laura on holiday from her boarding school where she was in her last year, Hugh on holiday from the boarding school where he had just started as a teacher, Vaughan finally free from school and waiting to go to the London Hospital as a medical student — though this wouldn't be for some months and my mother had proposed that before then he should go to stay with a family in Heidelberg to improve his German. One evening I arrived home late after a visit to Richard in Kensington and found Hugh awake in the bedroom, which was the same one that we had shared as children, and he told me Vaughan had been behaving very strangely and after supper had suddenly asked my father, 'Why did you never tell me about sex?' This had sounded like an accusation, but our father — who in fact had never thought it necessary to tell any of us about sex — had simply asked Vaughan sympathetically what was the matter, and then Vaughan had repeated 'Why did you never tell me about sex?' and he had gone on repeating this at intervals throughout the evening and neither our father nor Hugh had been able to get anything else intelligible out of him. 'It was obvious,' Hugh said to me, 'that there's something psychologically the matter with him, and it's serious.' We began to remember and to tell each other of odd things Vaughan had done recently before this, though none had seemed as abnormal as this at the time, one of them being his not informing anyone in the family that he had at last got through the School Certificate Examination which previously he had twice failed solely because of his Maths — his English and Modern Languages were well above average — and which he needed to get through in order to be accepted as a medical student. And Hugh told me that when Vaughan had gone to bed our father had described how after accompanying him for his interview at the London Hospital — where our father had been a medical student himself — he had noticed as they were leaving the hospital that one side of Vaughan's face was streaming with blood, which could only have been caused by his digging his nails deeply into his cheek. My recent reading of Freud prevented me from thinking that Vaughan's psychological trouble might be due to his not wanting to become a doctor: I assumed it must be due to sex — his question to our father seemed to prove it must be — and I hoped to be able to discover from him what exactly his sexual problem was and perhaps (through what knowledge I had of Freud's theories) to be able to help him. In the morning I asked him to play golf with me. On the small two-stroke Triumph motor-bicycle which our father had used after the war and had given to Hugh and me when he had bought a car, we rode up to the golf-club, Vaughan long-legged astride the pillion, and from the moment we arrived until the moment we came off the course after finishing our game I could get hardly a word out of him. There was nothing wrong with his golf, though: he had always been a good player — so good that our father had even thought of his becoming a golf professional if he failed to get his school certificate — and that morning, in spite of frost which made the ground hard, he played at least as well as usual, but seemingly without interest. As we were coming into the clubhouse to put away our golf-bags in the locker room he did briefly show interest, however, at the sight of a small bird which was on the door-mat in front of the entrance, unmoving though not dead. I picked it up. 'It's a blue tit', I said. 'I suppose it's like this because of the cold.' He seemed to look at it, and said 'It's a blue tit', as if he recognised that this was what it was and not merely as if repeating my words unmeaningly. I carried it up to the locker-room, which was warm, and though I did not hold it upside down it did not struggle at all. I put it on the window-sill, where it soon showed signs of revival; so I opened the window, and it flew out. Vaughan took little notice of its going; but his having said before we'd come upstairs 'It's a blue tit' may have been what enabled him to go on talking now. He told me his genitals had become black and he knew they would rot away and drop off. While I was trying to think what Freudian significance there might be in this, he held out his hand towards me with its knuckles uppermost and said 'That consumption? Sure thing.' He went on to name several more diseases he believed he was suffering from, though he never once mentioned mental illness. I tried to question him about them but he did not answer me. Then he forgot about diseases and spoke of other dangers: it was as if he knew there was something gravely wrong and was trying to discover what. 'I'm in the sea,' he said. 'What sea?' I asked, and for once he did answer. 'The sea of water,' he said. After this he talked almost without pause, more and more confusedly and fantastically and whenever I managed to ask him a question he either ignored it or misinterpreted it. Fear grew in me, and when we left the club-house to ride back home I knew that not only I, who in my silly intellectual conceit had thought that my reading of Freud might enable me to help Vaughan in his agony (and agony it was, as I was soon to realise) but even the most expert psychoanalyst, even Freud himself, would be unable to reach through to him past his delusions, let alone to cure him; and from this time my distrust of Freud began, though I did not yet recognise how anti-scientific his concepts mainly were — the Oedipus complex, penis envy, the Id, the Unconscious, the castration complex and all the rest of his inventions which have pleased so many poets, novelists and painters — nor for a long while yet was I to recognise that in his ideas on women and on society he had been a reactionary even among his contemporaries. My fear and grief for Vaughan deepened during the next few days. It was as though I foreknew everything that he would be doomed to, his forty years in mental hospitals, his dreadful end at the age of sixty in one of them where because of understaffing he was allowed to choke himself to death. An eminent alienist whom my father got to our house told us — after mentioning as one sign of abnormality the fact that unlike his own son of the same age Vaughan had not become a lance corporal in the school O.T.C. — the illness was dementia praecox, from which there was no likelihood of recovery. My mother refused to accept this prognosis, but the rest of us accepted it and before long we became resigned to it, and it even gave me — though I was ashamed to feel this — a kind of relief. Another effect it soon had on me was to convince me that my plan to write anti-tragic poetry had been mistaken. In face of what had happened to Vaughan an anti-tragic attitude was as utterly untenable as a classically tragic one would have been. A false picture of reality, no matter how aesthetically appealing it might seem to be, could never be made into a good poem. I reminded myself of Wilfred Owen's saying; 'The true poets must be truthful.' Only by aiming to write truthfully might I at last be able to solve my creative problem.

Let me remind myself now that my first aim in my present poem too should be truthfulness rather than poetic richness. And since the poem is mainly about the defeat of the hopes I once fixed on the Party, it is bound to be bleak if it is truthful. Don't let me be afraid of bleakness. There is a need anyway for poetry to break with the over-richness of twentieth-century bourgeois modernism, to get rid of literary allusiveness, clotted imagery, deliberate ambiguities. A revolt against modernism is as necessary to-day as a revolt against eighteenth-century poetic conventions was in Wordsworth's time. Nevertheless I must not let my poem become any bleaker than it already is, or I would find that what I would be writing would not be poetry but a political tract. I shall still need to strengthen poetic feeling in myself by remembering my past imaginative life — and by taking notice of my surroundings during my afternoon walks. Since I walked through the woods above the sea two hours ago I have noticed almost nothing until this moment when I see that I am within a few hundred yards of home. I must make a point of doing the same walk on another afternoon quite soon and of really looking at things all the way.

9

I have finished the poem at last, six years after I began it. Only two hours ago this morning when I opened the French windows and came out from the drawing-room to sit on the verandah here in the sun I had a fear that I would never be able to write the ending, that perhaps there had been no wholeness, no unity, in my initial conception of the poem and it would therefore be unfinishable, that in all its seven sections it might prove to have been misconceived. As I sat down I looked at the flint wall under the holly tree where an oblong of sunlight was reflected from one of the windows of the house, and I remembered the morning soon after my retirement from teaching when I told myself I must start work on this poem without fail, and the memory helped me to finish work on it to-day. I have succeeded, I have done what I aimed six years ago to do. I wish it had been quicker, but it has been achieved and my life since I retired has not been wasted. Even if I am never able to get the poem published I shall at least have been myself during these years, a poet not a slave. Nothing in my future can alter the fact that this has happened. How different the reflected sunlight on the alternate banded rows of grey and white flints seems to-day from when I so apathetically stared at it that morning six years ago. And the dark summer house in the corner of the garden, 'the soul's dark cottage' as Elsie and I have named it, with its honeysuckle-covered unglazed latticed windows and its octagonally pyramidal roof topped by a green wooden spike pointing up at the red-gold leaf-buds of the sycamore above it, never seemed more wonderful, not even in my childhood.

Or am I lying to myself? The truth is that there was no

occasion in my childhood when I was able to see this garden at this time of year; and the wonderfulness of the summerhouse is impaired for me now by a misgiving I am trying not to feel about the quality of my poem. And because I am trying not to feel it I am not clear what it is, and while it remains vague I shall not be able to rid myself of it. I don't think it is about the political passages in the poem, which have so often worried me previously. I am as convinced as I can be that the bleakness of these is necessary and artistically right, and that any attempt to make them scintillate verbally would falsify the description they give of the painful time when Elsie and I were forced out of the Party for continuing to uphold the Marxist-Leninist principles which the revisionist leaders of the Party were abandoning. No, my misgiving is not about the political passages but about the climax of the poem where I glorify the life I have been living since my retirement, the new poetic life, the free life of imaginative activity and poetic creation with political action as my secondary aim. And one reason why this worries me is that the new poetic life has had so little strength of its own, has needed to be constantly sustained by my remembering the imaginativeness I was capable of in the years before I joined the Party; another reason is that when I tried in the past to live for imagination and poetry, I failed so utterly at last that I came near to madness and suicide. Yet need I have failed? Certainly the poetic life as Richard and I thought of it forty years ago, a life not only of poetic creativity but also of romantic love and of freedom from enforced work, was an economic impossibility for me; nevertheless after I had abandoned my delusive half-hopes of somehow being able to live it somewhere and had become permanently a schoolmaster, couldn't I have lived primarily for imagination and poetry at least during my spare time and my school holidays, if I had also taken part secondarily in the political struggle as I have since my retirement?

Admittedly it would not have been easy for me to go on trying to live for poetic creation beyond the period of almost four years when I did still try to after leaving Cornwall, a period of cumulative defeat beginning with my failure to write poetry in the London lodgings which Richard helped me to find. But each new attempt I made to write during those years was bringing me nearer, as I believe now though I couldn't know then, to achieving a poem good enough at last to justify my aim of living primarily for poetry; and each defeat revealed to me, and enabled me to avoid when I made my next attempt, some serious fault either in my writing or in one of the subsidiary activities that at various times I regarded as component parts of my life for poetry.

My failure in my London lodgings to start work on the long realistic non-tragic poem which I intended to write there, and which I had been so optimistic about when I had conceived it after Vaughan's illness had caused me to reject my previous intention of writing an anti-tragic poem, was due to the revulsion aroused in me by my first experience of the kind of sexual activity that I had imagined would be one of the chief attractions of the urban poetic life I meant to live. The frustration of my love for Tessy in Cornwall had made me decide that I would stop futilely searching for a girl who would be my poetic soul-mate, and that I would find someone like Rosetti's Jenny (fond of a kiss and fond of a guinea) or at worst like Dowson's Cynara (last night, ah, yesternight, betwixt her lips and mine/There fell thy shadow, Tessy) or at best like Baudelaire's Jeanne Duval, who would give me sexual joy. London seemed a place where even if I didn't succeed in meeting a woman who would be as physically appealing to me as Jeanne Duval had been to Baudelaire I would anyway have no difficulty in losing my unhappy virginity at last. And Richard was keen to accompany me in looking for a woman, not because he himself needed one — his tastes weren't heterosexual at all

— but because for my sake he wanted to see me 'properly equipped' as he put it.

The bed-sitting room he helped me to find was on the second floor of a semi-detached Victorian house and had a big window that let in plenty of light from the sky and in front of the window was a heavy-looking old-fashioned table at which a poet like John Davidson might, I imagined, once have sat; I believed I would be eager to settle down every morning to write in this room. On the evening of the day when I installed myself there I had an outing with Richard to Soho where, even before we had had anything to drink, the lights and the dark seemed warm with a sensual invitation which I found all the more exciting because of the slight apprehensiveness it caused in me. After having a meal and plenty of wine in a French restaurant, we went for more drinks into the ornate bar of a large Victorian-style pub, and as we came out of it half an hour later into the cooler street I had a moment when sexual desire rose like an ecstasy in me. Soon we picked up two girls, whom we took into a cheaper restaurant than the one we had already eaten in. They were dressed alike, and were of the same height, and their faces were alike. They looked the sort of teenagers that Desmond and I had taken out on the river at Cambridge, and I began to doubt whether they were prostitutes after all. They were not very responsive to my or Richard's alcoholically-inspired talk. Before long I had to leave the restaurant to search for a public lavatory, which I found down a subway some way off, in Cambridge Circus it may have been, and when I came up out of it I saw roads radiating in every direction and I walked down one after another of them without rediscovering the restaurant till nearly an hour later, by which time Richard — taking my hat and umbrella with him — had left, and the girls had too.

I assumed he would have abandoned them by now and gone home, but I was determined that the evening should not end in frustration for me, so instead of going by the Underground back to my lodgings I walked down Shaftesbury Avenue and picked up the first obvious whore I saw there. She took me into a house through an inconspicuous-seeming doorway and we went up bare wooden stairs at the top of which I heard a man — who was unobtrusively visible to me for a moment in the gap of a half-opened door — say to the whore, 'Nellie has gone to sleep'. I thought that Nellie must be another whore, but I didn't think about the kind of relationship there might be between this man and these women. My whore and I had to sit on the stairs and wait. I didn't ask her what her name was, nor did I look closely at her face. I told her in Publicschoolboyishly obscene words how eager I was to copulate with her. She smiled, encouragingly. But suddenly in alarm she said, 'What's that?' She pointed to the palm of my hand on the upper part of which there was a strip of sticking-plaster. I told her I had got a blister from playing golf. 'Oh, golf,' she said in a mock upper-class accent and with evident relief. I too felt some relief: I supposed she had suspected that the plaster might be covering a chancre — my talk could have given her the impression that I often went whoring — and her alarm seemed to indicate that she herself was not already diseased. My father's medical books had given me a fear of syphilis which neither my being drunk nor my having taken the precaution earlier in the evening of going into a chemist's to buy a sheath and a packet of permanganate-of-potash crystals could wholly free me from. I was almost free from it, however, when at last she stood up and led me — though I hadn't heard anyone tell her that Nellie had now woken up — along a short passage into what I remember, probably wrongly, as a dimly red-lit room where nearly everything, the walls and the carpet and the bedspread over the double bed which was in a corner of the room, was dark red. With no delay she took off her skirt, but she apparently did not intend to take off any of her clothes above the waist. When I told her I wanted to see her breasts she said in a tone of regret which sounded oddly shy to me, 'I'm afraid I haven't got any'; nevertheless she removed her upper clothes, and the breasts she exposed were certainly very flat and triangular. In a moment she was lying on her back on the bed, at right-angles to its length, raising her legs in the air and waggling them crudely far apart, while I squeamishly tried to avoid seeing her vulva too clearly: the effect this exhibition had on me was the opposite of enticing, and I waited there without making any move towards her until at last she got me to lie on the bed and began to pull off my trousers. I searched quickly in their pockets before they went, and then desperately and still more quickly in the pockets of my jacket, trying to find the sheath I had bought at the chemist's, but it seemed to be lost; I told her, and she got off the bed to fetch her handbag from which she brought out a sheath that was already unrolled and had the look, to my fright, of having been previously used, though it also looked as if it had been rinsed out and dried and I did not resist when she slipped it on me. The actual copulation, during which I was the passive partner, was brief and was locally pleasurable for a few seconds in spite of my fears. When it was over and we had got off the bed I said to her with a cynicism which I didn't think she detected, 'You're the first I've ever done this with. Does that interest you?' Instead of answering she said, 'When you saw me in the street — did you fancy me?' I thought I could see she really hoped I had fancied her, and I felt there was a pathos in this. I did not answer her with a direct lie but I looked at her in a way which was meant to make her think I might have been attracted by her. I wondered how old she was and I noticed as I had not previously done the very even colouring of her cheeks and the deep blackness of her hair. 'We must meet again,' she said. The proposal instantly made me aware that I needed to get away from her without a moment's

252

further delay and to go back to my lodgings and disinfect myself. I paid her and, not saying good-bye, I found my way out of the house and hurried to the Underground station and within half an hour, after discovering during the journey that the sheath and permanganate crystals I had bought were in one of the pockets of my jacket after all, I was in the bathroom at my lodgings washing myself with hot water which the dissolving crystals had turned dark purple. I also dipped parts of my woollen vest and of my pants and shirt into the disinfectant, though I must have known this was unnecessary since I had read in one of my father's medical books that spirochetes and gonococci couldn't normally survive for long apart from the human body, and anyway I would be changing into other underclothes to-morrow; no doubt I was desperately trying not merely to disinfect my body and my clothes but to wash off the whole soiling experience I had just been through. I took a long time getting to sleep that night and I wasn't helped by feeling additionally anxious lest staying awake might make it more difficult for me to get down to work at my writing in the morning.

When I woke to see daylight through the long curtains of my bed-sitting room I immediately knew not only that I wouldn't be capable of writing poetry that morning but I wouldn't be capable of it here on any other morning either. These London lodgings were inseparably associated for me with what I had experienced in Soho the night before, and the longer I stayed here the worse my apprehension and self-disgust would become. I would have to go home. This decision, by the time I was up and dressed, was firm enough not to need the further strengthening it got when I opened a cupboard I had not yet looked into and saw on the floor of it a heap of used sanitary towels, presumably not noticed by the landlady when she cleaned up the room after the previous occupant had left. I could not go home at once, however, because I had arranged to meet Richard again in the evening. And after visiting the bathroom to try to wash out the permanganate stain from the vest, pants and shirt I had disinfected the previous evening I realised that, also before returning home, I would have to dispose of them somewhere, because the stain proved to be irremovable and my mother would certainly discover it if I took them back with me. I was briefly tempted to add them to the heap of sanitary towels in the cupboard; but finally, having cut off the name tabs which my mother had attached to them (she still bought clothes for me) I carried them with me wrapped in newspaper when I went to meet Richard that evening, and after we had had a meal together in a restaurant again we went down to the Thames Embankment, where according to him there would be fewer people about — it was for this reason that homosexuals used to seek one another out in public lavatories here at this period until the police made it too dangerous — and I left the newspaper parcel under the arch of a bridge. My having to spend a second night at my lodgings was made tolerable for me both by my being drunk again and by the knowledge that Richard would be arriving in the morning — as we had arranged over our meal at the restaurant — to tell me and the landlady that he had had a phone call from my home (she was not on the phone) saying that my brother was seriously ill and asking me to return at once. When he did tell her she obviously did not believe him, but I paid her for a fortnight's lodging in advance before I left the house, and she was not aggrieved. As I walked out of the front door with Richard and down the steps which bridged the basement area, the relief I felt expanded into a confidence that home when I arrived back to live there again would be less unfavourable to my getting on with my poem than it might have been if I had never tried to live in these London lodgings.

Home, almost as soon as I walked into it again by the morning-room door at the back of the house, did seem a place where writing poetry would be easier for me. Even before I opened the door the sight of the room through the windows gave me the idea of a new and more attractive beginning for my realistic poem: I would describe the lounge at the local golf-clubhouse as seen from outside in the early evening with members playing cards at green baize tables in a tobacco-hazy brightness. During the next fortnight at home I was able to concentrate on this idea and to make several attempts at starting the poem, in spite of Vaughan's illness which had become worse since the Christmas holidays. My mother had got Mademoiselle Radigue, who had formerly been his and Laura's French governess for a while, to come over from Paris to help her look after him: one advantage my mother no doubt had in mind when engaging her rather than an Englishwoman was that she would be unlikely to gossip in the town, and this was important because having a case of insanity in the family was still regarded — at least among the middle-classes — as a disgrace. (And perhaps those present-day psychiatrists who hold that madness is primarily the fault of the family in which it occurs rather than the fault of society or of the sufferer's own physiological constitution are helping to perpetuate the opinion that it is a disgrace to the family.) Vaughan was not easy to manage; I could no longer persuade him to play golf with me, and it appeared to me he took a pleasure in giving the impression that he might at any moment become violent: at lunch one day he got hold of the carving knife and grinningly refused for a while to hand it over to me after I'd told him I wanted to carve the joint with it; he was obviously enjoying the alarm he guessed I and the rest of us must be feeling. Nevertheless his illness did not prevent me, whenever I wanted to think about my intended poem, from finding somewhere in the house where I could be alone for a while, and I believe I might have succeeded in starting the poem if I hadn't received from the Scholastic Agency, about a fortnight after

I'd abandoned my London lodgings, a notice of a job that I could apply for at a minor Public school in a cathedral town. The Agency used to send me frequent notices which I always showed to my parents when I was at home, and usually I was able to point out convincingly to them that the jobs were not good enough to be worth my applying for, but this latest job looked not too objectionable; and as I didn't want my parents to think I planned to live off them permanently, especially now that they would have to keep Vaughan probably for the rest of their lives, I applied for it — and I got it. One unobjectionable thing about it was that it was temporary and would last for only three weeks. I consoled myself also by forming a resolution to think about my poem, if not actually to make a start on it, in the evenings after teaching.

I was aware however that I might be so miserable at the school as to be incapable of thinking of anything at all except the immediate actuality there. What interested me most about the coming three weeks was whether I would be able to exist as a schoolmaster. I knew that I didn't want to be a Public school-type authoritarian, but the problem was how could I be a rebel against the system and at the same time keep order among the boys I would have to teach? I would be in an educational no-man's-land, belonging neither with the authorities nor with the pupils. And certainly I did feel isolated on my first day at the school as I followed other members of the staff into the assembly hall for morning prayers and went up the steps on to the platform in front of two hundred watching boys. Another new master, who stood next to me in the back row behind the senior masters on the platform, whispered to me 'Isn't this ghastly?' — but though I liked him for saying so I doubted whether he felt as out-of-place as I did up there among the staff or as out of sympathy with the prayers which were being conducted by the Headmaster (wearing a clerical white tie) to whom I by my presence on the platform was giving my support.

I did not have to do any teaching that morning, and apprehension had time to grow in me as I sat in the Common-Room looking at newspapers. After lunch when I found my way to the upper fourth form-room where I was due to give a French lesson I felt still more isolated than I had at assembly. As I came into the room and saw to my left the boys sitting at their desks and to my right the master's desk which was raised on a dais, I had no impulse to go and sit among the boys, but neither did I want to oppose myself to them by stepping up on to the dais; nevertheless I did step up on to it because there seemed no other way for me to start the lesson. I asked them to get out the French reading book that was used in this form, and while they did so I had almost the same sensation of momentary panic I had had as a learner car-driver when for the first time I had set the car in motion by my own use of the controls. I soon knew I had made a mistake: there were not enough books to go round, so some of the boys had to share, and this led to talking between them which became steadily louder, and before long I had to use my whole energy continuously to try to prevent the talk from becoming riotously noisy. I decided briefly that I would never be able to survive as a schoolmaster. But the action was too quick for emotion to reach any depth in me. One boy whom I tried to be mildly sarcastic to when he asked me for a third time whether 'ne . . . plus' meant 'no more' went on to ask whether I came from Bromsgrove school (he was confusing me with the other new master) and I answered 'No, Mr Donald came from there,' and then I said with a foolishness which later experience as a teacher makes me find almost incredible now, 'I am only here for three weeks.' 'You'll be glad when it's over, sir?' the same boy asked. 'That depends,' I said, ludicrously trying to sound sinister, 'on how you behave.' 'We'll make it pretty lively for you, sir,' the boy said, and when I finally turned away from him he added, 'We killed the last master we had' — (a remark which may not have been such a commonplace in the baiting of inexperienced teachers forty years ago as it has probably become nowadays.) My next period was with the lower fourth who were younger, quieter and less impudent, though towards the end of the period one startlingly percipient boy said to his neighbour loudly enough to make it obvious that he intended me to hear, 'Film-star or mad poet?' When afternoon school was over I walked back to my lodgings in some despair, but that soon passed — without my having to give myself a philosophical lecture on the need for keeping up my morale. My recovery was constitutional, physical. Within two hours I felt I *wanted* to take the upper fourth again the next day. This was because I had been attacked — for the first time since I had left my own Public school (except on the one occasion of the messing up of my room by the poshocracy at Cambridge). I realised that to be attacked was better for me, more bracing, than to be aided, flattered, smarmed.

I also realised that teaching during these three weeks was going to leave me in no state for writing poetry in the evenings, and I was glad to go out to pubs either with the two high-spirited young colleagues whose lodgings I temporarily shared — they had placed on their landlady's dining-room mantelpiece a cardboard ink-bottle case slotted to take coins and inscribed 'He who swears most pays most' — or with the other new man, Donald, who found the teaching almost as exacting as I did. He appreciated the appropriateness of the account I gave him of a comic film I had recently seen in which the hero took a job as a gym instructor at a rurally-situated girls' boarding-school where the girls made life hell for him and as soon as the day's work was over he walked exhaustedly out of the school grounds to go to the village pub and to order 'a clothes brush' — cocktails in those days had all sorts of fancy names so this one didn't surprise me much — and the barman after setting down the filled cocktail glass on the bar counter laid an ordinary clothesbrush beside it. The hero, watched impassively by two bearded and besmocked yokels on a bench, drank the cocktail immediately and within a second or two his face changed, became contorted, his body trembled, he tottered, he fell down flat on the floor, he writhed in convulsions, while the yokels continued to watch him impassively, and at last he stopped writhing and stood up and, looking completely recovered and renewed, he took the clothesbrush from the bar-counter and brushed the dust off his clothes with it. Donald and I more than once got fairly drunk; and once we picked up two girls in the town, a rash thing for him to do since unlike me he hoped that his job at the school would be permanent. My three weeks, because they were so full of dislikeably stimulating incidents at the school, seemed to go on for months, and by the end of them I had managed to gain some control over most of the forms I taught, but I had gained it at the expense of such extreme and such humiliating effort that I would almost have preferred to have had no control at all. I decided that I could not possibly live as a schoolmaster. However, the unpleasantness of my experiences at the school made the prospect of my return home all the more pleasing to me and helped to heighten my hope that when I got back there I would find poetry-writing easy in comparison with teaching.

Within my first week back at home I did write a poem. The idea for it, and also the first line of it, came to me a moment after I walked out of the railway station and looked down South Street into the town. The afternoon was wet and grey, and for the first time something which my mother had said in a letter to me during my last week at the school, and which my experiences there had prevented me from thinking much about, became significant for me. She had said that Mademoiselle Radigue had returned to Paris and that a male nurse was now living in the house to look after

Vaughan. There was a suggestion in the letter that Mademoiselle Radigue had found Vaughan too much for her, and as I walked out of the station I remembered how even before my three weeks away from home Vaughan had once raised his hands towards her neck pretending that he meant to strangle her. I was relieved when I arrived home to find he was no worse if no better than when I had left, and he got on well enough with the male nurse, an amiable though sad-looking cockney who didn't appear to be much younger than forty. My poem, which took me five days to write, began with the line, '*On what new disaster does the rain fall*'. I intended it to have something of the atmosphere of Poe's *The Fall of the House of Usher,* but in spite of the genuine feeling which had given rise to my first conception of the poem its form became more important to me than its content, and this priority was evident in the finished product. It consisted of two very long sentences in 'speech rhythm', which were designed to bear a resemblance to the octet and the sestet of a sonnet except that the first sentence occupied ten lines instead of eight and the second sentence seven instead of six, and the few rhymes I introduced were either internal or when they came at the ends of lines they were never more than half-rhymes, vowel-rhymes only or consonant-rhymes only. When I'd finished it I knew it would give an impression of being over-contrived and deficient in feeling, but the fact that I had finished it was encouraging to me. It made me confident that I would very soon be able to begin writing the long realistic poem which would prove to me that I was something better than a minor versifier. I believe I might have begun if Rabbitarse and String hadn't sent me, within three weeks of my return home from my brief first school-teaching experience, a notice of a tutoring job which I could think of no convincing grounds for telling my parents that I didn't want to apply for. It was in a country house occupied by a family named Parkin in the north of England and the pay offered was good. When in answer to my application Mr Parkin wrote accepting me for the job I told myself that this time whatever else happened I would force myself to start work on my long poem in the evenings. Surely, I thought, with only one boy for me to teach — and he was recuperating from an illness so he would probably not be too obstreperous — I would be unlikely to find the new job as unfavourable to my writing as real schoolmastering had proved to be.

During my first ten days with the Parkins I neither started nor even gave any thought to my realistic poem, but on the tenth evening soon after getting into bed in the pleasant bedroom which had been allotted to me — a large one with two armchairs and an ottoman as well as a capacious old-fashioned bed and with wallpaper that I described in a consciously amazing letter to Richard as 'birded' — I conceived a poem which was not realistic but surrealistic, as I would now call it, though at the time I thought of it as a dream poem since I hadn't yet read anything surrealist and hadn't even come across that word. The conceiving of a dream poem came easily to me in this strange household where Stokes, the chauffeur, seemed the dominant person, 'a kind of lay Rasputin without, so far as I know, Rasputin's expensive vices' was how I described him to Richard. He had invented an emulsion which had helped as nothing else had to soothe the pain of Mr Parkin's bad knee and which Mr Parkin believed could have made Stokes a millionaire if he had put it on the market instead of preferring to reserve it exclusively for Mr Parkin. In contrast to Stokes, who always looked loftily calm, and whom Mr Parkin would never have dared to treat with anything but deference, Mr Parkin himself in his attitude towards other members of the household had at times something of the ill-temper of a dictator's assistant — the pain of his knee had no doubt contributed to this — though his outbursts of fury against them, I noticed, would usually be released not directly at them but to be overheard by them, as when one morning while he and I were alone in the dining-room together with the door open he went over to the sideboard and eyeing the levels of the whisky and brandy in the cut glass decanters inside the tantalus, which he had forgotten to lock after last using it, he said loudly enough for any servant who might be anywhere near the dining-room to hear, 'Some drunken devil has been stealing the brandy again'. Whenever he wanted to attack me he didn't do so directly either but by abusing education generally and by pointing out how much better a man Stokes was for being without it. Mrs Parkin who unlike her husband could spell properly was very watchful of me and didn't hesitate to correct what she considered my bad English when she noticed that I pronounced the word 'again' as 'agen' and not as 'agane'. However she spent much of her time in bed, and Mr Parkin explained to me that this was only what was to be expected at her time of life: 'all women have to go through it, just like horses,' he said. There was an eccentricity in him which sometimes seemed near to madness, as when one evening he borrowed the boy's air-gun to shoot at bats out of the bedroom window. The boy was the most normal member of the family, though he was in the habit of having long talks with the dog, a pure-bred terrier that he insisted to me seriously was a human being. I got on well enough with him, inventing activities for him such as making model-railway lines out of three-ply wood with his fretsaw, and life in the house was fairly luxurious, there was beer at meals and often hare-soup and Scotch cheddar — it's true I had to change into evening dress with a starched shirt every evening but I soon became so used to this that I ceased to feel the discomfort of it — and the grounds outside the house were exciting, four lawns all at different levels, tall trees with rooks' nests in them, a blue-faced and gold-figured stable clock in a square turret against a dark maze of boughs high in the background. But what really made living in this household tolerable for me was the dream poem I had been able to begin here, and when I found that writing it only at nights after I was in bed prevented me, because of sleepiness, from getting on with it as fast as I wanted, I didn't hesitate to tell Mr Parkin that I would like to have an hour and a half off every afternoon away from the boy. If he had refused me this I would have given him notice, but to my surprise he agreed very readily, as though he thought my request quite reasonable.

I have never found more pleasure in writing than during those free afternoon intervals, and I was glad that the poem as I'd conceived it was to be a long one which I calculated might take me two months to finish. It was to be a dream narrative beginning with the narrator going into a lavatory at the back of a football stadium. While he is there he hears from the closet next to his a sound as if the man occupying it is scraping his body with a strigil. This man and the narrator come out of their respective closets at the same moment, and the man looks just like Snell at Marchfield — with the same big yellow teeth and prominent adam's apple though without the clerical collar — so the narrator hurries away, but after getting into the stadium and finding a place to stand among the enormous crowd of spectators he is soon aware that Snell's double is standing beside him. The football game which has already begun appears very far off because the stadium is so huge, and when suddenly something goes wrong in the game and a number of the players start expostulating with the referee the narrator has no idea what they are indignant about, but a voice from nearby in the crowd says 'It's the blackest foul of our times.' At once the whole crowd in its tens of thousands surges forward down from the stands on to the football pitch, taking the narrator with them. They are pursuing someone who has got away through a wide gap which has appeared at the far end of the stadium, and the narrator goes with them, trying to run less fast than they do and succeeding when the crowd begins to

thin out and not to press so much upon him as they get out
into open country. He finds himself running at an easier
pace — the sort of pace he had learnt to run at years before
as a boyscout — beside Snell's double, who as if trying to
explain to him the reason for all that is happening tells him
about a boys' club in the East End of London and how
poverty-stricken the families are from which the boys come,
and — with a sob in his throat — about one boy whom he
calls Froggie's little brother. Then he talks about people in
the West End of London who think nothing of spending
twenty pounds each on a single meal. The narrator gets the
impression that it's people like these who are being pursued
by the crowd. But then the landscape changes and so does
this impression; he and Snell's double -- who is transformed
abruptly into someone else whose identity the narrator is
unsure of — are running with great difficulty across Nilotic
mud among papyrus reeds and the air has become very
warm and he begins to suspect that he and his new
companion are not the pursuers but the pursued. This
seems certain when the landscape changes again and
becomes an Amazonian rain-forest — the poem would
describe this scene and the Egyptian scene very richly,
extravagantly, fantastically — a forest in which as they run
the narrator hears behind them the cracking of twigs caused
by Indians who have been hired by the twenty-pound diners
and who are carrying bows with curare-tipped arrows, but
just in time the scene changes yet again, he is among snowy
mountains, his companion at his side is a dark-faced
hooded pilgrim holding a long staff as he runs, and the
narrator is aware of being a pursuer once more, not hunting
anyone down now but pursuing something glorious and
exalted. At last he comes out, quite alone, on to an
immense plain in the middle of which there stands a
towering obelisk cylindrical in shape and rounded at the top
and obviously a phallus. Eagles are circling above it, and at
its base there is an inscription in huge letters: The One

Valid Assertion. But though this dream poem gave me so much pleasure to write, by the time I was nearing the end of it I felt that life in the Parkin household was becoming intolerable. My position was a slavish one, bound to the boy. I was one of the servants, though less free if more pampered than the rest of them were, and the grim-looking Scottish chambermaid showed clearly that she resented having to bring tea up to me in my bedroom every morning. Mr Parkin increasingly revealed himself to me as an ignorant eccentric whose money gave him the power not only to buy up an expensively educated young man as an attendant for his boy but also to exert an influence over the whole district here, and who, besides showing contempt for the local village schoolmaster as an upstart earning far too large a salary, succeeded in making some of the farm labourers behave towards him like the simple rustic toadies he wanted them to be. He, and the household as a whole, helped to revive socialist ideas in me such as I had not had since my boyhood in the Sixth Form at my Public school. Two things above all else, however, made me decide to give notice: one was my not being able to meet girls, and the other was the realisation that my dream poem was a product of the unnatural and servile life I'd been leading and was not a serious work of art, and that I would never be able to get started on my long realistic poem here. So, after two and a half months, I told Mr Parkin one morning that I wanted to leave in order to work in films. This was untrue; what gave me the idea of saying it was that Richard had just got a job in a film studio, but Mr Parkin seemed to believe me and didn't try to dissuade me.

A distressful event within a week of my returning to my home in Essex after leaving the Parkins for good turned me even more decisively against dream poetry. I went with my father and Hugh to see Vaughan in the private mental home where he had been sent three weeks before because, as my mother had said in a letter to me at the Parkins', he had run away from his male nurse who had been taking him for a walk near our home and he had not been found till after midnight when a phone call came from a police station twenty-five miles away on the other side of London to say he was there. The private mental home, as we drove up the curving shrubbery-bordered gravel drive towards it in my father's Ford car, looked not unpleasant — a large Edwardian house built of red brick with white-painted window frames and Virginia creepers up the walls — and the proprietress, an ex-hospital nurse, came to meet us at once at the front door. Her considerate attentiveness, however, appeared in a new light when after a brief conversation with us about Vaughan's illness which she viewed not un-optimistically, she forewarned us that we should see he had had a slight accident: he had attacked one of the male nurses who had had to defend himself and had hit back. She took us to a comfortably furnished room where she left us to wait for Vaughan, who soon came in. He had a black eye. He gave no obvious sign of recognising us, yet we sensed he did recognise us. He did not speak. He did not answer our questions. Soon the male nurse who had hit him came into the room and gave us his own account of what had happened: it was the same account as the proprietress had given us. Then he laid a friendly, even a seemingly affectionate, hand on Vaughan's shoulder, but Vaughan showed no response. The nurse was wearing white plimsolls, and they reminded me of those worn by boys in the boxing matches which I had apprehensively watched and sometimes taken part in when myself a boy at school. From my experience of the times when Vaughan had used his strength on me since he had been ill I couldn't believe he had 'attacked' this man other than half-playfully or that the man had been justified in punching him in the eye. After a while the man unlocked a door which led out of the room where we were into a billiard room: he wanted us to be aware of the amenities of this private and expensive mental home. The lights within the big green shade over the billiard table were not switched on, and the shade had the effect of making the billiard room look sombre. Several patients were standing about in silence, one of them holding a billiard cue but not as though he had any thought of playing billiards with it. I had the impression of a misery there so deep that no one who was not himself mentally ill would have been capable even of imagining its depth. After we had said goodbye to Vaughan and had come out of the building to go to the car again I saw that my father was weeping. I don't remember why my mother was not with us. From the day when Vaughan's illness began until her death twenty-three years later she was to care far more deeply about him than the rest of the family did and to continue to visit him in various hospitals as long as she was physically able to and long after we — with the exception of Laura — had ceased to do so: perhaps she did not want to be with my father when he visited Vaughan on this occasion, as there had been recriminations between her and my father about him, each accusing the other of having been the cause of his illness. One effect on me of this visit to the mental home was to make me lastingly recognise that in a world in which things like his illness could happen I could never get satisfaction from dream poetry, no matter how technically ingenious it might be: only a realistic poem such as the one I had wanted to write about my home town, and had so inexcusably and so long delayed making an effective start on, could have any validity at all for me now. And I was getting older and I would not for ever be able to live by finding temporary jobs between which I would have months of poetic leisure: sooner or later I would be forced to take some slavish permanent job, and if I hadn't started the poem by then what hope would I have of ever starting it after then? And if I never started it what would I have been alive for all these years from my imaginative childhood onwards? But this time, now that I was free from the

Parkins, I would start, and I would not take another job until I had started.

Would I live at home for a while, and start while I was here? What tempted me most to stay here was that two days before the visit to Vaughan I had been introduced by Richard in London to a new literary friend he had made, a woman writer whom he called Selina, twenty years older than ourselves, a widow — he spoke to me jokingly of her as the 'wappened widow', a quotation from one of our favourite passages in *Timon of Athens.* He had talked to her about me and my sexual plight, and the third time I met her I went to bed with her. I knew I would be welcome to go to bed with her again when I wanted to, and while I lived at home I would be able to get to her house within three-quarters of an hour. Nevertheless I soon decided that I must not risk trying to write at home. I had failed here before; and, though there might be a good chance that because my sexual problem was now solved at least on a physical and friendly level I might succeed here this time, I would do better to find somewhere entirely new to me — not her house, however, because too much sensuality would be likely to be even more unfavourable to my writing than too much asceticism. I put an advertisement in the *Daily Herald* describing myself as a student who wanted somewhere to work which would be quiet and in the country. I chose the *Daily Herald* because I supposed it to be a socialist paper, and the socialist ideas which while I had been with the Parkins had revived in me from my Sixth Form schooldays were still active in my mind. The first answer came from Broxbourne in Hertfordshire, but when I went to look at the house I saw that it was a small asbestos-tiled bungalow which looked as though I wouldn't find much privacy in it to get on with my writing, so I did not even ring the doorbell. The second answer came from a semi-detached house at the end of a row of similar houses on top of a low hill at Buxted in Sussex: the sitting-room I was offered there was very small, but its window gave a westward downhill view over a wide meadow at the bottom of which were a spinney and a stream. I arranged to take this room, and the equally small bedroom above it.

As soon as I settled in I had a conviction that I would be able to write here, and I liked the young landlady and also her husband, a cheerful and tubbily-built rosy-faced traction-engine driver. I talked with her only when she brought me my meals, however, and with him never at any length or about anything seriously except once when there was an otter hunt in the district, and then he gave me his opinion of the hunters as much by his expression of face as by the words he used about them. They certainly were a weird lot, some of them from county families he said, and they would have caused despair to the kind of lower-middle-class snob who at that period hoped by dressing smartly to be taken for a member of the upper class. During three weeks or more I was alone most of the time, writing in the mornings, walking in the afternoons, reading in the evenings. My writing, as I had expected, went well; that's to say I got down from five to ten lines of my projected long poem on paper every morning, and their quality seemed satisfactory. I was employing a new technical device which pleased me and which consisted of avoiding as much as possible the use of the definite article: the avoidance produced an effect of curtness which I thought appropriate to the realism I was aiming at in the poem. But a suspicion that this device might be too artificial, even that it might savour of preciosity, began to develop in me when I was half-way through my second week of writing at Buxted. I tried to suppress the suspicion and I was partly successful in this, but during my third week I had the beginnings of a more serious doubt, so serious that I would not allow myself to focus it clearly in my thoughts. One afternoon, while I was walking along a footpath which was a public right of way through the grounds of a country house, I saw beyond some low iron fencing a group of exceptionally big trees with dark foliage tumescent like thunder-clouds against the bright blue sky, and simultaneously the words 'Since by man came sin' arose in my mind. I felt an extreme exaltation which was painful as well as happy, more painful than happy. A few days later I became unable any longer to prevent myself from recognising clearly not only that my device of avoiding the definite article was reprehensibly precious but also that the poem was no more than an accumulation of successive images without any development in them. The poem — or at least the present version of it — would have to be abandoned. But I knew I would never be able to conceive a new version of it if I remained at Buxted. This place had become associated for me with defeat and the longer I stayed here trying to work in my small room every morning and walking alone every afternoon the deeper I should sink into melancholia. If I was to clamber out of the pit I must leave here at once. I must go home again.

My first day back home did bring me a hope of re-conceiving the poem, but the hope soon dwindled. I did not hide from my mother that I had failed in what I had set out to do at Buxted, and she was sympathetic though she did not know what to suggest I should do next. After breakfast in the morning-room one day I caught her looking at me with something like terror: she evidently thought I might be going the same way as Vaughan. I told her I was not, but I realise now that the strain I had been putting on myself might well have upset my mental balance if my nervous constitution had been less strong than it was. After several weeks at home I believed I knew for certain I would never write poetry again, and I saw nothing ahead of me except having to take another job. In my diary at this time I made an entry which I can still remember every word of:

'Reasons at best can be no more than clues to feelings. My reasons for shooting myself are a mere accompaniment to my feelings. I record them here in order to prove that I am still capable of thinking coherently.

'I am not unhappy. But I foresee clearly that if I do not shoot myself I shall be forced to earn my living by doing work which I regard as dishonest. To present my case in psychological jargon: I am unable to adapt myself to reality. There is nothing discreditable in this. It's true that the majority of human beings do manage to adapt themselves: but their lives seldom emerge from the common quag of boredom and anxiety. I have been at times extraordinarily happy. I have been, in my own estimation, a genius. I have no grievance either against life or against myself or against anyone else. But I prefer not to sell myself into slavery. I do not envy the great majority of those I leave behind me.'

The rational and magnanimous tone I had achieved in this would-be final statement helped me to persuade myself that I really meant it. I decided to buy a powerful air pistol — this would be cheaper and a less conspicuous thing to carry about with me than the kind of air gun that Uncle Edmund had shot himself with — and remembering that there had been a shop in Cambridge which had shown air pistols in its window I took a day trip up to Cambridge and bought one of these pistols from this shop. When I got it back to my home I tested its strength by firing it at a notebook, not a very thick one, which I placed on a well-upholstered sofa: the lead pellet went right through the notebook but made no mark on the sofa. I spent several days planning the details of my suicide and decided I would do it in a rowing-boat far out to sea. I consulted one or two of my father's medical books in vain to try to find which part of the head it would be best for me to shoot into in order to stun myself. I thought out how I would sit in the boat so that my body would fall into the water immediately after I was stunned. I considered various dates when I might put my plan into practice and decided that the most appropriate day would be my birthday, though this was more than two months ahead. One reason why I didn't choose a much nearer date for my suicide was that I was getting a satisfaction, almost a creative satisfaction, out of thinking about it, and I didn't want this to end too soon. Before long I began to ask myself whether I might not be able to find some other kind of imaginative satisfaction, short of trying to write poetry, without the limitation in it that this one had. I thought I might try reading some philosophy. I found a book of translated selections from Epictetus. He appealed immediately to me with his saying 'You may be unconquerable, if you enter into no combat in which it is not within your own power to conquer'. I read the book through slowly, dwelling on every paragraph, and it improved my morale far more than my planning of suicide had done. Next I began to read Jung's *Psychological Types*. I'm not sure why, unless the fact that he had broken with Freud recommended him to me. Soon I felt he would help me to counter B. K. Wilshaw's view that poetry was merely 'emotive' and that unlike science it did not refer to anything. Jung held that the newly born brain of an infant is an ancient instrument in active command of experience outside itself, that the 'Unconscious' (Jung had not abandoned this Freudian concept) is a 'Collective Unconscious' and disposes of a whole world of imagery representing all experiences which have ever happened on this planet and having a boundless range which yields in nothing to the claims of the world of 'real' things. Though Jung's putting the word 'real' into inverted commas seemed to imply a degree of contempt for external reality, and though I couldn't quite bring myself to believe that primordial ideas could be born with the brain, I felt that his theory gave a new and strengthened status to poetic imagery and could be used as a weapon against Wilshaw's argument that poetry is made up of 'pseudo-statements'. The excitement aroused in me by Jung's book led me to start writing down notes which I headed in my notebook with the title 'Towards a refutation of B. K. Wilshaw's theory of Meaning as he applies it to poetry'. Before I had completed more than five or six pages of these notes I began to lose confidence in the Collective Unconscious as an idea that could give reliable support to my argument that poetic statements were not pseudo but were just as much about reality in their way as scientific statements were. I abandoned the notes. However the act of writing them had had something in it not totally different from the feeling which imaginative creation would have brought me, and it gave rise in me to the faint beginnings of a renewed hope that I might one day start to write poetry again after all.

But for this hope my will might have become so paralysed that I would have been incapable of writing a letter of application for a job as a teacher again (I didn't even think of trying to get work of a different kind, mainly because no other way of earning a living was any less unappealing to me than teaching). I am sure that only this hope enabled me to apply for the job I actually got — in the north of England at a Public school which, though it offered a better salary than other schools I was notified of by Rabbitarse and String, had a special reputation for the severity of its discipline. The word 'Sparta' was in the Latin motto under the school crest, and the only punishment allowed was caning. In the letters I wrote to Richard from this school the name I gave it was Lacedaemon. But though the boys there were treated fairly severely, the conditions for the staff were not so Spartan. I had a comfortably furnished sitting-room to myself in the lower-school building, and there was free beer at meals just as when I had been with the Parkins. The boys I taught gave me no trouble, partly because they were younger and fewer to each class than they had been at the school where I had had my first brief experience of teaching, but also because the general discipline had accustomed them not to be impudent to members of the staff. I was unexhausted in the evenings and there seemed a

273

possibility that before long I might be able to think about how I could start writing poetry again. Several of my colleagues, I discovered, were not indifferent to poetry, though even the younger among them were under the influence of religion and would seriously discuss the sermons we heard in the school chapel. I used sometimes after the Sunday morning service to go to the rooms of one of the younger classics men, Anderson, and usually Bartlett who was one of the younger maths men would be there too. I remember the sort of conversation we had on one of these occasions:

Anderson: Have a drink.

Bartlett: Yes. Thanks.

A.   Sherry? It's all I've got as a matter of fact. We finished off the whisky last night. It's really very good sherry.

B.   How much was it?

A.   Six and Six.

Myself: The same as mine, but mine was dark.

A.   Yes, I've tried that. I don't think it's as good.

M.   (sipping from the glass he has handed me): It isn't.

B.   Cheerioh.

A.   Ditto.

M.   Something to take away the taste of the sermon.

A.   I thought he was rather good.

B.   So did I.

A.   I should have liked to give him a sound caning for his voice but I thoroughly approved of what he had to say.

B.   'Vaguely benevolent' was a good phrase.

A.   Yes. It describes a certain type of person perfectly.

M.   I call it commonplace.

A.   You would. But if I may say so, old boy, I think your enthusiasm for literary language rather biases your judgement.

M.   Literary balls. What I objected to was the falseness of the man's attitude. Real simplicity I admire, but

274

commonplaces are never simple. They are confused, they may mean anything.

A. Not to the ordinary commonsense person.

M. Then tell me what that sentence of his about 'school patriotism' meant. Apparently we are not to run down other schools but we are to consider our own school as far and away the best.

B. Well that seems to me reasonable enough. Though you don't exactly quote his words.

M. It seems to me that the first part of the sentence is a mere pious guard — like putting sixpence into the poor-box and then stealing two pounds out of it. If we consider our own school to be much the best how can we do anything but look *down* on other schools.

A. It all depends what you mean by 'look down'. Presumably we can admire other schools and at the same time *prefer* our own. Loyalty to one school doesn't imply contempt for all others.

B. Hear, hear.

M. Well, I'll admit that a boy's loyalty expands a bit after he leaves school. He extends it from one Public school to Public schools in general.

A. A kind of 'vague benevolence'?

M. Perhaps. Only this time the effects are rather more serious. He 'looks down' on everyone who hasn't been to a Public school.

A. That comes straight out of Hyde Park.

M. No, it doesn't.

A. Anyway it's pure balls. The Public schools don't breed snobs. If anything, they err on the other side — they encourage modesty and suppress self-esteem.

Not all of our Sunday after-chapel discussions were as unintellectual as this. One of them for instance began with Anderson's stating 'I've never known any book which sufficiently stressed the influence of the Eleusinian mysteries on Greek religion.' From this, via ancient Egypt, he and

Bartlett got on to the subject of Gothic arches, Anderson asserting that the reason why the Romans didn't build these was that they weren't mystics, and Bartlett counter-asserting that they didn't build them because they didn't know how to, they couldn't solve the technical problems. I felt that Anderson and Bartlett were not arguing just for the sake of it: they were both of them seriously interested not only in religion but also in architecture and in art. I felt too that they would have been interested to read my poems if I had had any that I'd thought good enough to show them. Nevertheless their company did not stimulate me imaginatively.

It was another of the younger masters, much less interested in the arts than Anderson and Bartlett were, who unwittingly inspired the poem I was suddenly able to write at the end of my second term. He was Lloyd, whom I got to know better than any other of my colleagues because we lived in the same building and usually had our evening meals in his sitting-room (I suppose in order to save the servants the trouble of carrying meals separately to each of our rooms). Like me he taught only the junior boys but unlike me he had a real vocation as a schoolmaster and was possibly the most capable and devoted one among the whole of the staff. He had an unartificial heartiness which went down well with the junior boys, and though he unquestioningly accepted the Public school system, the Anglican religion and the British Empire, he did so tacitly and was not constantly lecturing the boys about them. Once when he was trying to persuade me to help him run the junior Scout troup — which I didn't want to do but which in the end he succeeded in persuading me to do — and I protested I couldn't see myself giving straight talks to the boys about the Empire or about bad language as the Scouting handbook recommended, he answered that he was not very keen on that sort of thing himself and that though it was all right in its way he did not think it was 'altogether suited to the type of boy we get here'. He was persistent in his aim of trying to make me more efficient. He wanted me always to change into proper football clothes when I refereed junior rugby games, and once, as I was returning towards the junior school buildings after refereeing a game and he was standing in the ash yard wearing football shorts and holding a rugger ball in the crook of his arm, he took one disapproving look at the flannel trousers I was wearing and then, swinging the rugger ball swiftly from his left to his right hip, he began to run at top speed away from the buildings. As though he was taking part in a rugger match he swerved, sold the dummy, fended off a tackle, punted the ball well over the head of the imaginary opposing full-back so that it fell among the far group of trees in front of the tennis courts. He sprang, he raced towards the tennis courts, bucking, heavily agile with jerking shoulders, going all out, broad-backed in a tight sweater; he plunged, he touched down, stumbling among tree roots. I was filled with revulsion and simultaneously with an irresistible admiration. I saw him momentarily as the incarnation of everything I most disliked and feared about the Public school system and at the same time I had a passionate temptation to applaud him. It was as though I had had a vision. I went back to my room and even before I got there I had already conceived a poem about what had happened. I finished writing it within a week.

It described my vision of Lloyd's run and his punting of the rugger ball and it ended with the thought that from now on I would be able voluntarily to have other visions — in the night, at lunch, everywhere. I had received an award of power, an award which was a reward for all I had been forced to do and would continue to be forced to do at this school and at similar schools where I would be spending the rest of my life. The poem compared my vision of Lloyd to Bunyan's hallucination that he could see mountains shining above the houses. The final words of the poem were: 'A

277

genuinely religious delusion. I am very glad.' But two or three days after I had written these words the idea of a life of sporadically ecstatic resignation began to arouse an antagonism in me — perhaps partly because of my having expressed the idea definitively in the poem. On a Sunday afternoon I was sitting alone in my room half-wishing to go out of the school grounds for a brief walk but being deterred by a slight fear that, if I did, someone connected with the school would see me wandering about the town on no definite errand, and suddenly I decided that I would nevertheless go out, and as I walked along the pavement to the sound of a Salvation Army band I told myself, 'In future I must resist trivial impulses to submit.' Antagonism against resignation arose more strongly in me one evening not long after this when I was taking prayers — Lloyd and I took them on alternate evenings — and was reading a prayer from the Anglican prayerbook in an unnatural voice to the boys who were on their knees with their heads bowed: in an instant the hypocrisy which my job at this school had led me into became so repulsive to me that I couldn't imagine how resignation could ever bring me ecstasy again. And I despondently knew that my poem about Lloyd, in spite of certain technical merits I believed it had, would not do at all.

A few days later I asked the newsagent to deliver the *Daily Herald* to me at the school instead of *The Times*: I expected that Lloyd for certain and probably other members of the staff too, none of whom were socialists, would discover the change, and it would be a minor act of rebellion. I began to get books I thought to be socialist out of the Public library, one of the first of them being an account of a visit to the U.S.S.R. by the American novelist Theodore Dreiser, which greatly impressed me. I bought the first volume of Marx's *Capital* in the translation by Eden and Cedar Paul and started reading it during the summer term, continued reading it throughout the summer holidays, finished it before the end of the Christmas term. I didn't hesitate to tell Lloyd, and the two or three other younger members of the staff whom I knew best, how highly I thought of it. No doubt older members too got to hear of the opinions I was expressing, just as they can hardly have failed to hear previously that I had cancelled *The Times* in favour of the *Daily Herald* (which, however, I soon came to realise was not a genuinely socialist paper). The equivocal reputation I had probably begun to get with the Headmaster also cannot have been improved when he came to see me one morning in my room just after breakfast — why he came I forget, but it wasn't to criticise me about anything — and noticed I was still in bedroom slippers though he knew I had been having breakfast with the junior boys in their dining-room. Lloyd's view of me, friendly though he remained, wasn't becoming any more favourable, either, in my fourth term at the school: his doubts about whether I would ever be a good junior school schoolmaster with the right attitude to games and scouting seemed to be hardening. And then a young nurse from a private nursing home whom I met by chance at a cinema — and with whom I soon found I had only one real interest in common — indiscreetly rang me up at the school. She had the wrong kind of accent, and the news may well have got about subsequently that I was a 'womaniser' as well as a socialist. Not long after the beginning of my second Easter term I had another morning visit from the Headmaster. He said he wondered how I felt I was getting on in the junior school and he wished he could offer me a job with the seniors but unfortunately there was no vacancy in the senior school nor was there likely to be one in the near future. He was a nice man and he was embarrassed as he said this, and perhaps he had not come with the fixed intention of giving me the sack: if I had told him I would make every effort to improve he might have been willing to give me another chance. But I told him I was ready to leave as soon as he liked. He asked me to stay on for another term, till the end of the academic year, so that he would have plenty of time to find someone to replace me. As he spoke, the thought came dazzlingly to me that if I left at the end of this Easter term I would have a whole summer of freedom before me. I told him I did not want to stay on, and he had to accept this. During the remainder of the term I not only became increasingly incautious in my womanising but I also started to plan a long poem — a Marxist poem — which I told myself I must begin to write when I got my freedom.

My Essex home when I returned there seemed once again a promising place to write in. Because I had earned my living for five terms at Lacedaemon I had fewer scruples about letting my parents keep me at their expense for a few months. And they were quarrelling less: having blamed each other constantly for Vaughan's illness during the earlier weeks after he became ill — my mother said my father's wanting to make a doctor of him had caused it, and my father said it obviously came from her side of the family — they had recognised that no amount of mutual accusation could bring him back to us in renewed health from the private mental home where he still was. The comfort that my living at home again gave me, in spite of Vaughan's being away with an illness I now thought of as incurable, was modified however by a feeling of urgency about my writing. The idea was growing in me that my last chance of success might be now. I couldn't go on taking teaching jobs and then throwing them up again after a few terms: the man at Rabbitarse and String's had strongly hinted that unless I stayed at least five years in my next post an impression might be given which would not encourage other headmasters to employ me in future. But if I had to take a permanent job what hope would there be of my finding the time and energy for the huge effort I knew would be required to produce a poem which would prove incontrovertibly to myself and to others that I was a real poet? The tension caused in me by the thought that my last chance had come was increased when after two or three weeks at home I recognised that I would not be able to write the Marxist poem I had been planning: it had seemed feasible enough in the atmosphere of the school, but now that I was back again in the comparative civilisation of home I no longer felt it to be relevant. After a further two or three weeks — more anxious than the first — I was able to begin to plan another long poem: I intended it to be about my home town, like the Marxist poem I had abandoned; but in reaction against that poem I decided it must be as free as possible from general ideas, and it must be full of the vividest concrete particulars. I did at last make a start on the poem, and was quite pleased with it; nevertheless after I had been working on it for nearly a month I began to have increasingly serious doubts about it. The descriptions in it were so static, mere accumulations of detail. My progress with it became slower and slower. When I woke in the mornings I had anxiety symptoms, heart-palpitations, moments when all the feeling seemed to retreat out of my arms and legs and to become burningly concentrated in my solar plexus. I had glimpses in my mind of an abyss ahead of me — total and everlasting failure, the final defeat of what I believed I had been born for. I was rescued from a state of deepening fear by a letter from Richard, who had gone to live in a seaside village where he was getting on very well with the poetry he was writing. The letter was extremely enthusiastic about the place and invited me to come down and live the poetic life with him there. I sent him a telegram to say I would come at once.

Need I have turned against the poetic life as utterly as I did there in the end? I found it promising enough when my visit to Richard began. On my very first evening at his lodgings, where he had been able to arrange for me to stay too, hopefulness about my poetry was revived in me by the decision he helped me to take, as we sat talking together on the verandah with the darkness of the garden in front of us and the white glow behind us from the glass-shaded oil lamp in the sitting-room, that I must abandon the latest version of my poem and must conceive a new and less statically pictorial version with ideas in it and a unifying central theme. My hopefulness was strengthened within the next three days by the place itself, in which there seemed to be almost all the aids I had ever day-dreamed that the poetic life at its finest would give to my poetry-writing, one of the aids being the opportunity to meet likely and beautiful girls, several of whom Richard told me he already knew in the village, and I glimpsed two of them — beautiful even beyond my expectation — in the moonlight from the windows of the Britannia pub on the evening of my arrival. I was poetically excited by the house in which we were staying ; by our sitting-room where the ottoman and the chairs were upholstered in red plush and a big gilt-framed mirror over the mantelpiece had swans in green reeds painted on its lower corners; by the white front gate under the arched hawthorn tree, and the sandy lane outside which led to the bay; by the small unrepaired esplanade that the sea, so calm now, had formerly broken, and the concrete groyne with the sunlight reflected in shifting reticulations all along it from the gently undulating water; by the cliffs and the sands and the images we invented to describe them during a morning walk on the shore; by my meetings with the friends he had made among the working-class inhabitants, whom I became friendly with too as I had long wanted to become with working-class people but hadn't dared or known how to until he showed me the way, and who were to be a main cause of my being able to discover, ten days after my' arrival, the unifying central theme I needed for a new version of my poem.

There may seem to have been something patronising, inwardly if not outwardly, in Richard's and my attitude towards these inhabitants — towards Mr Peel (the Tripper, as Richard privately named him to me, though he was a genuine enough inhabitant, having retired to this place after winnning a prize in a newspaper competition) who was wobble-bellied in large-girthed cream-coloured flannel trousers and who affably recommended excursions to various beauty spots; towards Mr Lillicrap, the jobbing gardener, whom Richard had nicknamed the Hedger and who on my first meeting him talked slowly and pauselessly for a long while about eggs and about the special tactics which different animals, such as rats, hedgehogs, rooks, adopt when stealing them; towards Basher — 'a hero of our own time' Richard described him as to me — who worked in the still-room at the big hotel on the cliff and told us that he had been a sailor and had been all over the world, that he had learnt to box because he was fond of women, whom he believed in giving 'a good turn-over', that he had found Australia to be the best country. Yet though we laughed about these local friends of ours (but seldom at them as they sometimes did at us) we laughed about them affectionately in much the same way as we did sometimes about living or dead poets we admired, and as we did at each other. There may seem to have been something a little heartless in our enthusiasm for the religious maniac who turned up at the bay one morning, but he was so ebullient that I couldn't think of him as a sufferer. Perhaps he was an actor, deliberately playing a part, and not insane at all, though this is unlikely. I can't be sure in detail of what he said, because of a short story Richard wrote three years later about him and other people at the bay: several of the imagined details in this story may have become permanently substituted in my mind for the reality. He arrived by charabanc, wearing a check suit with brown and white squares which were so large that I could only suppose he had hired it from a theatrical costumier's. He came and stood near the edge of the esplanade and began to preach in a powerful uncultured voice: 'You'll never get this day again

283

as long as God Almighty is God Almighty'. A number of holiday makers grouped near him to listen as he went on, 'I've seen a good many charabancs in my time but I've never seen one called Mount Vesuvius. In a hundred years' time that charabanc will be no more than a blade of grass. Aha, that's got some of you.' He brought a dandelion out of his pocket, the earth still clinging to its roots. 'Why, a flying machine can't pick up what I picked out of a railway carriage this morning.' He looked up at the sky. 'When England can produce a black man she can produce the sun.' He pointed with his stick at a concrete buttress against the sea wall below the esplanade. 'The man who built that must have thought he was in Egypt.' His listeners, except Richard and myself, soon became embarrassed and moved away from him. He gave us a smile, seemingly of gratitude for staying with him. Then two young poshocrats from the big hotel on the cliff came walking confidently by — a tall and handsome young man with wavy yellow hair and a prominent well-moulded cleft chin whom Richard had once overheard saying to the local curate 'Of course, if one leads a pretty full life. . . . ,' and an earnest-looking girl with a singsong voice whom he had heard saying that somebody or something was 'fearfully stimulating'. He urged the maniac, 'Couldn't you tell us about those two?' To my alarmed delight the maniac immediately called out after them, 'Adam and Eve, Adam and Eve. There you go, there you go. And all you've got is nothing.' We had the satisfaction of seeing them quicken their pace for a moment before continuing to walk on as though nothing had happened, and then the maniac, guffawing, turned from us and walked away in the opposite direction from them up the road that led inland. But it was not the maniac, nor Basher, nor any of the inhabitants I made friends with in the bar of the Britannia, who finally enabled me to conceive a new and more promising version of my poem. It was the young men and girls I saw taking part in an open-air dance one evening on a sunken stretch of grass near the esplanade.

I can't deny that the central unifying theme in the new version could be regarded simply as a resurrection of the doom idea which I had used in my later Rugtonstead poems and had repudiated even before I came down from Cambridge. As I stood with Richard watching the couples dancing to the music of the local brass band, I saw that several of the girls were beautiful; and all at once they, and their partners, and the other couples also, were more than merely beautiful, were transfigured. The unambiguous emotional music, the soft strong movement of limbs beneath the dresses, the happy seriousness of faces, the pride and the gliding erectness of body and of head, made me feel that in these dancers I was seeing the human race as it truly was, sublime, infinitely finer than all the gods and goddesses it had ever invented. Soon afterwards on our way back to our lodgings when I was trying to describe exactly to Richard the effect the dancers had had on me, I suddenly thought I understood what made them so fine — it was that they were doomed, that in ten to fifteen years' time most of those girls we had seen dancing would be prematurely middle-aged and ugly, and that they were dancing in defiance of their inevitable fate: we had been looking at the first or second act of the historic tragedy of woman played over again in sight of a small bay and still cliffs. As we came up the path from the white front gate towards the verandah of our lodgings I developed this idea further: not only were those girls fine but so were all the working-class inhabitants of this seaside village, and for the same reason — they were all doomed. 'What makes people vile is being successful and comfortably off,' I said. 'Only the doomed are good, and we must be on their side always.' By the end of the evening I had decided that in the new version of my poem the ordinary working people of my home town would be shown as the doomed and good. Nevertheless I think now that however much of a retrogression this central unifying theme may have been, it was an advance on the earlier doom idea in that it strongly took the side of the working-class. Also it enabled me to start writing the following day, and the new version I began then was an improvement on any that I had begun previously.

At breakfast the next morning something happened which made my starting to write, only two hours afterwards, all the more of an achievement. Richard, as soon as he came downstairs from his bedroom, told me to my bitter surprise that he couldn't bear staying in this place a single day longer and had been wanting almost from the moment of my arrival to go back to London in order to be with a boy he had talked a lot to me about who had been down here on holiday just before me. Although by the time Richard left for London, an hour after breakfast, I had got over my resentment, recognising that he had every right to leave and that the relation between us had always been one of mutual independence, I did have a suspicion that the poetic life I had been invited down here to lead might not be so possible without him. But my success that same morning in starting to write helped to weaken this suspicion, and I was able to forget it entirely a few days later when I first met Peg. I had seen her before, and she had seen me, watching the dancers at the open-air dance, and Richard had urged me to go and ask her to dance with me, but everything about her appearance had been so appealing to me — she was not unlike Tessy, though her hair had a pale coppery colour instead of being deep black — that I was overcome with a romantic timidity of a kind I ought to have outgrown after my experience with Tessy, and I dared not ask her to dance. Later that evening, the pain of the injury which my timidity had inflicted on me made me promise Richard, whom I had been telling how I felt about her, that next time I saw her I would without fail go and speak to her. I did not see her again till nearly a week later, at the next open-air dance. Within a few minutes of my asking her to dance with me she seemed the girl I had daydreamed of since my boyhood — she was not only beautiful but she liked poetry, and said she had written some herself, and she gave every indication of being as much attracted by me as I was by her. Not more than two or three days later I went at night to her aunt's house, where she was staying on holiday from her secretarial job in London, and I climbed in through the scullery window which, as she had told me beforehand, had a broken catch. When we were in bed together I held her in my arms for a long time without movement, as though movement would have been a sacrilege. After the climax I told her that I had been in love with other girls before and had been to bed with other girls before, but that I had never before been to bed with a girl I had been in love with. I loved her not just because she was beautiful but also because she was a person in her own right who could be independent of any man; and as a physical human being she aroused my senses more keenly than any other girl had ever done. The sight especially of the dimpled skin of the popliteal space (a name I found later in one of my father's anatomy books) at the back of her knees, with no sign of the hamstring tendons which are often very noticeable behind male knees, could cause a sensual ecstasy in me so intense that it seemed almost spiritual.

I should have accepted the advice she gave me, in words that she quoted from Yeats, to 'take love easy/As the leaf grows on the tree'. She had warned me, at the open-air dance when we first met, that she had a fiancé who was a successful business man in London, though she had added that this would make no difference to us and that she intended to go on having men friends even after she was married to him. I should have accepted her love in the spirit in which she offered it — a spirit of poetic make-believe, evident within a few minutes after we first met when she decided she would call me by my fancy second forename of Thorwald and she wanted me to call her by her fancy name of Althea rather than by the name of Peg which she said her family used for her. But I, already feeling a need to bring her down to earth from the heights of her half-playful romanticism, said I would call her Peg. And after we had made love together I asked her not to marry her fiancé but to marry me instead. Next day she told me that I was taking our affair too seriously, and that we should have to stop going to bed together, though she wanted us to go on being friends. I said that this would make me even more miserable than if she abandoned me totally. I desperately and abjectly begged her to change her mind, but she would not; and after she returned to London I never saw her again. I should have been able, when she had gone, to adopt Swinburne's attitude: 'Hast thou not given me above all that live/Joy, and a little sorrow shalt not give?' Yet though I couldn't adopt that attitude my misery was not so great as to put an end to the poetic life for me. Love was not essential to the poetic life. If I was to be able to live for poetry the one indispensable thing was that I should be able to write it, and I did manage to go on with my poem after Peg left for London, and I continued to think that it was more effective both technically and in its content than any previous version of it I had begun.

The content of the poem, not its technique, was what I began to have misgivings about after I had been working on the new version for three or four weeks. I had believed at the start that the central unifying theme was distinguished essentially from the doom idea of my Rugtonstead poems by being in praise of ordinary working people; but I made less and less headway with the new version, and at last the suspicion came to me that to think of working people as being good because they were doomed might not be very different from thinking of doom as being good for working people, and that my new theme might be even more objectionable than my Rugtonstead view of doom as being good for me. I tried to force myself to go on writing, not with any confidence that I would be able to introduce some improvement into the central theme but in fear of what would happen if I stopped. Once again, as at home before I got Richard's invitation to come and live the poetic life, I had anxiety symptoms when I woke in the mornings and I glimpsed an abyss of everlasting failure ahead of me. One afternoon, as I was lifting the latch of the gate under the hawthorn arch on my way out from the garden towards the beach, I knew I would have to stop trying to force myself to continue the new version. Yet the terror that came upon me then gave way a moment later, strangely, to a feeling which was not far from relief. This may have been partly because of my having been freed at least temporarily from the painful struggle of the last few weeks, but it was mainly because even before my finally recognising that the new version was no good a hope had already been half-formed in my mind that I might still be able to write the Marxist version I had wanted to towards the end of my time at Lacedaemon. Marxism, which had seemed to lose relevance after I had escaped from the reactionary atmosphere there, was relevant again for me owing to my awareness that the time was drawing nearer when I would have to apply for another and perhaps worse teaching job.

I failed during the next ten days to write a tolerable beginning of the Marxist version of my poem: I produced nothing but platitudinous abstractions, and at last I told myself there was no point in my trying any more. A morning came when I stood looking into the big gilt-framed mirror over the mantelpiece in the sitting-room and saw with detestation and then with fear the face of a person who — whatever allowances I might make for him on the grounds of his genetic inheritance or of the poisoning he had got from his upper-class education — was worthless, a would-be genius who assumed he was altogether different from other people and ought not to have to earn his living in an ordinary slavish job, whereas the truth was that he had no talent at all, that he was a pampered young or no longer quite so young shirker, useless to society. Why didn't I realise then that during the last ten days I had come nearer than I had ever yet been to solving my poetic problem? I had not been wrong in thinking a Marxist theme was what I needed in order to write a poem which would satisfy me at last, and my recognition of abstractness as the chief fault in the attempt I was abandoning ought to have suggested to me that I might still succeed in writing a satisfactory Marxist poem if first of all I got some practical experience of Marxist political activity, and that even though I would have to leave this seaside village to get the experience there would be no necessity for me to cease trying to live primarily for poetry. But I was sure I had failed for ever as a poet. I futilely decided to kill myself, and I walked up the path towards the highest part of the cliff above the bay. Perhaps my believing that I would be able to use the appalling method of throwing myself over the cliff proves that my state of mind was sufficiently abnormal to have made me slightly more likely to kill myself this time than I had been two years before when on my return home from Buxted I had planned to do it by a combination of shooting and drowning. And there was an automatism in the way I still went on walking towards the edge of the cliff even after I had become convinced that I would be as incapable of deliberately throwing myself over as I would have been of jumping from the bottom of the cliff to the top. What stopped me within a few yards of the edge (though I suspect now that I was much less near to it than I thought then) was not horror only — it was also the desire which the sight of the sea's utter calmness, sunny and unwrinkled from the horizon inwards towards the very beach below the cliff, had re-aroused in me to go on living. But I knew I could not go on living as I had been, in a state which had demonstrated to me at last what being doomed was really like and had taught me how hatefully false my idea was that working-class people were fine because they were doomed. I understood that it was necessary to fight against being doomed. I knew I must become politically active on the side of the working-class, though I decided that before becoming so I would return to my home in Essex to recover from the sick demoralisation I had fallen into and to prepare myself for political activity by reading more of the Marxist classics. I walked back to my lodgings, and on the same day I travelled home. Some while later — a much longer while than I had intended — I contacted the Communist Party in London. And after that for twenty years I put politics first. So I gave up trying to live for poetry just at a time when living for it could have enabled me to write it satisfactorily at last, if secondarily I had begun living for politics also as I have been doing since my retirement.

I am lying to myself. There was no possibility at all of my continuing to try to live for poetry after that walk up the cliff path. I am lying to myself because I know that to admit the total failure of the poetic life in the past is to cast doubt on the possibility of the new poetic life in the present. After the agony of that failure — and don't let me think I can persuade myself I'm exaggerating in calling it agony — how could I have found the will to make yet another attempt? And suppose I had found the will, and suppose after I had had some experience of the working-class movement in London my continuing to make poetic creation my main objective had not prevented me from writing a few fairly good poems, how could I later on in the nineteen thirties have regarded the advance of fascism and the approach of war as matters of only secondary concern to me? The truth is there wasn't the least chance that my aim of living primarily for poetry could ever have been realised then. So what hope can I have that by persisting in deliberately remembering my past poetic and imaginative activities, which were brought near to total defeat by my trying to live for them, I might still be able to give strength to the imaginativeness and creativity I have been living for since I retired? And without this remembering how can the new poetic life be sustained? Certainly during these last six years my taking part secondarily in the political struggle through the work Elsie and I have done for C.N.D. and the meetings we have helped to organise against American imperialism's Vietnam war, and also through the politically militant ideas I have introduced into my poem, has invigorated my imagination and my creativity; but what possibility is there that the struggle can remain secondary for me in future as the deepening crisis of capitalism causes the external world to become yet grimmer and stormier than now? This morning I must recognise at last that the new poetic life — which already showed signs of enfeeblement during my first days of full freedom here, though it had seemed almost a success when I had begun living it in my spare time before I retired — cannot go on any longer.

If I am to write poetry at all in future I must turn once more to a life which is primarily in support of the political struggle. I was near to knowing this a year ago when I was walking along the disused railway track one afternoon in early spring, but I was still afraid that to put politics first again would have the effect it had eventually had in the nineteen thirties of bringing my poetry to a stop. I ought to have remembered that my decision to live for the political struggle had enabled me, within a few months of my return to my Essex home after the seaside failure of the poetic life, to begin at last to write poems which I was not dissatisfied with. The stop did not come till several years later, and it came because I put the Party not the political struggle first: my believing .the Party's general policy to be Marxist-Leninist, wholly unaware as I was that there were already the beginnings in it of the revisionism which was to become so blatant after the war, led me to accept the Party's line on literature too, though I found that my poetry was increasingly restricted and impoverished by my attempts to follow the line in practice. I shall not repeat that mistake now. Nor shall I give most of my energy to directly political activities, though I must never neglect those: I shall make my main contribution to the struggle in the way I am best fitted to make it, through poetic creation, unless political circumstances arise in which the interests of the struggle absolutely require me to do otherwise. I shall live the new political life.

But in the poem which I have been working on for six years and have written the final lines of to-day my central intention has been to glorify the new poetic life. And yet I feel far less misgiving about the quality of the poem than I did an hour ago when I was still trying to believe that the new poetic life could and must go on. My deciding to bring that life to an end has led me to remember that at its beginning it had the function of restoring importance to poetry for me after my years of Party work had accustomed me to regard direct political activity as the one thing that really mattered. In trying to live once again for imagination and poetic creation I was going through a necessary phase and was motivated by the love I have felt for these throughout most of my life and will never repudiate, though I know now that the only way I can bring poetic vitality into the poetry I want to write in future is by writing it to serve the political struggle. And only by making the struggle my first concern always, and by being prepared to lose everything for it if necessary, shall I become capable of finding more often in my surroundings here something of the same marvellousness that my imagination helped to give them years ago, and that I am already beginning to find again now as I sit out on the verandah this morning in April, looking at the summer house beneath the sycamore tree, and with my completed poem in my notebook on the small table beside my chair.